WITHDRAWN

**THE ROUGH GUIDE TO**

# Singapore

written and researched by

Richard Lim

with additional contributions by

Hanna Butler

**ROUGH GUIDES**

roughguides.com

# Contents

# Introduction to
# Singapore

"The handiest and most marvellous city I ever saw", wrote the natural historian William Hornaday of Singapore in 1885, "as well planned and carefully executed as though built entirely by one man. It is like a big desk, full of drawers and pigeonholes, where everything has its place, and can always be found in it." This succinct appraisal seems apt even now, despite the tiny island's transformation from an endearingly chaotic colonial port, one that embodied the exoticism of the East, into a pristine, futuristic shrine to consumerism. In the process, Singapore acquired a reputation, largely deserved, for soullessness, but these days the place has taken on a more relaxed and intriguing character, one that achieves a healthier balance between Westernized modernity and the city-state's traditional cultures and street life.

The foundation for Singapore's prosperity was its designation as a tax-free port by Sir Stamford Raffles, who set up a British trading post here in 1819. The port plays a key role in the economy to this day, though the island now also thrives on high-tech industry, financial services and tourism, all bolstered by a super-efficient infrastructure. All these achievements were accompanied by a major dose of **paternalism**, with the populace accepting heavy-handed management by the state of most aspects of life in exchange for levels of affluence that would have seemed unimaginable a couple of generations ago. Thus it is that since independence much of the population has been resettled from downtown slums and outlying *kampongs* (villages) into new towns, and the city's old quarters have seen historic buildings and streets bulldozed to make way for shopping malls.

Yet although Singapore lacks much of the personality of some Southeast Asian cities, it has more than enough elegant temples, fragrant medicinal shops and grand colonial buildings to captivate visitors. Much of Singapore's fascination springs from its

**ABOVE** STREET DINING

**multicultural population**, a mixture of Chinese, Malay and Indian, which can make a short walk across town feel like a hop from one country to another, and whose mouthwatering cuisines are a major highlight of any visit. The city also rejoices in a clutch of fine historical **museums** that offer a much-needed perspective on the many successes and sacrifices that made Singapore what it is today, plus a lively arts **scene** featuring no shortage of international talent and local creativity.

# What to see

Shaped like a diamond, Singapore's main island is 42km from east to west and 23km from north to south, compact enough to explore in just a few days. The southern corner of the diamond is home to the main part of the city – "downtown", or just "town" to locals – which centres on the **Singapore River**, the creek where Raffles first landed on the island in 1819. After a full day's sightseeing, it's undoubtedly the top place to unwind, lined with former warehouses that are now home to buzzing restaurants and bars.

The main draws for visitors are the city's historic ethnic enclaves, particularly **Little India**, a couple of kilometres north of the river. Packed with gaudy Hindu temples, curry houses and stores selling exotic produce and spices, the district retains much of its original character, as does nearby **Arab Street**, dominated by the golden domes of the **Sultan Mosque**. South of the river, **Chinatown** is a little sanitized though it still has a number of appealing shrines; an immaculately restored Chinese mansion, the **Baba**

## TOP 5 DISHES

Singapore has no national dish – but that's because it has any number of dishes that could happily qualify for that title. As many travellers never graduate beyond extremely predictable fried rice and noodle plates, here's our selection of five of the best things to try.

**Satay** A mainly Malay dish of mini-kebabs on twig-like sticks, barbecued over coals and eaten dipped in a peanut-based sauce, accompanied by glutinous rice cakes and cucumber and onion slices.

**Fish-head curry** Many Indian restaurants offer this fiery stew containing a large fish head – eyes and all; the cheeks are the best bits.

**Chicken rice** Widely available at hawker centres, this Hainanese speciality features steamed chicken served atop rice cooked in chicken stock, served up with chicken consommé – the simplest of concepts, but incredibly satisfying.

**Chilli crab** Whole crabs wok-fried and served in a gloopy gravy made with tomato, chilli, garlic and a little egg. It's mainly served at seafood outlets, though some ordinary Chinese restaurants offer it too.

**Laksa** A Peranakan classic of rice noodles, prawns and other morsels steeped in a rich, spicy, curried coconut soup; not hard to find at hawker centres and food courts.

**ABOVE** CHILLI CRAB **OPPOSITE** TRISHAW RIDE

## SINGLISH

Singapore is the only country with an ethnic Chinese majority not to use Chinese as its main language of education and business. English enjoys that role – but here it's often upstaged by the entertaining, though often baffling, **Singlish**, a mash-up of English together with the grammatical patterns and vocabulary of Chinese and Malay. Pronunciation is staccato, with final consonants often dropped, so "cheque book" would be rendered "che-boo". In two-syllable words the second syllable is lengthened and stressed by a rise in pitch: ask a Singaporean what they've been doing, and you could be told "slee-PING".

Conventional **English syntax** is twisted and wrung, and tenses and pronouns discarded. If you ask a Singaporean if they've ever seen a Harry Potter film, you might be answered "I ever see", while enquiring whether they want to go out to buy something might yield "Go, come back already". Responses are almost invariably reduced to their bare bones, with words often repeated for stress; request something in a shop and you'll hear "have, have", or "got, got".

Exclamations drawn from **Malay** and **Hokkien Chinese** complete this pidgin, the most ubiquitous being the Malay suffix "lah", used to add emphasis to replies, as in: "Do you think we'll get in for free?" "Cannot lah!" If Singlish has you totally confused, try raising your eyes to the heavens and crying "ay yor" (with a drop of tone on "yor") – an expression of annoyance or exasperation.

Although these linguistic quirks often amuse foreigners and locals alike, there is much official hand-wringing that poor English could compromise Singapore's ability to do business globally, so much so that a government-backed **Speak Good English** movement has been set up to try to shore up standards.

**House**; plus a heritage centre documenting the hardships experienced by generations of Chinese migrants in Singapore. Wherever you wander in these old quarters, you'll see rows of the city's characteristic **shophouses**; compact townhouse-like buildings that are the island's traditional architectural hallmark.

Of course, the British left their distinctive imprint on the island as well, most visibly just north of the Singapore River in the **Colonial District**, around whose grand Neoclassical buildings – including City Hall, Parliament House and the famed **Raffles Hotel** – the island's British residents used to promenade. Also here are the excellent **National Museum**, showcasing Singapore's history and culture, and **Fort Canning Hill**, a lush park that's home to a few historic remains. All these are constantly being upstaged, however, by the newest part of town, **Marina Bay**, built on reclaimed land around a man-made reservoir into which the Singapore River now drains. Around it are arrayed the three-towered **Marina Bay Sands** casino resort, the spiky-roofed **Esplanade – Theatres on the Bay** arts centre and **Gardens by the Bay**, with its two huge arch-shaped conservatories.

Nearly as modern as Marina Bay, but steeped in tradition as far as Singaporean consumerism is concerned is **Orchard Road**, a parade of shopping malls that begins just a few minutes' walk inland from the Colonial District. Just beyond is the finest park on the whole island, the **Botanic Gardens**, featuring a little bit of everything that

## SINGAPORE'S CLIMATE

The table below shows the average maximum and minimum **temperatures** in Singapore, and average **monthly** rainfall.

|  | Jan | Feb | Mar | Apr | May | Jun | Jul | Aug | Sep | Oct | Nov | Dec |
|---|---|---|---|---|---|---|---|---|---|---|---|---|
| Max/min (°C) | 30/23 | 31/24 | 32/24 | 32/24 | 32/25 | 31/25 | 31/25 | 31/24 | 31/24 | 31/24 | 31/24 | 30/23 |
| Max/min (°F) | 86/74 | 88/75 | 90/75 | 90/75 | 90/77 | 88/77 | 88/77 | 88/75 | 88/75 | 88/75 | 88/75 | 86/74 |
| Rainfall (mm) | 244 | 262 | 185 | 179 | 172 | 162 | 158 | 176 | 170 | 194 | 256 | 289 |

makes Singapore such a verdant city, though most tourists make a beeline for the ravishing orchid section.

Downtown Singapore is probably where you'll spend most of your time, but the rest of the state has its attractions too. North of downtown is the island's last remaining pocket of primary rainforest, the **Bukit Timah Nature Reserve**, and the splendid **zoo**, where the animals are confined in naturalistic enclosures rather than cages. There's more fauna of the avian kind on show in the west of the island at the excellent **Jurong Bird Park**, while eastern Singapore is home to some sandy beaches and a museum recalling the infamous **Changi Prison**, where so many soldiers lost their lives in World War II. Among the many smaller islands and islets that lie within Singapore waters, the only one that is close to being a must-see is **Sentosa**. Linked to the main island by causeway and cable car, it boasts Southeast Asia's only **Universal Studios** theme park and several slick beach hotels.

# When to go

Singapore's **climate** is simplicity itself: hot and humid. The island experiences two monsoons, from the southwest (May–Sept) and the northeast (Nov–March), the latter picking up plenty of moisture from the South China Sea. Consequently, December and January are usually the rainiest months, though it can be wet at any time of year; during the southwest monsoon, for example, there are often predawn squally showers sweeping across from the Straits of Malacca. The inter-monsoon months of April and October have a tendency to be especially stifling, due to the lack of breezes. At least it's easy enough to prepare for Singapore's weather – have sun cream and an umbrella with you at all times.

**OPPOSITE** CRICKET ON THE PADANG, WITH THE FINANCIAL DISTRICT BEHIND

# 19

## things not to miss

Unless you're in town for a while, it's not possible to see everything Singapore has to offer in one trip. What follows is a selective taste of the city-state's highlights – the most vibrant neighbourhoods, best museums and most captivating events. Each entry has a page reference to take you straight into the Guide, where you can find out more.

## 1 CHINATOWN
Page 58

Chinatown's once characterful shophouses have been rendered improbably perfect by restoration, but the area is still home to many shrines and shops specializing in Chinese food, medicine and other products.

## 2 THE SINGAPORE SKYLINE
Page 70

The towers of the Financial District are amazing viewed from the Singapore River or Marina Bay.

## 3 CLUBBING
Page 141

Singapore's clubbing scene is small but seriously happening, with space-age decor and regular visits by world-famous DJs.

## 4 THE ARTS SCENE
Page 143

From ballet in the ultramodern Esplanade complex to street performances of Chinese opera, Singapore's entertainment scene has something for everyone.

### 5 THE BUDDHA TOOTH RELIC TEMPLE
Page 62

Chinatown's biggest, newest and brashest temple has its own museum, roof garden and, most memorably, thousands upon thousands of Buddha figurines.

### 6 LITTLE INDIA
Page 50

Little India is easily the most atmospheric of Singapore's historic quarters, with colourful south Indian-style shrines, spice shops and outlets blaring Tamil music.

### 7 MARINA BAY SANDS
Page 75

The striking *Marina Bay Sands* hotel and casino includes its own museum and a vast rooftop deck where you can eat or drink while enjoying stunning views of the Colonial District.

### 8 BUKIT TIMAH NATURE RESERVE
Page 84

Crisscrossed by several easy trails, this pocket of primary rainforest offers an authentic jungle experience, minus leeches but with the prospect of coming face-to-face with hyperactive macaques.

### 9 BOAT QUAY
Page 67

Boat Quay is alfresco dining at its best, the reflected lights of its myriad riverside bars and restaurants dancing on the waters of the Singapore River by night.

### 10 THIMITHI
Page 59

The annual fire-walking festival is centred on the Sri Mariamman temple, a Hindu shrine that, in true multicultural Singapore style, happens to be in the heart of Chinatown.

### 11 CHANGI PRISON MUSEUM
Page 95

Centred on a replica wartime chapel, this is a hushed and moving memorial to the horrors perpetrated in Singapore during World War II.

### 12 ARAB STREET
Page 54

Dominated by the golden-domed Sultan Mosque, the area around Arab Street is a fascinating mix of carpet-sellers, curio shops and alternative boutiques, and its informal Arab and Malay restaurants are a great place to chill out in the evening.

### 13 ZOO AND NIGHT SAFARI
Page 88

Spot polar bears and Malayan tigers at this excellent zoo; one section is entirely devoted to nocturnal animals and open, appropriately, at night.

### 14 TEKKA MARKET
Page 50

The closest thing Singapore has to a central produce market, selling everything from halal goat meat to exotic vegetables, and featuring its own superb food centre.

### 15 AN ORCHARD ROAD SHOPPING SPREE
Page 151

Think Oxford Street, Fifth Avenue or Ginza: Orchard Road has enough famous brands to impress even the most jaded shopaholic.

### 16 UNIVERSAL STUDIOS
Page 106

Packed with hair-raising rollercoaster rides and fantastic re-creations of everything from big-city America to ancient Egypt.

### 17 NATIONAL MUSEUM
Page 41

Take stock of Singapore's transformation from rustic island to hi-tech metropolis, a story enlivened by plenty of oral-history clips.

### 18 STREET FOOD
Page 123

Enjoy Malay and south Indian curries and a bewildering range of Chinese rice and noodle dishes – mainstays of Singapore's delightful and inexpensive street food – in myriad food markets called hawker centres and in the *kopitiam* diner.

### 19 THE BOTANIC GARDENS
Page 81

Genuinely world-class, Singapore's Botanic Gardens feature everything from jungle and ornamental tropical shrubs to a dazzling collection of orchids.

MARINA BARRAGE

# Basics

# Getting there

**Reaching Singapore by air is straight-forward: the island is one of the main air hubs of Southeast Asia and is often a stopover on one of the world's busiest long-haul routes, between Europe and Australasia, so fares can be much more competitive than you might expect. There are also budget flights linking the country with the rest of Southeast Asia, with southeastern Chinese cities including Hong Kong, with India and with many cities in Australia.**

Whether you book your flight from a regular or an online travel agent or with the airline directly, it pays to buy it as far in advance as possible. Fares shoot up for travel during **high season** – from mid-June to early September, and over Christmas and New Year. It's also a little more expensive to fly at the weekend; the sample fares below are for midweek travel.

## Flights from the UK and Ireland

There are daily flights to Singapore from the UK. Singapore Airlines and British Airways all offer **nonstop** flights out of London Heathrow, a journey time of twelve to thirteen hours, with Singapore Airlines also flying daily from Manchester via Munich. Many European, Middle Eastern and Asian airlines offer **indirect** flights to Singapore, which involve a change of plane at their hub airport en route and thus take at least a couple of hours longer, though they are generally also cheaper if you're starting from one of the London airports. Conveniently, a few airlines, such as Air France, KLM or Lufthansa, can also get you to Singapore from a UK regional airport or from Ireland.

**Fares** from London to Singapore start at around £550 during low season, climbing to at least £650 in high season. If you're flying from a UK regional airport, it may cost you very little extra to go via a hub in mainland Europe rather than London; otherwise reckon on an extra £50–100. Fares from the Republic of Ireland come in at around €700 in low season, while in high season reckon on at least €800. All prices mentioned here include taxes.

A good time to book your tickets is during the autumn and winter as this tends to be when the airlines advertise promotional fares, valid for travel within the next six to nine months and shaving at least ten percent off regular prices. Besides the usual online agents, it may be worth contacting Lee's Travel (UK ☎0800 811 9888, ✆leestravel.com) or Rex Air (UK ☎020 7439 1898, ✆rexair.co.uk), both of which specialize in Far Eastern flights.

## Flights from the US and Canada

Singapore is roughly halfway around the world from North America, which means that whether you head east or west towards Southeast Asia, you have a long journey ahead. Setting off from the west coast, you'll invariably fly west across the Pacific; it's faster to fly the transatlantic route if you're departing from the east coast, though sometimes it can cost less to fly via the Pacific.

Unsurprisingly, the most comprehensive service is provided by Singapore Airlines, which operates daily **direct flights** from New York (nonstop from Newark – the longest scheduled passenger flight in the world at 19hr – or from JFK via Frankfurt), Los Angeles (18hr nonstop, or via Tokyo) and San Francisco (via Seoul or Hong Kong), plus several flights a week from Houston (via Moscow). **Indirect flights** on other airlines might not add more than a couple of hours to your journey if you're lucky with connections, and will often cost less.

From **New York**, you'll pay at least US$1100 in low season for the round trip, or US$1500 in high season; fares from the west coast tend to be slightly lower. From Canada, the best fares are from **Vancouver** – Can$1100 in low season, rising by 30 percent or so in high season; fares from other Canadian airports are at least twenty percent higher.

---

### A BETTER KIND OF TRAVEL

At Rough Guides we are passionately committed to travel. We believe it helps us understand the world we live in and the people we share it with – and of course tourism is vital to many developing economies. But the scale of modern tourism has also damaged some places irreparably, and climate change is accelerated by most forms of transport, especially flying. All Rough Guides' flights are carbon-offset, and every year we donate money to a variety of environmental charities.

## Flights from Australia and New Zealand

The **budget carriers** JetStar, Tiger Airways and Scoot (an offshoot of Singapore Airlines) offer some of the best deals **from Australia** to Singapore. JetStar has the best coverage, with flights from cities including Melbourne, Perth, Cairns and Darwin, while Tiger Airways only flies directly between Singapore and Perth, though it offers connections from other cities; Scoot serves only Gold Coast airports. at the time of writing. **From New Zealand**, it's possible to fly to Singapore with JetStar from Auckland. Otherwise, the usual full-cost airlines, including quite a few Southeast Asian carriers, operate to Singapore from major cities. Flights from Auckland to Singapore take just over ten hours nonstop, while from Sydney and Perth the journey takes eight and five hours respectively.

**Fares** in high season are generally up to a third higher than in low season. In general, a low-season return ticket from Melbourne to Singapore can start from as little as Aus$600 on JetStar, while the same flights on a full-cost airline cost around Aus$900. From Auckland, you're looking at fares of around NZ$1300 in low season with JetStar, or nearly NZ$2000 on a full-cost carrier if you pay for flights with prompt connections.

## Flights from South Africa

There are nonstop flights **from Cape Town to Singapore via Johannesburg** with Singapore Airlines, taking around eleven hours from Jo'burg. These tend to be expensive though, costing around twenty percent more than indirect flights with a Middle Eastern airline, for which you can expect to pay around ZAR7500 in low season, ZAR9000 in high season.

## From Southeast Asia

Thanks to the **low-cost airlines**, it's easier than ever to visit Singapore as part of a wider Southeast Asian trip. AirAsia, JetStar, Tiger Airways and the Malaysia Airlines offshoot Firefly provide low-cost links with several Malaysian cities, while Berjaya Air connects Singapore with the Malaysian resort islands of Redang and Tioman. JetStar, Tiger and AirAsia, between them, also fly from many major cities and holiday destinations in Thailand, Indonesia and further afield.

### Buses, trains and ferries

Travelling to Singapore by land or sea might seem more interesting than flying, but the range of places you can do this from is surprisingly limited. At least there's a plethora of buses from Peninsular Malaysia, no major town in which is more than 12 hours from Singapore. The largest of the Malaysian bus companies is Transnasional (Ⓦtransnasional.com .my), which is both reliable and good value. Other companies that stand out from the crowd are the premium operators Plusliner (Ⓦplusliner.com.my) and Transtar (Ⓦtranstar.com.sg) which mainly serve the largest Malaysian cities, including Kuala Lumpur and Penang. Finally, there are also buses from Hat Yai in southern Thailand, a fourteen-hour slog.

The Malaysian **rail** network is inefficient and actually slower than the buses. Schedules change frequently (check the latest timetables at Ⓦktmb .com.my), but in general there are a few services daily from Kuala Lumpur to Singapore's Woodlands station, complemented by a couple more from Kelantan state in Malaysia's northeast. And if you've got money to burn, you could embark on the plush Eastern & Oriental Express, a fantasy evocation of what a colonial-era luxury train service might have been like had it existed in this part of the world; it chugs between Bangkok and Singapore at least monthly (Ⓦorient-express.com).

### Ferries

No long-distance international **ferry** services sail to Singapore at all. The only ferries that exist operate from nearby Indonesian islands, including Bintan and Batam, plus the small southern Malaysian town of Kampung Pengerang in Johor, all of which are mainly visited from Singapore rather than being on the tourist trail in their own country. You can get a reasonable overview of Indonesian ferry services on Ⓦsingaporecruise.com.sg.

# Arrival

**Singapore's Changi International Airport is gleaming, modern and ridiculously efficient – the country in microcosm. Arriving by bus or train is a slightly less streamlined experience thanks to border formalities and occasional jams at the two causeways connecting Singapore to the southernmost Malaysian state of Johor. Wherever you arrive, the island's well-oiled infrastructure means that you'll have no problem getting into the centre.**

## SINGAPORE ADDRESSES

Premises within high-rise towers, shopping complexes and other buildings generally have an address containing two numbers preceded by #, as in "#xx-yy". Here xx refers to the floor (ground level is 01, the next floor up 02, and so on) while yy refers to the unit number. So a restaurant whose address includes #04-08 can be found in unit 8 on the building's fourth storey. Note that the term "ground floor" is also used in some older buildings to refer to the floor at street level. It's also worth noting that all buildings within municipal housing estates have a block number displayed prominently on the side, rather than a number relating to their position on the street on which they're located.

To look up an address on a **map**, enter the street, building name or six-digit postal code into ⓦstreetdirectory.com and you will usually get a precise fix on the location.

## By air

**Changi Airport** (ⓦchangiairport.com) is at the eastern tip of Singapore, 16km from the city centre.

The three main terminals each has a **tourist office** (daily 6am–midnight, or until 2am in terminal 3) which can make hotel bookings, plus separate hotel reservation counters which represent the major hotels. There are also the usual exchange facilities/ATMs and plenty of shops, restaurants and food courts. But chances are you'll not linger long – baggage comes through so quickly that you can be heading to the city centre within twenty minutes of arrival.

The airport's **MRT** (metro) station is beneath terminals 2 and 3. Trains run between 5.30am (6am on Sun) and midnight daily to Tanah Merah MRT, two stops away, where you transfer to trains on the main East West line into town. Note that the last downtown train leaves from here around 11.30pm. A one-way ticket for the half-hour downtown trip costs just under $2, though unless you buy a stored-value card you will also have to pay a $1 deposit which is refunded at your destination station when you return the ticket. All the three main terminals are served by the **#36 bus** (every 10min, 6am–midnight; around $2), which passes through the suburb of Katong and Marina Centre before heading to the Orchard Road area. For more on the public transport system and the complexities of ticketing, see p.22.

Whether you take the MRT or a bus, lack of room for luggage (especially on the bus) may be a hindrance. To get round the problem, consider taking the **Airport Shuttle** bus ($9/$6), which calls at downtown hotels, or the **Beesybus** shuttle, which serves backpacker lodges and budget hotels in Katong, the Arab Street area and Little India (☎6396 6694, ⓦbeesybus.com; $8). As for **taxis,** reckon on at least $20 to get downtown, though note that airport departures command a surcharge

of a few dollars on the metered fare, with a fifty-percent surcharge between midnight and 6am. For more on taxi tariffs, see p.24.

## By bus

Most buses from Malaysia and Thailand use the main causeway to reach Singapore from Johor, and terminate at one of three locations. Local buses from **Johor Bahru** (JB) in **Malaysia** arrive at the Queen Street terminal, a couple of minutes' walk from the Bugis MRT station. Buses from further afield in Malaysia and from **Thailand** may terminate at the Golden Mile Complex on Beach Road, or at a number of other locations used by individual companies, some of which are based near Lavender MRT. Bus #100 southwest along Beach Road will take you close to City Hall and Esplanade MRT stations.

Arriving at the causeway, you will have to get off the bus on the Malaysian side to clear immigration and customs, then get back on board – if you're on a local #170 bus, hang on to your ticket and use it to continue on any vehicle on this route – to reach the Singapore side of the bridge, where you go through the same rigmarole. When major jams build up at the causeway, as they often do, follow the crowd and get off the bus a little way before the checkpoints; it's much faster to walk.

## By train

For decades **trains** from Malaysia used the Art Deco Singapore Railway Station on Keppel Road, southwest of Chinatown, but in mid-2011 the terminus moved to a building next to the Causeway immigration complex in Woodlands. From here, bus #170 or #170X will get you to Kranji MRT nearby, with the #170 continuing all the way to Little India.

## LEAVING SINGAPORE

Leaving Singapore presents no special issues except that if you wish to head to Malaysia or Indonesia around the time of a major festival or during the school holidays, try to buy your travel tickets at least a couple of weeks in advance.

### BY AIR

When **flying** from Changi (flight enquiries ☎6542 4422 or on ⓦchangiairport.com) during rush hour, be sure to set off early to allow for traffic. Air tickets can be purchased directly from the airlines or from a travel agent such as STA Travel, 534a North Bridge Rd (near Bugis MRT; ☎6737 7188, ⓦstatravel.com.sg), Chan Brothers, 150 South Bridge Rd (Chinatown; ☎6438 8880, ⓦchanbrothers.com) or Zuji (ⓦzuji.com.sg).

### BY RAIL

**Malaysian rail** tickets can be bought at ⓦktmb.com.my or at Woodlands station (daily 5am–11pm; ☎6765 0076). Note that it is much cheaper to buy your ticket at Johor Bahru's train station, as fares from Singapore are numerically almost the same as those from Johor Bahru, but the latter are priced in Malaysian ringgit, worth half as much as the Singapore dollar.

### BY BUS

**Long-distance bus companies** are based either at the Golden Mile Complex on Beach Road or at their own offices scattered around downtown. At Golden Mile, Transtar (☎6299 9009, ⓦtranstar.com.sg) has some luxury services to the west coast of Malaysia, while Grassland Express ( ☎6293 1166, ⓦgrassland.com.sg) serves the west coast as well as southern Thailand. The most comprehensive services to both coasts of Malaysia are operated by Transnasional from a basement office at The Plaza on Nicoll Highway, close to Arab Street (☎6294 7034, ⓦtransnasional.com.my). For Malacca specifically, you can also try the Singapore–Malacca Express at 101 Lavender St (☎6292 2436).

If you simply want to pop across to Malaysia briefly, perhaps to get a fresh visa upon your return or take advantage of much lower prices in the shops, the easiest way is to head to **Johor Bahru** on the local #170 bus, the Singapore–Johor Express bus or a yellow Causeway Link #CW2 service; all of these leave fairly frequently from the Queen Street bus terminal (near Bugis MRT) and tickets cost only $2–3 single. Having cleared Malaysian formalities at the causeway, you can head into the city on foot rather than get back on the bus unless you wish to end up at the Larkin Terminal outside the centre, from where there are buses to all parts of the country. You can head back on the #170 or #CW2 at the causeway.

## By sea

Boats from Indonesia's **Riau archipelago** dock either at the HarbourFront Centre, off Telok Blangah Road at the southern tip of Singapore, or at the Tanah Merah Ferry Terminal in the east of the island. The former is on the MRT's North East and Circle lines, while the latter is linked by bus #35 to Tanah Merah and Bedok MRT stations. Most ferries from the resort island of Batam end up at HarbourFront Centre, though a few of these boats plus all services from the other resort island, Bintan, use the Tanah Merah terminal. If you see a reference to "RFT" in schedules, it means the HarbourFront Centre.

The only ferry service from **Malaysia** comprises humble "bumboats" from Kampung Pengerang just northeast of Singapore in the Straits of Johor. These moor at Changi Point, beyond the airport, from where bus #2 travels to Tanah Merah MRT station and on to Geylang, Victoria Street and New Bridge Road in Chinatown.

# Transport

**Downtown Singapore is best explored on foot and is compact enough to be tackled this way: for example, Orchard Road is only just over 2km end to end, and it's a similar distance from the Padang to the middle of Chinatown. Of course you'll need a high tolerance for muggy heat to put in the legwork, and tourists tend instead to rely on the underground MRT trains. At some point you may also end up taking buses, which are just as efficient as the trains but a**

**little bewildering, such is the profusion of routes. Both trains and buses are reasonably priced, as are taxis.**

For public transport information, contact either **SBS Transit** (☎ 1800 287 2727, ⓦ sbstransit.com.sg) – historically a bus company, though it's now responsible for two MRT lines – or **SMRT** (☎ 1800 336 8900, ⓦ smrt.com.sg), which runs the bulk of the MRT network and has some bus services of its own.

## The MRT

Singapore's **MRT** (Mass Rapid Transit) metro network is a marvel of engineering – the island's remarkably soft subsoil made it a real challenge to drill train tunnels – and of cleanliness, efficiency and value for money, though the network is often overcrowded. The system has four lines. SMRT operates the **North South** Line, which runs a vaguely horseshoe-shaped route from Marina Bay up to the north of the island and then southwest to Jurong; the **East West** Line, connecting Boon Lay in the west to Pasir Ris and Changi airport in the east; and the **Circle** Line which, despite its name, is a long arc rather than a circle. It passes through little of downtown, since it runs from the Colonial District out to the eastern suburbs, then curls north and west before heading south to the HarbourFront Centre; there's also a short side extension from Promenade station to Marina Bay via Bayfront station (for *Marina Bay Sands*). Finally, the **North East** Line, linking the HarbourFront Centre with Punggol in the northeast, is operated by SBS Transit. They will also run the new **Downtown** Line, whose first stage, from Chinatown to Bugis via Bayfront, should open in 2013.

Trains run every five minutes on average from 6am until midnight downtown, but, as you'll soon discover, overcrowding is a problem, not just during rush hour, and the last trains leave downtown as early as 11.30pm – which puts paid to getting back by train after an extended drinking or clubbing session. Your mobile phone will work on stations, trains, even in the tunnels, but you aren't allowed to eat, drink or smoke (the signs that appear to ban hedgehogs from the MRT actually signify "no durians").

The easiest and cheapest way of getting about is to buy a stored-value card (see box below). Otherwise, single **tickets** cost between $1.20 and $2.40, and can be bought from ticket counters or from automated machines at stations. Annoyingly, all such tickets require you to pay an additional $1 deposit, refunded when you return the ticket to the ticket counter or a ticket machine at the end of your journey.

## Buses

Singapore's **bus network** is comprehensive and slightly cheaper to use than the MRT system for short trips. Most buses operate from 6am, with services tailing off between 11.30pm and 12.30am, and the majority are air-conditioned. Both double- and single-decker buses are in use, and you always board at the front.

Fares rise in small steps with the distance travelled (cash fares are always between $1.10 and $2.20), so if you're paying cash you may well have to consult the driver on the precise fare for your destination. Cash should be dropped down the metal chute next to the driver; change isn't given, so have plenty of coins

---

### EZ-LINK CARDS AND TOURIST PASSES

You can avoid the rigmarole of buying tickets for every bus or MRT ride by purchasing a stored-value **EZ-Link card** (ⓦ ezlink.com.sg), available at MRT stations and bus interchanges. Besides offering convenience, the card shaves at least ten percent off the cost of every trip, and a journey involving up to five transfers (using trains, buses or both within 2hr) is treated as one extended trip if you use the card, again leading to a slight saving. The cards can be bought from post offices, 7-11 stores and some MRT stations for $10–12, of which $5 is the cost of the card and the remaining $5–7 is credit. Cards can be topped up with $10 or more of credit at ticket offices or ticket machines, and stay valid for at least five years. Note that in order to board a train, you need to have at least $3 credit on an EZ-Link card.

Alternatively, the **Singapore Tourist Pass**, valid for up to three days' unlimited travel, can be bought at Visitor Centres and a few MRT stations, including the one at the airport. It costs $10/$16/$20 for 1/2/3 days, plus a $10 refundable deposit. Once the pass expires, you can top it up at MRT stations for additional days' travel, though the pass will now behave like an EZ-link card, charging for journeys rather than offering unlimited travel. To claim the deposit back, be sure to return the card within five days of purchase. For more on the pass, see ⓦ thesingaporetouristpass.com.

to hand to avoid frittering money away – or buy an EZ-Link card or tourist pass. With an EZ-Link card, note that you must touch the card on the electronic reader not only on entering but also **at the exit**, otherwise the maximum fare will be deducted.

A few buses have **fixed fares**, chiefly services within new towns, limited premium services (which run express for much of their route, always have route numbers of the form "5xx" and cost $3 or $3.50) and **night buses**, which operate late on Fridays, Saturdays and before a public holiday and connect downtown with the new towns. SMRT's night buses (11.30pm–4.30am; $3.50) start from Resorts World Sentosa, while SBS night buses (midnight–2am; $4) operate from Marina Centre; they can be useful for downtown travel after the MRT shuts, but note that they may run express in certain parts of town.

Both the SBS Transit and SMRT websites have detailed breakdowns of their bus routes, including journey planners and maps. A pocket-sized guide to the network, the *Singapore Bus Guide*, is also available from bookshops for a few dollars.

## Taxis

Singapore's **taxis** are seemingly without number and they keep on proliferating; indeed some locals joke that in uncertain economic times the authorities probably license yet more taxis to keep jobless figures down. While this means flagging down a taxi generally isn't a problem, it can be tricky at night or during a storm. If you have difficulty finding a cab, it's best to join the queue at the nearest taxi rank – hotels and malls are your best bet. Note that in the downtown area, queueing at a taxi is supposed to be compulsory, though some drivers will ignore this rule to pick up passengers on quieter roads after dark. If you want to book a taxi over the phone, you'll pay a fee of at least $2.50 (or at least $8 if you want a vehicle at a specific time, rather than the next available one). To book a taxi, either call ☎6342 5222, which represents all of the taxi operators, or try individual firms such as Comfort/CityCab (☎6552 1111), Premier Taxi (☎6363 6888) or SMRT Taxis (☎6555 8888).

Taxis come in various colours, but all are clearly marked "TAXI" and have a sign or display on top indicating if they are available for hire. Regular cabs (as opposed to premium/"limousine" vehicles) charge $3 for the first kilometre and then 22c for every 400 metres travelled, with a slightly lower tariff kicking in after you've gone 10km.

There are **surcharges** to bear in mind: 25 percent extra on journeys during rush hour (which, for taxis, means Mon–Fri 6–9.30am & 6pm–midnight, Sat & Sun 6pm–midnight), and fifty percent extra between midnight and 6am. Then there are charges arising from Singapore's **electronic road pricing (ERP)** scheme, which means a $3 surcharge on taxi journeys starting from the ERP zone downtown between 5pm and midnight, *plus* passengers being liable for the actual ERP charge their trip has incurred (shown on the driver's ERP card reader). Journeys from Changi Airport incur a $3 surcharge ($5 Fri–Sun 5pm–midnight), trips from Sentosa $3. On the whole, Singaporean taxi drivers are friendly and honest, but their English isn't always good, so if

---

## USEFUL BUS ROUTES

Below is a selection of handy bus routes. Note that one-way systems downtown mean that services that use Orchard Road and Bras Basah Road in one direction return via Stamford Road, Penang Road, Somerset Road and Orchard Boulevard; buses up Selegie and Serangoon roads return via Jalan Besar and Bencoolen Street; and services along North and South Bridge roads return via Eu Tong Sen Street and Hill Street.

**#2** From Eu Tong Sen Street in Chinatown all the way to Changi Prison and Changi Beach, via the Arab Quarter and Geylang Serai.

**#7** From Holland Village to the Botanic Gardens and on to Orchard Road, Bras Basah Road and Victoria Street (for the Arab Quarter), continuing to Geylang Serai.

**#36** Orchard Road to Changi Airport via Marina Centre and the Singapore Flyer.

**#56** Little India to Marina Centre via *Raffles Hotel*.

**#65** Orchard Road to Little India and then up Serangoon Road.

**#170** From the Ban San Terminal at the northern end of Queen Street to Johor Bahru in Malaysia, passing Little India, the Newton Circus food court, the northern end of the Botanic Gardens, Bukit Timah Nature Reserve and Kranji War Cemetery on the way.

**#174** Runs between the Botanic Gardens and Baba House in Neil Road, via Orchard Road, the Colonial District, Boat Quay and Chinatown.

you are heading off the beaten track, it's worth having the address written down for them to digest. If a taxi displays a destination sign or "Changing shift" above, it means the driver is about to head home or that a new driver is about to take over the vehicle, and that passengers will be accepted only if they are going in the right direction for either to happen.

## Driving

Given the efficiency of public transport, there's hardly any reason to **rent a car** in Singapore, especially when it's a pricey business. Major disincentives to driving are in place in order to combat traffic congestion, including large fees for a permit to own a car and tolls to drive into and within a large part of downtown. This being Singapore, it's all done in the most hi-tech way using electronic road pricing **(ERP)**: all Singapore cars have a gizmo installed that reads a stored-value card or EZ-Link card, from which the toll is deducted as you drive past an ERP gantry. **Parking** can be expensive, though at least every mall has a car park (displays all over town will tell you how many spaces are left at nearby buildings) and many car parks offer the convenience of taking the fee off your ERP card, failing which you will have to purchase coupons from a licence booth, post office or shop. If you are still keen to rent a car, you can contact Avis (Ⓦavis .com.sg) or Hertz (Ⓦhertz.com), both of which have offices at Changi Airport – and note that in Singapore, you drive on the left.

## Cycling

Though largely flat, Singapore is hardly ideal cycling country. Main roads have furious traffic and few bike lanes, and there have been some much-publicized fatal accidents involving cyclists, though this doesn't put off the few dedicated locals and expats whom you'll see pedalling equally furiously along suburban thoroughfares such as Bukit Timah Road. Cycling downtown isn't such a great idea though, and bicycles aren't allowed at all on expressways.

Where bikes come into their own, in theory, is in out-of-town recreational areas and nature parks, which are linked by a park connector network that it's possible to cycle. The reality, however, is that most of these rides involve some stretches along busy suburban roads, and anyway you're unlikely to be visiting any of these parks on a short stay. For more on the network, see the Visitors' Guide section of the Singapore National Parks website (Ⓦnparks.gov.sg). As for bicycle-friendly areas that tourists are likely to

visit, there are really only four: the Bukit Timah nature reserve (see p.84), Changi Beach (see p.96), Pulau Ubin (see p.96) and Sentosa (see p.105). Bike rental outlets exist at all except Sukit Timah. Wherever you cycle, you'll need a high tolerance for getting very hot and sweaty – or drenched if you're caught in a downpour. For more on the local cycling scene, including details of bike shops, try the Singapore Mountain Bike Forum at Ⓦsmbf.com .sg/forum.

## Organized tours and trips

If you're pushed for time, consider taking a **sight-seeing tour**. Various offerings are available, either taking in the obvious downtown districts or, in some cases, focusing on specialist themes as World War II sites and Peranakan culture. It's also possible to do trips down the Singapore River (see p.26) or take a spin in a trishaw, a three-wheeled cycle rickshaw. Once **trishaws** functioned like taxis, but these days they exist only to give tourists a spin on certain routes (they aren't allowed on many major roads). In Chinatown, freelance trishaw men may congregate near the Buddha Tooth Relic Temple, though you'll have to bargain to arrange a ride; alternatively you can book a trip with the operator listed below.

For details of other tour options, contact the STB (see p.31) or check the Tours and Guides section of Ⓦyoursingapore.com. It's also possible to arrange a tour with one of the country's registered tourist guides, each of whom will have their own fees and specializations; again, contact STB for details or use the directory at Ⓦguides-online.yoursingapore.com.

If you will be staying in Singapore for any length of time and have an interest in Singapore's wilder side, consider joining the Singapore Nature Society (❶6741 2036, Ⓦnss.org.sg). This veteran group undertakes conservation projects and organizes guided walks for birdwatchers, plant lovers and so forth, sometimes in areas genuinely off the beaten track; annual membership costs $40. Similarly, the Singapore Heritage Society (❶6345 5770, Ⓦsingaporeheritage.org; $60 per year) organizes regular talks on history and conservation as well as tours of buildings of architectural interest.

### TRIPS AND OPERATORS

**DuckTours** ❶ 6338 6877, Ⓦ ducktours.com.sg. On which an amphibious vehicle takes you around the Colonial District and Marina Bay; fun for families. Hourly 10am–6pm; $33.

**Harbour cruises** ❶ 6533 9811, Ⓦ watertours.com.sg. Offering views of the Financial District and the Singapore Flyer, these trips supposedly evoke the spirit of journeys made by the fifteenth-century

Chinese mariner Cheng Ho, though the boats used look not so much like a traditional junk as a mini palace stuck on top of a floating platform. Boats depart daily from the Marina South Pier, 1500m southeast of Marina Bay MRT station, with prices starting at $27 including light refreshments; free pick-up from the station and a few downtown hotels.

**The Original Singapore Walk**s ☎ 6325 1631, ⓦ www .singaporewalks.com. Guided walks of downtown and Changi, generally lasting 2hr 30min; around $30.

**Singapore River cruises** ☎ 6336 6111, ⓦ www.rivercruise.com. See the city from river level in tarted-up versions of bumboats (daily 9am–10.30pm; 3–4 hourly): choose from the Singapore River Experience (40min; $17), which takes in Clarke Quay, Boat Quay and Marina Bay, and the New River Experience (1hr; $22; until 5pm), which adds Robertson Quay. Probably the most popular trip with tourists; tickets from any of the booths which line the final stretch of the river.

**Trishaw Uncle** Booth on Queen St, close to Bugis MRT ☎ 9012 1233, ⓦ www.trishawuncle.com.sg. The only trishaw cooperative at the time of writing, it charges $39 for a half-hour ride around the immediate vicinity and Little India, or $49 with Clarke Quay included. Daily 11am–10pm.

# The media

**Singapore boasts plenty of newspapers, TV channels and radio stations serving up lively reportage of events, sports and entertainment in the four official languages, though don't expect to come across hard-hitting or healthily sceptical coverage of domestic politics.**

The media are kept on their toes by a legal requirement that they must periodically renew their licence to publish, and most newspapers have actually been herded into a conglomerate in which the state has a major stake. Likewise radio and TV are dominated by Mediacorp, a company which is effectively stated-owned; satellite dishes are banned; and, while many international broadcasters are available on cable, the sole cable provider is a company in which Mediacorp is a major shareholder.

While a wide range of foreign newspapers and magazines are available from bookstores, there are occasional bans on editions containing pieces that displease the authorities, and Singapore's leaders have a long history of winning defamation suits against foreign publications in the island's courts. Given these circumstances, it's no surprise that in the 2011/12 World Press Freedom Index, issued by the pressure group Reporters Without Borders, Singapore was far down the rankings at no. 135 – some way below much poorer nations not exactly noted as exemplars of free speech, such as Albania and Paraguay.

If this seems an unremittingly bleak picture, it should be said that the advent of **independent news websites** and **blogs** has been a breath of fresh air in recent years. Elsewhere in cyberspace, it's possible to turn up various YouTube clips of discussion forums and interviews with activists, offering an alternative take on local issues.

## NEWSPAPERS, MAGAZINES AND ONLINE NEWS

**Straits Times** ⓦ straitstimes.com. This venerable broadsheet was founded in 1845, though, sadly, its pedigree isn't matched by the candour of its journalism; not so dull when it comes to foreign news, however.

**The Online Citizen** ⓦ theonlinecitizen.com. Delivers a rather less sanguine picture of Singapore than you'll find in the mainstream media.

**Today** ⓦ todayonline.com. A free paper from the state-owned broadcaster Mediacorp, *Today* is less bland than the *Straits Times* and carries worthwhile arts reviews at the weekend.

**TR Emeritus** ⓦ tremeritus.com. Formerly the Temasek Review, this website boasts fine independent reporting of the island's affairs.

## RADIO AND TV

**BBC World Service** ⓦ bbcworldservice.com. 88.9FM, 24hr.

**Channel News Asia** ⓦ channelnewsasia.com. Mediacorp's CNN-like diet of rolling TV news, via cable.

**Channel 5** ⓦ 5.mediacorptv.sg. The main terrestrial channel for English programming, with plenty of imported shows.

**Mediacorp Radio** ⓦ mediacorpradio.sg. Several English-language radio stations, including the speech-based 938 LIve (93.8FM) and Symphony (92.4FM) for classical music.

# Health

**The levels of hygiene and medical care in Singapore are higher than in much of the rest of Southeast Asia. Tap water is drinkable throughout the island and all food for public consumption is prepared to exacting standards.**

**No inoculations** are required for visiting Singapore. However, it's a wise precaution to visit your doctor no later than four weeks before you leave to check that you are up to date with your polio, typhoid, tetanus and hepatitis A inoculations.

It pays to use mosquito repellent in Singapore, particularly if you're in a nature reserve or beach area. This isn't because Singapore is malarial – it isn't – but because mosquitoes may carry **dengue fever**, an illness which is seldom fatal but can be debilitating while it lasts. Note that DEET-based repellents are not available in Singapore, so if you prefer these you will have to buy them abroad.

Travellers unused to tropical climates periodically suffer from **sunburn** and **dehydration**. The easiest way to avoid this is to restrict your exposure to the sun, use high-factor sunscreens, drink plenty of water, and wear sunglasses and a hat. Heat stroke is more serious: it is indicated by a high temperature, dry red skin and a fast pulse and can require hospitalization.

**Medical services** in Singapore are excellent, with staff almost everywhere speaking good English. **Pharmacies** are well stocked with familiar brand-name drugs, though only the largest outlets have pharmacists dispensing prescription medication; the two main chains are Guardian and Watsons, both ubiquitous.

**Private clinics** are found throughout the city, even inside shopping malls such as the Tanglin Shopping Centre (19 Tanglin Rd) and Paragon (290 Orchard Rd). A consultation costs from $50. You can find a list of dentists at Ⓦ yellowpages.com.sg. If you require emergency treatment, dial ☎ 995 or get to one of the **hospitals listed below, all of which have 24-hour casualty/emergency facilities.** Don't forget to keep any receipts for insurance claim purposes.

### HOSPITALS

**Mount Elizabeth Hospital** 3 Mount Elizabeth, off Orchard Rd ☎ 6250 0000, Ⓦ mountelizabeth.com.sg. Private.

**Raffles Hospital** 585 North Bridge Rd ☎ 6311 1111, Ⓦ rafflesmedicalgroup.com. A stone's throw from Bugis MRT; private.

**Singapore General Hospital (SGH)** Outram Rd ☎ 6222 3322, Ⓦ sgh.com.sg. The main state-run hospital, near Outram Park MRT.

### MEDICAL RESOURCES FOR TRAVELLERS

#### AUSTRALIA, NEW ZEALAND AND SOUTH AFRICA

**The Travel Doctor** ☎ 1300 658 844, Ⓦ traveldoctor.com.au. Lists travel clinics in Australia, New Zealand and South Africa.

#### US AND CANADA

**Canadian Society for International Health** ☎ 1 800 454 8302, Ⓦ csih.org. Extensive list of travel health centres.

**CDC** ☎ 1 800 232 4636, Ⓦ cdc.gov/travel. Official US government travel health site.

**International Society for Travel Medicine** Ⓦ istm.org. Has a full list of travel health clinics.

#### UK AND IRELAND

**Hospital for Tropical Diseases Travel Clinic** ☎ 020 7388 9600, Ⓦ thehtd.org.

**MASTA (Medical Advisory Service for Travellers Abroad)** Ⓦ masta.org. Travel clinics throughout the UK.

**Travel Medicine Clinic** Northern Ireland ☎ 028 9031 5220.

**Tropical Medical Bureau** Ireland Ⓦ tmb.ie.

# Travel essentials

## Costs

Singapore is one of the more expensive Asian cities, especially for accommodation, and many items are priced at Western levels. On the other hand, with budget dormitory accommodation in plentiful supply, and both food and internal travel cheap, it's possible to survive on £20/US$32 a day, though that would leave little for sightseeing. If you want to share a double room in a lower-mid-range hotel and enjoy one restaurant meal a day in addition to hawker-cooked food, your budget is likely to soar to £60/US$95 at least.

Note that Singapore has a 7 percent Goods and Services Tax **(GST)**, which is levied by all companies except small businesses. Prices in shops include GST (see p.151 for details of refunds for tourists), but it's not uncommon for hotels and restaurants to leave it out, quoting prices with **"++"** at the end. In this case, the first plus indicates that they levy a ten percent **service charge** (as all mid-range and upmarket hotels and restaurants do) and the second plus indicates GST on the combined cost of the room or food and the service charge, that is, a 17.7 percent surcharge in total.

Where two prices are given for a museum or other attraction in this book, the second price is for a child ticket unless otherwise stated.

## Crime and personal safety

If you lose something in Singapore, you're more likely to have someone running after you with it than running away. Nevertheless, you shouldn't be complacent – muggings have been known to occur and theft from dormitories by other tourists is not unknown. Singapore's police, recognizable by their dark blue uniforms, keep a fairly low profile but are polite and helpful when approached.

Singapore is notorious for the **fines** that people found guilty of various misdemeanours are liable to pay. Though these fines aren't often enforced – their severity has the intended deterrent effect on an already compliant public – it reveals something of the micro-managed state the island has become that, in principle, someone can be fined hundreds of dollars for smoking in certain public places and shopping malls, "jaywalking" (crossing a main road within 50m of a designated pedestrian crossing or overhead bridge) and littering. Even **chewing gum** has been banned (for the mess it creates when not disposed of properly), except when the gum contains prescribed medication.

While the above might seem amusing, the penalties for possession or trafficking illegal drugs are no laughing matter (foreigners have been executed in the past), and if you are arrested for drugs offences you can expect no mercy and little help from your consular representatives.

## Culture and etiquette

The rules of thumb often trotted out concerning behaviour in Asia apply much less to Singapore, given how Westernized the island can be. Nonetheless, appearances are deceptive, and it pays to bear a few points in mind to avoid causing offence.

Although Singaporeans are not especially prudish when it comes to **dress**, they may well frown upon public displays of affection, which aren't really the done thing. It's also not appropriate to pat children (or even friends, for that matter) on the head – the head being considered sacred in Buddhist culture. Conversely, the soles of the feet and, by extension, the soles of your shoes, are regarded as unclean, hence the need to **remove footwear** before stepping over the threshold when visiting people at home, at just about every guesthouse and before entering a temple or mosque.

One cliché about Asia that does still hold in Singapore concerns the importance of not losing face. A mistake or problem that might be regarded as trifling elsewhere might, here, be rather humiliating for the person responsible. The most likely situation in which visitors might need to bear this particular sensitivity in mind is when making a **complaint**. Rather than raising your voice and making a scene, it's best to state your case politely but firmly; this will help preserve the dignity of whomever you are complaining to, and improve the chances of a speedy resolution of the issue.

To avoid losing face yourself, note that when it comes to meetings, the old Singaporean habit of nonchalantly showing up half an hour late for social and other engagements has been replaced by pretty stringent **timekeeping**, so be sure to set off early.

Finally, while there are generally few restrictions about what you can and can't **photograph**, staff at some temples and other places of worship take a dim view of snapping pictures on their premises; when in doubt, always ask.

## Electricity

Singapore's **power supply** is at 230 V/50 Hz, and British-style sockets – taking plugs with three square pins – are the standard.

## Entry requirements

British citizens, and those of the Republic of Ireland, the United States, Canada, Australia, New Zealand and South Africa, don't need a **visa** to enter Singapore. Regulations change from time to time, though, so check with the embassy before departure. You'll normally be stamped in for at least thirty days.

It is possible to extend your stay by up to three months. This being Singapore, you can apply online: check the section on extending short-term visit passes at ⓦica.gov.sg, or call the Immigration and Checkpoints Authority on ☎6391 6100 for more details. Otherwise, there's always the option of taking a bus up to Johor Bahru, across the border in Malaysia, and then coming back in again with a new visit pass.

For a list of embassies in Singapore, as well as a list of Singapore embassies abroad, see the Missions section of ⓦmfa.gov.sg.

### Customs

Upon entry from anywhere other than Malaysia you can bring into Singapore up to three litres in total of spirits, wine and beer **duty-free**; duty is payable on all tobacco. For up-to-the-minute customs information, including how the alcohol allowance works in practice, go to ⓦwww.customs.gov.sg. Under certain conditions, tourists can reclaim the Goods and Services Tax (GST) of seven percent on the cost of items they have bought in Singapore; for more on the red tape this involves, see p.151.

## Insurance

Before you set off, it's a good idea to arrange **travel insurance** to cover medical expenses as well as loss of luggage, cancellation of flights and so on. A typical policy usually provides cover for

---

**ROUGH GUIDES TRAVEL INSURANCE**

Rough Guides has teamed up with WorldNomads.com to offer great **travel insurance** deals. Policies are available to residents of more than 150 countries, with cover for a wide range of **adventure sports**, 24-hour emergency assistance, high levels of medical and evacuation cover and a stream of **travel safety information**. Roughguides.com users can take advantage of their policies online 24/7, from anywhere in the world – even if you're already travelling. And since plans often change when you're on the road, you can extend your policy and even claim online. Roughguides.com users who buy travel insurance with WorldNomads.com can also leave a positive footprint and donate to a community development project. For more information go to ⓦ**roughguides.com/shop**.

---

the **loss of baggage**, tickets and – up to a certain limit – cash or cheques, as well as cancellation or curtailment of your journey. Most of them exclude so-called dangerous sports unless an extra premium is paid. When securing baggage cover, make sure that the per-article limit will cover your most valuable possession. If you need to make a claim, you should keep receipts for medicines and medical treatment, and in the event that you have anything stolen, you must obtain an official statement from the police.

## Internet access

The best place to look for **internet cafés** is Little India, where they are ubiquitous and charge as little as $2 per hour. Chinatown and Orchard Road have a sprinkling of internet cafés too, though they may charge quite a bit more. Several café chains offer free wi-fi, too. It's also possible to sign up for the free **Wireless@SG** wi-fi service available in the lobbies of many shopping malls; though not always reliable, it's mighty convenient when it works. One site where you can sign up is at bit.ly/dw6fFX. The snag is that you will need a friend with a Singapore mobile phone, as the system can only send your password by SMS to a local number.

## Mail

Singapore's **postal system** is predictably efficient. The island has dozens of **post offices** (typically Mon–Fri 9.30am–6pm & Sat 9.30am–2pm), including one conveniently off Orchard Road at 1 Killiney Rd (near Somerset MRT) that keeps extended hours (Mon–Fri 9.30am–9pm, Sat 9.30am–4pm, Sun 10.30am–4pm). Poste restante/general delivery (bring proof of ID) is at the Singapore Post Centre, 10 Eunos Rd (near Paya Lebar MRT; Mon–Fri 8am–6pm, Sat 8am–2pm). For more on the mail system, contact SingPost (☏1605, ⓦwww.singpost.com).

## Maps

The best **maps** of Singapore are those at ⓦstreet directory.com, also accessible via the Singapore Maps app (see p.31). Besides being totally up to speed with the constant rebuilding and reshaping of Singapore, these maps include handy features such as the ability to view shops inside buildings by clicking, and clicking on bus stops to reveal which buses serve them and when the next services will arrive. Bookshops sell printed versions of these maps as street atlases, with new editions regularly published. Otherwise, the maps in this book should be sufficient for most of your exploration, and you can back them up with free foldout maps available from the Singapore Tourism Board.

## Money

Singapore's **currency** is the Singapore dollar, divided into 100 cents. Notes are issued in denominations of $2, $5, $10, $20, $50, $100, $500, $1000 and $10,000; coins are in denominations of 1, 5, 10, 20 and 50 cents, and $1. At the time of writing, the exchange rate was around $2 to £1 and $1.25 to US$1. All dollar prices in this book are in local currency unless otherwise stated.

Singapore **banking hours** are generally Monday to Friday 9.30am to 3pm (although some open until 6pm), Saturday 9.30am to 12.30pm. Major branches on Orchard Road are open Sunday 9.30am to 3pm as well. Outside of these hours, currency exchange is available at moneychangers, whose rates are comparable to those at banks. Major hotels also offer currency exchange, though don't expect their rates to be competitive.

ATMs are plentiful around Singapore and take most types of debit and credit card, usually charging a fee for each withdrawal. Larger retailers and companies accept all major cards, and there are often adverts in the press offering discounts on shopping and meals if you pay with your card.

# Opening hours and public holidays

Shopping centres are open daily 10am to 9.30pm, while offices generally work Monday to Friday 8.30am to 5pm and sometimes on Saturday mornings (see p.29 for banking hours). In general, Chinese temples open daily from 7am to around 6pm, Hindu temples 6am to noon and 5 to 9pm, and mosques 8.30am to noon and 2.30 to 4pm.

Singapore has numerous **public holidays**, reflecting its mix of cultures. Dates for some of these vary; with Muslim festivals, we've given the months in which they fall during 2013–15. For more on traditional festivals, see chapter 000.

It's worth noting the dates of local **school holidays**, at which time Sentosa and other places of interest to kids can be inordinately crowded: schools take a break for one week in March and September, throughout June and from mid-November until the end of December.

### PUBLIC HOLIDAYS

**January 1** New Year's Day
**January/February** Chinese New Year (2 days)
**March/April** Good Friday
**May 1** Labour Day
**May** Vesak Day
**July/August** Hari Raya Puasa (the end of Ramadan)
**August 9** National Day
**September/October** Hari Raya Haji (also called Eid al-Adha)
**October/November** Deepavali (Diwali)
**December 25** Christmas Day

# Phones

**Local calls** from private phones in Singapore cost next to nothing; calls from public phones cost 10c for three minutes. Nearly all phone numbers have eight digits (except for a few free or premium-rate numbers, which start with 1800 or 1900 respectively). Land-line numbers always begin with 6 and mobile numbers with 8 or 9; there are no area codes.

Local SIM cards are available from any 7-11 store or Singtel/Starhub shop. Prices vary depending on what packages are being promoted, though expect to pay at least $10, and bring your passport to complete the registration process. Note that on Singapore networks, receiving calls and texts on your phone incurs a charge.

# Sports

Singapore has a good range of sports facilities, including one of the best networks of **swimming** pools anywhere – almost every new town has its own open-air 50m pool. A full list of state-run sports centres appears at 🌐 ssc.gov.sg; some venues, including privately run facilities, are listed below.

### SPORTS FACILITIES

**Golf** The Marina Bay Golf Course at 80 Rhu Cross (☎ 6345 7788, 🌐 mbgc.com.sg), next to the Bay East garden, is one of the most central and reasonably priced golf facilities, and as such it tends to get booked up quickly – best to reserve a slot at least a couple of weeks in advance (mornings are less busy). Nine holes costs $83 on weekdays, including use of a golf buggy. Bus #158 from Aljunied MRT.

**Gyms** The main operators are California Fitness (🌐 californiafitness.com), True Fitness (🌐 truefitness.com.sg) and Fitness First (🌐 www.fitnessfirst.com.sg). All have gyms downtown, though you will need to take out membership to use them.

**Swimming** The most conveniently located of the island's Olympic-sized pools is at the Jalan Besar Swimming Complex on Tyrwhitt Rd (☎ 6293 9058). Farrer Park or Lavender MRT. Daily 8am–9.30pm (Wed from 2.30pm). Other pools are listed at 🌐 singaporeswimming.com.sg.

**Tennis** Farrer Park Tennis Centre, 1 Rutland Rd ☎ 6299 4166 (daily 7am–10pm; Farrer Park or Little India MRT); Kallang Tennis Centre, 52 Stadium Rd ☎ 6348 1291 (daily 7am–10pm; Mountbatten MRT).

# Time

Singapore is eight hours ahead of Universal Time (GMT) year-round, and therefore two hours behind Sydney (when daylight saving time is not in effect there) and thirteen hours ahead of Eastern Standard Time.

# Tipping

There are a few cases where you might want to tip someone offering you a personal service, for example a hairdresser or barber, but these are the exception rather than the rule – tipping is seldom the custom in Singapore. The better restaurants add

---

## DIALLING CODES

To call home **from Singapore**, dial ☎ 00 plus the relevant country code (see below), then the number (omitting any initial zero).
**Australia** ☎ 61
**Ireland** ☎ 353
**New Zealand** ☎ 64
**South Africa** ☎ 27
**UK** ☎ 44
**US & Canada** ☎ 1

## SINGAPORE APPS

A variety of mobile apps can help you get the most out of your visit to Singapore. At the time of writing, all of the following were free and available for both iOS and Android devices.

**myENV** Official weather forecasts, flood and dengue alerts, plus – so Singaporean – a hawker-centre locator.

**SBS Transit Iris** Service information and journey planner for the North East and Circle MRT lines, and all of SBS's buses.

**Singapore Maps** Don't bother with Google Maps while in Singapore – this app features super-accurate home-grown maps, based on state cartography, and includes real-time bus information and detailed business listings for each address.

**SMRT Connect** Does the same for the rest of the MRT network, plus SMRT's buses.

**YourSingapore** The official app of the Singapore Tourism Board repackages content from their website and lets you locate nearby points of interest.

a ten percent service charge to the bill anyway, and the inexpensive *kopitiam*-type diners don't expect tips, nor do taxi drivers.

## Tourist information

In a place as organized and wired-up as Singapore, it's usually straightforward to get hold of accurate and comprehensive information of use to travellers: everything from public transport to sales taxes is extensively documented online, some companies provide toll-free ☎1800 helplines, and many restaurants and shops have websites that are kept up to date.

The **Singapore Tourism Board** (**STB**; information line Mon–Fri 9am–6pm ☎1800 736 2000, Ⓦyour singapore.com) and operates Visitors' Centres at Changi Airport and downtown on Orchard Road, diagonally across from the 313@Somerset mall (daily 9.30am–10.30pm). Two smaller Visitors' Centres exist on the ground floor of the ION Orchard mall (above Orchard MRT; daily 10am–10pm), and behind the Buddha Tooth Relic Temple in Chinatown (Mon–Fri 9am–9pm, Sat & Sun 9am–10pm).

If you have a particular interest In Singapore's past and architectural heritage, you can get booklets providing background on downtown districts from the Singapore City Gallery (see p.64), or download them from Ⓦura.gov.sg/rediscover.

A number of **publications** offer entertainment listings plus reviews of restaurants and nightlife. The best of these are the weeklies *I-S* (Ⓦis-magazine .com; free) and the monthly *Time Out* (Ⓦtimeout singapore.com.sg; $4). Other freebie publications available from Visitors' Centres and hotels contain similar information, and the "Life!" section of the *Straits Times* also has a decent listings section. Geared towards the large expat community (though with some information of interest to tourists) are *The Finder*, a free monthly magazine

available at some downtown bars and restaurants, and the website Ⓦexpatsingapore.com.

### SINGAPORE TOURIST OFFICES ABROAD

**Australia** Level 11, AWA Building, 47 York St, Sydney ☎02 9290 2888.
**UK** Grand Buildlings, 1–3 Strand, London ☎020 7484 2710, Ⓔstb_london@stb.gov.sg.
**US** 1156 Avenue of the Americas, Suite 702, New York ☎212 302 4861, Ⓔnewyork@stb.gov.sg; 5670 Wiltshire Blvd Suite 1550, Los Angeles ☎323 677 0808, Ⓔlosangeles@stb.gov.sg.

## Travellers with disabilities

Singapore is a moderately **accessible** city for **travellers with disabilities**. Many hotels and even a handful of guesthouses make provision for disabled guests, though often there will be only one accessible room in the smaller establishments – always call ahead and book in plenty of time.

Getting around Singapore is relatively straightforward. MRT stations and trains are built to assist passengers using wheelchairs or with impaired sight or hearing, while around 100 bus routes are now fully served by accessible buses, though some stops may not be suitable for wheelchair users. For more details, check the "Accessibility" section of Ⓦsmrt.com.sg, and the "WAB services" section of Ⓦsbstransit.com.sg. If you can afford to use taxis all the time, so much the better; SMRT taxis (☎6555 8888) are wheelchair-accessible, and Comfort Taxis and CityCab (both on ☎6552 1111) have drivers trained to assist wheelchair-bound passengers.

The best people to talk to for pre-trip advice are the Disabled People's Association of Singapore (☎6899 1220, Ⓦdpa.org.sg) or the Singapore Tourism Board. You may also want to consult one local tour operator, the Asia Travel Group (☎6438 0038, Ⓦasiatravel group.com.sg), which can arrange customized tours of the island in suitably equipped minibuses.

RAFFLES HOTEL

# The Colonial District

North of the old mouth of the Singapore River is what might be termed Singapore's Colonial District, peppered with venerable reminders of British rule set back from the vast lawn that is the Padang. The area still feels like the centrepiece of downtown, even though modern edifices in the surroundings constantly pull focus from it – notably the towers of Marina Bay Sands and the Financial District, away to the south, and the Esplanade – Theatres on the Bay complex to the northeast. Despite the district's historical associations, there are not that many high-profile sights. Chief among these are the excellent National Museum and Peranakan Museum, both nestling beneath verdant Fort Canning Hill – itself worth a look, as are the dignified St Andrew's Cathedral and the diminutive Armenian Church of St Gregory the Illuminator. By far the district's most famous building, however, is the grand old Raffles Hotel.

## The Padang

Bounded by St Andrew's Rd to the west and Stamford Rd to the north

The **Padang** ("field" in Malay), earmarked by Raffles as a recreation ground shortly after his arrival, is the very essence of colonial Singapore. Such is its symbolic significance that its borders have never been encroached upon by speculators and it remains much as it was in 1907, when G.M. Reith wrote in his *Handbook to Singapore*: "Cricket, tennis, hockey, football and bowls are played on the plain". Once the last over of the day had been bowled, the Padang assumed a more social role: the image of Singapore's European community hastening to the corner once known as Scandal Point to catch up on the latest gossip is pure Somerset Maugham.

The brown-tiled roof, whitewashed walls and green blinds of the **Singapore Cricket Club**, at the southwestern end of the Padang, have a nostalgic charm. Founded in the 1850s, the club was once the hub of colonial British society; today its membership is more diverse, though the place remains a fairly exclusive affair, catering not just to cricket but also to rugby and, less strenuously, bridge and darts. Right at the opposite end of the Padang is another clubhouse, the grandiose **Singapore Recreation Club**, founded in 1883 by Eurasians who were barred from the Cricket Club by the prejudices of the era.

## Esplanade Park

Connaught Drive · Unrestricted access

**Esplanade Park** feels somewhat overlooked today, though back in 1907 G.M. Reith recommended it as "a strip of green along the sea wall, with a footpath, which affords a cool and pleasant walk in the early morning and afternoon". Even a few decades ago, it drew flocks of locals to its seafront promenade, **Queen Elizabeth Walk**. Now it's the fresh water of man-made Marina Bay that's on view, and the vista is slightly spoilt by the new Esplanade Bridge in the foreground.

The park itself has a handful of minor monuments. The most prominent of these is the central **Cenotaph**, commemorating the dead of World War I and somewhat reminiscent of the Cenotaph in central London. Rather more attractive is the cast-iron **Tan Kim Seng fountain** to the north, erected in tribute to the wealthy merchant who helped fund the island's first water treatment works. A delightful blue-and-white assembly of Roman mythological figures, it looks like it could have been purloined from a minor central European palace, though it was actually manufactured in northern England in the 1880s.

## The Supreme Court buildings and City Hall

St Andrew's Rd

On the west side of the Padang, across from the Cricket Club, Singapore's erstwhile **Supreme Court** was built in Neoclassical style between 1937 and 1939, and sports a domed roof of green lead and a splendid, wood-panelled entrance hall. Formerly the site of the exclusive *Hotel de L'Europe*, whose drawing rooms allegedly provided Somerset Maugham with inspiration for many of his Southeast Asia short stories, the building has itself been upstaged by Sir Norman Foster's **New Supreme Court** just behind on North Bridge Road – mainly thanks to its impressive, flying-saucer-shaped upper tier.

### City Hall

St Andrew's Rd

Next door to the former Supreme Court is **City Hall**, built in the 1920s. Its uniform rows of grandiose Corinthian columns lend it the austere air of a mausoleum and reflect its role in Singapore's wartime history: it was on the steps of the building that Lord Louis Mountbatten (then Supreme Allied Commander in Southeast Asia)

**1**

announced Japan's surrender to the British in 1945. Fourteen years later, Lee Kuan Yew chose the same spot from which to address his electorate at a victory rally celebrating self-government for Singapore. For now, couples still line up in their wedding finery to have their big day captured in front of one of Singapore's most imposing buildings, but both City Hall and the old Supreme Court have been vacated and are being renovated to jointly comprise the prestigious new National Art Gallery of Singapore (ⓦnationalartgallery.sg), due to open in 2015.

## The Victoria Theatre and Concert Hall

11 Empress Place

Across from the southern end of the Padang are two more fine examples of colonial architecture, the **Victoria Theatre** and, to the right, the **Victoria Concert Hall** (also called the Victoria Memorial Hall). The former was completed in 1862 as Singapore's town

### THE COLONIAL DISTRICT

0   200   metres

**◉ SHOPS**

| | |
|---|---|
| ARTrium | 8 |
| Earshot Café | 9 |
| Elliott's Antiques | 1 |
| Eng Tiang Huat | 1 |
| Funan DigitaLife Mall | 6 |
| Jim Thompson | 1 |
| MPH | 4 |
| Raffles City | 4 |
| Roxy Records | 5 |
| Select Books | 3 |
| Singapore Tyler Print Institute | 7 |

**■ DRINKING AND NIGHTLIFE**

| | |
|---|---|
| Bar Opiume | 5 |
| Crazy Elephant | 3 |
| The Long Bar | 1 |
| Timbre | 2/4 |

**● EATING**

| | |
|---|---|
| Bobby's | 2 |
| Brussels Sprouts | 8 |
| Cedele | 5 |
| Coriander Leaf | 9 |
| Flutes at the Fort | 6 |
| Indochine | 11 |
| Novus Café | 1 |
| Shiraz | 10 |
| Soho Coffee | 4 |
| Spinelli's | 7 |
| Tiffin Room | 3 |

**■ ACCOMMODATION**

| | |
|---|---|
| Fort Canning | 1 |
| Novotel Clarke Quay | 5 |
| Peninsula Excelsior | 4 |
| Raffles | 2 |
| Robertson Quay | 6 |
| Swissôtel The Stamford | 3 |

hall, while the concert hall was added in 1905. Both venues host a good many prestigious cultural events, a role that should be enhanced when they reopen in 2013 after a major refit.

During the Japanese occupation, the concert hall's clock tower was altered to Tokyo time, while the statue of Raffles that stood in front of it narrowly escaped being melted down. The newly installed Japanese curator of the National Museum (where the statue was sent) hid the statue and reported it destroyed. A copy can be seen by the river here at **Raffles' landing site**, where, in January 1819, the great man apparently took his first steps on Singaporean soil. Sir Stamford now stares contemplatively across the river towards the Financial District.

## The old and new parliament houses

Old Parliament House 1 Old Parliament Lane • New Parliament House 1 Parliament Place

The dignified white Victorian building up Parliament Lane, somewhat overshadowed by the Victoria Memorial Hall, is the **Old Parliament House**, built as a private dwelling for a rich merchant by Singapore's pre-eminent colonial architect, the Irishman George Drumgould Coleman. Relieved of its legislative duties, the building is now home to a contemporary arts centre called **The Arts House** and includes a shop stocking literature, DVDs and other works by home-grown talent. The bronze elephant in front of Old Parliament House was a gift to Singapore from King Rama V of Thailand (whose father was the king upon whom *The King and I* was based) after his trip to the island in 1871 – the first foreign visit ever made by a Thai monarch. Just across Parliament Lane from its predecessor is the back of the rather soulless **New Parliament House**, where it is possible to watch parliamentary debates in progress; check Ⓦparliament.gov.sg for details.

## Asian Civilisations Museum

1 Empress Place • Mon 1–7pm, Tues–Thurs, Sat & Sun 9am–7pm, Fri 9am–9pm • $8/$4 or $11/$5.50 joint ticket with the Peranakan Museum (see below) • ☎ 6332 2982

The **Empress Place Building**, very close to the mouth of the Singapore River, is a robust Neoclassical structure named for Queen Victoria and completed in 1865. Having long housed government offices, it is now home to the fine **Asian Civilisations Museum**, tracing the origins and growth of Asia's many and varied cultures, from Islamic West Asia through South and Southeast Asia to China. A bit of a misfit here, though most apt given the museum's location, is the excellent Singapore River gallery. It has displays of sampans and other river craft, and a diorama of a timber dwelling for coolies that recalls the grim lodging houses that once featured in London's docklands, but best of all are fascinating oral history clips featuring people who once worked on and lived by the river. In keeping with the river's renaissance as a major area for wining and dining, Empress Place also houses several slick restaurants, notably those run by the Indochine chain.

## Cavenagh Bridge

The elegant suspension struts of **Cavenagh Bridge** are one of the Colonial District's irresistible draws. Named after Major General Orfeur Cavenagh, governor of the

---

### MUSEUM PASSES

For $20, or $50 for a group of five, you can buy a **three-day pass** valid for, and available from, the National Museum, the Asian Civilisations Museum, the Peranakan Museum, the Singapore Art Museum, the Philatelic Museum (all covered in this chapter) and two war-themed museums, Memories at Old Ford Factory (see p.84) and Reflections at Bukit Chandu (see p.99).

Straits Settlements from 1859 to 1867, the bridge was constructed in 1869 by Indian convict labourers using imported Glasgow steel. Times change, but not necessarily here, where a police sign maintains: "The use of this bridge is prohibited to any vehicle of which the laden weight exceeds 3cwt and to all cattle and horses." Cross the footbridge to reach Singapore's former GPO (now the luxurious *Fullerton Hotel*; see p.70), with Boat Quay (see p.67) and Raffles Place MRT just a couple of minutes' walk away.

## St Andrew's Cathedral

In its own grounds next to Coleman St, west of the Padang, with a small visitor centre on North Bridge Rd • Mon–Sat 9am–5pm; free volunteer-led 20min tours Mon, Tues, Thurs & Fri 10.30am–noon & 2.30–4pm, plus Wed 2.30–4pm, Sat 10.30am–noon • ☎ 6337 6104

Gleaming even brighter than the rest is the final building of note close to the Padang, **St Andrew's Cathedral**, adjoining Coleman Street and North Bridge Road. Using Indian convict labour, the cathedral is the third church to be built on this site and was consecrated by Bishop Cotton of Calcutta on January 25, 1862. Constructed in high-vaulted, and neo-Gothic style, its exterior walls were plastered using Madras *chunam* – an unlikely composite of eggs, lime, sugar and shredded coconut husks which shines brightly when smoothed – while the small cross behind the pulpit was crafted from two fourteenth-century nails salvaged from the ruins of Coventry Cathedral in England, which was destroyed during World War II. During the Japanese invasion of Singapore, the cathedral became a makeshift hospital, with the vestry serving as an operating theatre and the nave as a ward. Today, closed-circuit TVs have been installed to allow the whole congregation to view proceedings at the altar – a reflection of the East Asian fascination with all things high-tech, since the cathedral's size hardly warrants it.

## Raffles City

252 North Bridge Rd

Dwarfing St Andrew's Cathedral is **Raffles City**, a huge development occupying a block between Bras Basah and Stamford roads and comprising two hotels – one of which is the 73-storey **Swissôtel The Stamford** – and a shopping mall. The complex was designed

### THE SINGAPORE RIVER

Little more than a creek, in the nineteenth century the Singapore River became the main artery of Singapore's growing trade, and was clogged with **bumboats** – traditional cargo boats, the size of houseboats, with eyes painted on their prows as if to see where they were going. The boat pilots ferried coffee, sugar and rice to warehouses called **godowns**, where coolies loaded and unloaded sacks. In the 1880s the river itself was so busy it was practically possible to walk from one side to the other without getting your feet wet. Of course bridges were built across it as well, mostly endearingly compact and old-fangled, apart from the massive new Esplanade Bridge at the mouth of the river.

Walk beside the river today, all sanitized and packed with trendy restaurants and bars, some occupying the few surviving godowns, and it's hard to imagine that in the 1970s this was still a working river. It was also filthy, and the river's current status as one of the leading nightlife centres of Singapore ultimately originates in a massive clean-up campaign launched back then, which saw the river's commercial traffic moved west to Pasir Panjang within the space of a few years. Several museums have sections exploring the role the river once played and the pros and cons of its transformation, with a particularly good discussion at the Asian Civilisations Museum, which states frankly: "[the project] also washed away … [the river's] vibrant history as a trade waterway. Its newly cleaned waters now appeared characterless and sterile." At least today various **boat rides** offer a view of the riverside restaurants and city skyline (see p.26).

## SIR STAMFORD RAFFLES

Despite living and working in a period of imperial arrogance and land-grabbing, Sir Stamford Raffles maintained an unfailing concern for the welfare of the people under his governorship, and a conviction that British colonial expansion was for the general good. He believed Britain to be, as Jan Morris says in her introduction to Maurice Collis's biography of Raffles, "the chief agent of human progress… the example of fair Government".

Fittingly for a man who was to spend his life roaming the globe, Thomas Stamford Raffles was born at sea on July 6, 1781 on the *Ann*, whose master was his father Captain Benjamin Raffles. By his fourteenth birthday, the young Raffles was working as a clerk for the **East India Company** in London, his schooling curtailed because of his father's debts. Even at this early age, Raffles' ambition and self-motivation was evident as he stayed up through the night to study and developed a hunger for knowledge which would later spur him to learn Malay, amass a vast treasure-trove of natural history artefacts and write his two-volume *History of Java*.

Raffles' diligence and hard work showed through in 1805, when he was chosen to join a team going out to Penang, then being developed as a British entrepôt. Once in Southeast Asia, he enjoyed a meteoric rise: by 1807 he was named **chief secretary to the governor in Penang**. Upon meeting Lord Minto, the governor general of the East India Company in India, in 1810, Raffles was appointed **secretary to the governor general in Malaya**, a promotion quickly followed by the **governorship of Java** in 1811. Raffles' rule of Java was liberal and compassionate, his economic, judicial and social reforms transforming an island bowed by Dutch rule.

Post-Waterloo European rebuilding saw the East Indies returned to the Dutch in 1816 – to the chagrin of Raffles. He was transferred to the **governorship of Bencoolen** in Sumatra, but not before he had returned home for a break. While in England he met his second wife, Sophia Hull (his first, Olivia, had died in 1814), and was knighted. Raffles and Sophia sailed to Bencoolen in early 1818. Once in Sumatra, Raffles found the time to study the region's flora and fauna as tirelessly as ever, discovering **Rafflesia arnoldii** – "perhaps the largest and most magnificent flower in the world" – on a field trip. By now, Raffles felt strongly that Britain should establish a base in the Straits of Melaka and in late 1818 he was given leave to pursue this possibility. The following year he duly sailed to the southern tip of the Malay Peninsula, where his securing of **Singapore** was a daring masterstroke of diplomacy.

For a man whose name is inextricably linked with Singapore, Raffles spent a remarkably short time on the island. His last visit was in 1822; by August 1824, he was back in England. Awaiting news of a possible pension award from the East India Company, he spent his time founding the London Zoo. But the new life Raffles had planned never materialized. Days after hearing that a Calcutta bank holding £16,000 of his capital had folded, his pension application was refused; worse still, the Company was demanding £22,000 for overpayment. Three months later, in July 1826, the brain tumour that had caused Raffles headaches for several years took his life. He was buried at Hendon in north London with no memorial stone – the vicar had investments in slave plantations in the West Indies and was unimpressed by Raffles' friendship with the abolitionist William Wilberforce. Only in 1832 was Raffles commemorated, with a statue in Westminster Abbey.

by Chinese-American architect I.M. Pei (the man behind the Louvre's glass pyramid) and required the highly contentious demolition of the venerable Raffles Institution, a school established by Raffles himself and built in 1835 by George Drumgould Coleman. The *Swissôtel* holds an annual vertical marathon, in which hardy athletes attempt to run up to the top floor in as short a time as possible: the current record stands at under seven minutes. Lifts transport lesser mortals to admire the view from the sumptuous bars and restaurants on the top floors.

## The Civilian War Memorial

In the green space east of Beach Rd and north of the Padang

The open plot east of Raffles City is home to four 70m-high white columns, nicknamed "the chopsticks" but actually the **Civilian War Memorial**, commemorating

**1**

those who died during the Japanese occupation. Each column represents one of Singapore's four main ethnic groups – the Chinese, Malays, Indians and Eurasians – while beneath the structure are remains reinterred from unmarked wartime graves around the island.

## Raffles Hotel

1 Beach Rd • ☎ 6337 1886, ⊕ www.raffleshotel.com

The *Swissôtel* was, for a time, the world's tallest hotel, but its short-lived fame never came close to that of the legendary **Raffles Hotel** just across from it. With its lofty halls, restaurants, bars and peaceful gardens, the hotel was practically a byword for colonial indulgence, and prompted Somerset Maugham to remark that it "stood for all the fables of the exotic East". Oddly, though, this most inherently British of hotels started life as a modest seafront bungalow belonging to an Arab trader, Mohamed Alsagoff. After a spell as a tiffin house, the property was bought in 1886 by the Armenian Sarkies brothers, who eventually controlled a triumvirate of quintessentially colonial lodgings: the *Raffles*, the *Eastern and Oriental* in Penang, Malaysia, and the *Strand* in Rangoon, Burma.

The brothers commissioned Regent Bidwell of local architecture firm Swan & MacLaren to convert the house into what became the *Raffles Hotel*, which opened for business on December 1, 1887. Despite a guest list heavy with politicians and film stars over the years, the hotel is proudest of its literary connections: Joseph Conrad, Rudyard Kipling, Herman Hesse, Somerset Maugham, Noël Coward and Günter Grass stayed here, and Maugham is said to have penned many of his Asian tales under a frangipani tree in the garden.

The hotel enjoyed its real heyday during the first three decades of the last century, when it established its reputation for luxury – it was the first building in Singapore with electric lights and fans. In 1902, a little piece of Singaporean history was made at the hotel, according to a (probably apocryphal) tale, when the last tiger to be killed on the island was shot inside the building. Thirteen years later bartender Ngiam Tong Boon created another *Raffles* legend, the Singapore Sling cocktail (still served for the princely sum of $31).

During World War II, the hotel became the officers' quarters for the Japanese, and after the Japanese surrender in 1945, it served as a transit camp for liberated Allied prisoners. Postwar deterioration earned it the affectionate but melancholy soubriquet "grand old lady of the East", and the hotel was little more than a shabby tourist diversion when the government finally declared it a national monument in 1987. A hugely expensive facelift followed and the hotel reopened in 1991.

### The museum

Daily 10am–7pm • Free

Though the hotel retains much of its colonial grace, the modern arcade on North Bridge Road lacks a certain finesse. The only part of *Raffles* open to people not staying or eating here, it includes a small **museum** of old photographs, hotel crockery and other paraphernalia.

## Hill and Coleman streets

A couple of blocks west of the Padang, **Hill Street** leads south along the eastern side of Fort Canning Park to the river. The brash building at no. 47 with the striking Chinese-temple-style roof is the **Singapore Chinese Chamber of Commerce**, dating from 1964 though remodelled since. Along its facade are two large panels, each depicting intricately crafted porcelain dragons flying from the sea up to the sky.

**OPPOSITE** STATUE IN THE GRAVEYARD OF THE ARMENIAN CHURCH OF ST GREGORY THE ILLUMINATOR (P. 40) >

**1**

## The Armenian Church of St Gregory the Illuminator

60 Hill St • Daily 9am–6pm • ⓦ armeniansinasia.org

One of the most appealingly intimate buildings in downtown Singapore, the **Armenian Church** of **St Gregory the Illuminator** was designed by George Drumgould Coleman and completed in 1835, which makes it among the country's oldest buildings. The white circular interior, fronted by a marble altar and a painting of the Last Supper, includes a framed photo of the few dozen Armenians who lived in Singapore in 1917, for whom the tiny church would have been room enough. Among the handful of graves in the tranquil garden, stretching between Hill and Armenian streets, is that of Agnes Joaquim, a nineteenth-century Armenian resident of Singapore after whom the national flower, the delicate, purple *Vanda Miss Joaquim* orchid is named; she discovered it in her garden and had it registered at the Botanic Gardens.

## Central Fire Station

Junction of Coleman and Hill streets • Galleries Tues–Sun 10am–5pm • Free • ☏ 6332 2996

The **Central Fire Station**, a stone's throw from the Armenian Church, across Coleman Street, is a pleasing red-and-white-striped edifice. When it was first built in 1908 the watchtower was the tallest building in the region and made it easy for firemen to scan the area for fires. Though the station remains operational, part of it is now taken up by the **Civil Defence Heritage Gallery**, which traces the history of firefighting in Singapore from the formation of the first Voluntary Fire Brigade in 1869. The galleries display old helmets, extinguishers, hand-drawn escape ladders and steam fire engines, all beautifully restored. Of more interest, though, are the accounts of some of the island's most destructive fires. One, not far from Chinatown in 1961, ripped through a shanty district and claimed sixteen thousand homes, a disaster which led directly to a public housing scheme that spawned Singapore's new towns. Nine years later a short circuit caused a blaze that gutted Robinson's department store, then in Raffles Place, with the loss of nine lives.

## The Freemasons' Hall

23A Coleman St, behind the Central Fire Station

Sir Stamford Raffles was a mason, apparently, and Singapore has had a Freemasons' Hall since the 1870s. Recently restored, the building is a little gem of colonial architecture, featuring a proud Palladian facade bearing the masonic compass-and-square motif.

## Singapore Philatelic Museum

23B Coleman St • Mon 1–7pm, Tues–Sun 9am–7pm • $6/$4 • ☏ 6337 3888

The **Singapore Philatelic Museum** occupies Singapore's former Methodist book rooms, which date back to 1906. Although clearly a niche destination, it manages to use its stamp collection imaginatively to highlight facets of the multicultural history and heritage of Singapore.

# Peranakan Museum

39 Armenian St • Mon 1–7pm; Tues–Sun 9am–7pm (Fri until 9pm) • $6/$3, or $11/$5.50 joint ticket with Asian Civilisations Museum (see p.35) • ☏ 6332 7591, ⓦ www.peranakanmuseum.sg

Dating from 1910, the beautifully ornamented three-storey building just west of Hill Street was once the Tao Nan School, the first school in Singapore to cater for new arrivals from China's Fujian province. Today it houses the worthy **Peranakan Museum**. While the museum boasts that the island's Peranakans are "fully integrated into Singapore's globalized society", in reality they are at best keeping a low profile, and in a country where ethnicity is stated on everyone's ID, "Peranakan" isn't recognized as a valid category – meaning they are inevitably lumped together with the wider Chinese

## THE BABA-NONYAS

From the sixteenth century onwards, male Chinese immigrants came to settle in the Malay Peninsula, chiefly in Malacca, Penang (both in what is now Malaysia) and Singapore, and often married Malay women. The male offspring of such unions were termed **Baba** and the females **Nonya** (or Nyonya), though the community as a whole is also sometimes called **Straits Chinese** or simply **Peranakan**, an umbrella term denoting a culture born both of intermarriage and of communities living side by side over generations.

Baba-Nonya society adapted and fused elements from both its parent cultures, and had its own dialect of Malay and unique style. The Babas were often wealthy and were not afraid to flaunt this fact in their lavish **townhouses** featuring furniture inlaid with mother-of-pearl and hand-painted tilework. The Nonyas wore Malay-style batik-printed clothes and were accomplished at crafts such as **beadwork**, with beaded slippers a particular speciality. However, it is their **cuisine**, marrying Chinese cooking with contrasting flavours from spices, tamarind and coconut milk, that is the culture's most celebrated legacy.

During the colonial era, many Baba-Nonyas acquired an excellent command of English and so prospered. Subsequently, however, they came under pressure to assimilate into the mainstream Chinese community despite often not speaking much Chinese (the Baba-Nonyas were sometimes labelled "OCBC" after the name of a local bank, though in their case the acronym meant "*orang Cina bukan Cina*", Malay for "Chinese [yet] not Chinese"). It is partly as a result of this assimilation that many of their traditions have gone into serious decline.

community. The museum should whet your appetite not only for the Baba House (see p.68) but also the Peranakan heritage of the Katong area (see p.92).

Singaporean Peranakans are **Baba-Nonyas**, and the galleries focus on their possessions (theirs was largely a material culture) and customs, in particular the traditional twelve-day wedding. Early on you reach one of the most memorable displays, showing the classic entrance into a Peranakan home, overhung with lanterns and with a pair of *pintu pagar* – tall swing doors; you'll see something similar if you visit the Baba House. Elsewhere, look out for artefacts such as the ornate, tiered "pagoda trays" used in the wedding ceremony, furniture inlaid with mother-of-pearl, and beautiful repoussé silverware, including betel-nut sets and "pillow ends", coaster-like objects which for some reason were used as end-caps for bolsters. It's also worth attending to the video interviews with members of the community, who speak eloquently about matters such as being a hidden minority, whether or not to "marry out" and the prognosis for the Baba-Nonya identity.

# Stamford Road

From the northern edge of the Padang, **Stamford Road** zigzags its way past the Colonial District's most important sight, the National Museum, passing three grand surviving examples of colonial commercial architecture: the 1930s **Capitol Building**, at the corner of North Bridge Road; **Stamford House**, built in 1904 at the corner of Hill Street; and the red-and-white **Vanguard House**, completed in 1908 at the corner of Armenian Street. Each has had an illustrious past – the Capitol Building as a theatre and cinema, Stamford House as an annexe to the *Raffles Hotel* (they were designed by the same architect) and as a major shopping centre, and Vanguard House as the headquarters of the Methodist Publishing House, then much later as home to the flagship store of the MPH bookshop chain. Despite regular maintenance that has kept their ornamented facades in tiptop condition, all now serve much more mundane roles hosting offices and run-of-the-mill shops.

### The National Museum

93 Stamford Rd • Daily 10am–8pm, History Gallery until 6pm • $10/$5, free after 6pm • ☎ 6332 3659, ⓦ www.nationalmuseum.sg

You can't fail to spot the eye-catching dome, seemingly coated with silvery fish scales, of the **National Museum of Singapore**. Its forerunner, the Raffles Museum and Library,

**1**

opened in 1887 and soon acquired a reputation for its natural history collection. In the 1960s, following independence, the place was renamed the National Museum and subsequently altered its focus to local history and culture, an emphasis retained after a recent overhaul that saw the original Neoclassical building gain a hangar-like rear extension larger than itself. That extension houses the mainstay of the new-look museum – the History Gallery – while the old building is home to the Living Galleries, focusing on various aspects of Singapore culture and society. If you have no interest in seeing the History Gallery, note that after it shuts there's **free admission** to the rest of the museum.

### The History Gallery

The History Gallery requires at least a couple of hours to see, thanks to the novel presentation with hardly any labelling; instead, textual descriptions and audio clips of extended commentaries or oral history are all stored on the "Companion", a device like a jumbo iPod which every visitor receives. The sound clips do enliven a collection of artefacts that is in part mundane, but they also take a frustrating amount of time to get through.

Things begin unpromisingly with a two-storey rotunda through which you descend on a spiral ramp while watching a 360° film projection of Singapore scenes that's accompanied by a bombastic choral soundtrack. Thankfully, you're soon into the first gallery proper, which focuses on Temasek (as the Malays called Singapore) before the colonial era. Pride of place here goes to the mysterious Singapore Stone, all that survives of an inscribed monolith which once stood near where the *Fullerton* hotel is today, though more memorable is beautiful gold jewellery excavated at Fort Canning in 1926 and thought to date from the fourteenth century. There's another film installation here, a cryptic affair depicting fourteenth-century conflict in Temasek.

From here the displays are split into a chronological **Events Path** and a human-interest-driven **Personal Path**, covering the same developments in parallel; you can switch from one to the other as you please. The Personal Path is often more entertaining, featuring, for example, a video reminiscence by a revue performer from Shanghai who arrived to perform in postwar Singapore and ended up staying. It's also worth keeping an eye out for the few items which the museum designates national treasures, some of which are truly worthy of the label, such as the gold jewellery mentioned above and some gorgeous Chinese watercolours depicting hornbills and tropical fruit, acquired by William Farquhar (see opposite).

Two aspects of the twentieth-century coverage are worthy of special attention: the dimly lit, claustrophobic area dealing with the Japanese occupation and the horrors of Operation Sook Ching (see p.86), and the sections on postwar politics in Singapore – even if most of the cast of characters is unfamiliar. From today's perspective it seems hard to believe that up until around the early 1970s, much was still up for grabs in Singapore politics, and the museum deserves credit for tackling the postwar period and devoting some space to former opposition figures.

### The Living Galleries

The most accessible of the museum's four Living Galleries focuses on **street food**, covering the history of and variations in local favourites such as *laksa* and *char kuay teow*, and displaying soft drinks and kitchenware that generations of Singaporeans remember from their childhood. Also appealing is the **photography** gallery which, under the banner of "Framing the Family", displays many Singapore family portraits made over the past 100 years, enriched with yet more oral history clips. It includes some interesting commentary on the prevalence of polygamy – not, as you might assume, in Muslim families but among the Chinese. The most edifying gallery tackles **film and wayang** (street opera) and includes plenty of memorabilia of the

Malay-language film industry which took off in Singapore in the middle of the last century; it's a sign of how the times have changed since the divorce from Malaysia that this cinematic flowering is news to many non-Malay Singaporeans today. Finally, there's the **fashion** gallery, using trends in women's clothing over the years as a bellwether of the changing status of Singapore women.

## Fort Canning Park

Entrances include Hill St (via a flight of steps) or at the back of the National Museum • Unrestricted access • Guided walk leaflets available from an information point on River Valley Rd, opposite the Liang Court shopping mall

When Raffles first caught sight of Singapore, the hill now taken up by **Fort Canning Park** was known locally as Bukit Larangan (Forbidden Hill). Malay annals tell of the five ancient kings of Singapura who ruled the island from here six hundred years ago, and unearthed artefacts prove it was inhabited as early as the fourteenth century. The last of the kings, Sultan Iskandar Shah, reputedly lies here, and it was out of respect for – and fear of – his spirit that the Malays decreed the hill off-limits. Singapore's first Resident (colonial administrator), William Farquhar, displayed typical colonial tact by promptly having what the British called Government Hill cleared and erecting a bungalow, Government House, on the summit; the fateful Anglo-Dutch treaty of 1824 was probably signed here. The building was replaced in 1859 by a fort named after Viscount George Canning, governor-general of India, but only a gateway, guardhouse and adjoining wall remain today.

Its jumble of colonial relics aside, Fort Canning Park offers a welcome respite from Singapore's crowded streets and is packed with shady, mature trees (which, unfortunately, also tend to put paid to panoramas over the Singapore River). If you use the National Museum approach, you enter the park down the slope from the grandiose and slightly incongruous **Fort Canning Centre**, a former British barracks now home to a dance company and other organizations.

### The Battle Box

Daily 10am–6pm, last admission 5pm • $8

On the right of the Fort Canning Centre, a path leads to the 1939 underground operations bunkers from which the Allied war effort in Singapore was masterminded. Now restored and called the **Battle Box**, these hold an animatronics-based exhibition that brings to life the events leading up to the British surrender of Singapore in February 1942.

### The keramat and Raffles Terrace

Back at Fort Canning Centre, turn left to reach a **keramat** (auspicious place), the supposed site of Iskandar Shah's grave, which attracts a trickle of local Muslims. Continue round the hill and you meet the staircase from Hill Street at **Raffles Terrace**, where there are replicas of a colonial flagstaff and a lighthouse – the hill was the site of an actual lighthouse that functioned up until the middle of the last century.

## Along River Valley Road

Fort Canning Park's southern boundary is defined by **River Valley Road**, which skirts below the park from Hill Street. At its eastern end is the **MICA Building**, with shuttered windows in striking bright colours. Formerly the Hill Street Police Station, it is now home to the Ministry of Information, Communications and the Arts, plus the Ministry of Culture – and its central atrium houses several galleries majoring in Asian artworks.

**1**

## GMAX

Daily 2pm till late · $45 · ☎ 6338 1146, ⓦ gmax.com.sg

Close to the Coleman Bridge is **GMAX**, billed as a "reverse bungy jump" though it's really more like a metal cage suspended from steel cables, allowing several screaming passengers to be tossed around in the air – best not sampled if you've already indulged at one of the many bars and restaurants nearby.

### Clarke Quay

3 River Valley Rd · ⓦ clarkequay.com.sg

The nineteenth-century godowns of **Clarke Quay**, painted in gaudy colours and housing flashy eating and nightlife venues, feel about as authentic as the translucent plasticky canopy built over them for shelter; nearby Boat Quay (see p.67) feels a bit homelier even when at its busiest. Further up the road is **Robertson Quay**, offering more of the same though less busy, except at weekends.

## Chettiar Temple

Turn right into Tank Rd off River Valley Rd · Daily roughly 8.30am–12.30pm & 5.30–8.30pm · Free · ⓦ www.sttemple.com · Bus #143 from Orchard Rd or Chinatown

Just west of Fort Canning Park and close to Robertson Quay is what is often still called the **Chettiar Temple** (officially the Sri Thendayuthapani Temple). The shrine, with a large, attractive *gopuram*, was built in 1984 to replace a nineteenth-century temple constructed by Indian *chettiars* (moneylenders) and is dedicated mainly to the worship of the Hindu deity Lord Murugan. It's also the target of every participant in the procession that accompanies the annual Thaipusam Festival (see p.148).

ABDUL GAFFOOR MOSQUE

# Bras Basah, Little India and Arab Street

Head a little way north of the Colonial District and you arrive at two of Singapore's most atmospheric old quarters: if you have time for little else on your stay, this is where to come. Centred on Serangoon Road, Little India has retained far more cultural integrity than Chinatown: here Indian pop music blares from shops, the air is perfumed with incense, spices and jasmine garlands, Hindu women promenade in bright saris, a wealth of restaurants serve up superior curries – and there are a couple of busy temples to visit, too. No more than a ten-minute stroll east is Arab Street, dominated by the domes of the Sultan Mosque and truly one of the island's most relaxed and appealing little enclaves, with interesting craft shops and plenty of inexpensive places to eat.

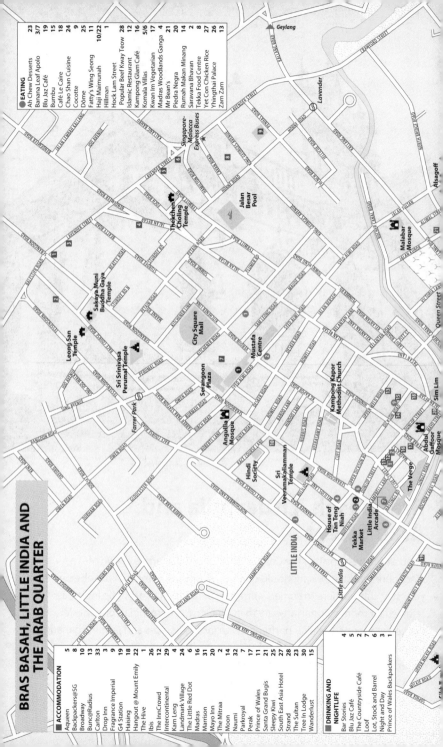

# BRAS BASAH, LITTLE INDIA AND THE ARAB QUARTER

Walking to either of these areas from the Colonial District means heading northeast across **Bras Basah Road**. The Singapore Art Museum aside, the surrounding area seems an uninteresting jumble of commercial towers at first, but look closer and you'll discover that a fair number of old buildings have survived, including a sprinkling of churches, temples and shophouses.

## Bras Basah Road to Rochor Road

**2**

**Bras Basah Road** – the main thoroughfare between Orchard Road and Marina Centre – supposedly got its name because rice arriving on cargo boats used to be brought here to be dried (*beras basah* means "wet rice" in Malay). The zone between it and **Rochor Road** at the edge of Little India has a transitional sort of feel, sitting as it does between the Colonial District and what were intended to be "ethnic" enclaves to the northeast. In recent times city planners have transformed the area into a nexus for the arts, with many distinguished old properties on and around Waterloo Street being turned over to arts organizations, including the **Singapore Art Museum**. The country's leading institutes in the field have also been lured here, among them the **Nanyang Academy of Fine Arts** (NAFA) on Bencoolen Street; and the **School of the Arts**, in a striking new building next to the Cathay cinema.

### CHIJMES

30 Victoria St • ⓦ chijmes.com.sg

**CHIJMES** (pronounced "chimes"), a complex of shops, bars and restaurants, is based in the restored neo-Gothic husk of the former Convent of the Holy Infant Jesus – from which name the acronym for the complex is derived. Its lawns, courtyards, waterfalls, fountains and sunken forecourt give a sense of spatial dynamics that is rare indeed in Singapore. Some locals, though, see it as rather crass that planners allowed this, one of several historic schools in the area, to assume its present role. If the idea of Bras Basah as an arts district had emerged earlier, things might have been very different for CHIJMES. A relic from CHIJMES' convent days survives on its Victoria Street flank, where local families left unwanted babies at the **Gate of Hope** to be taken in by the convent.

### Singapore Art Museum

71 Bras Basah Rd • Daily 10am–7pm, Fri till 9pm • $10, free Fri 6–9pm • Guided tours Mon 2pm, Tues–Thurs 11am & 2pm, Fri 11am, 2pm & 7pm, Sat & Sun 11am, 2pm & 3.30pm • ☎ 6332 3222, ⓦ singaporeartmuseum.com

The **Singapore Art Museum** has a peerless location in the venerable St Joseph's Institution, Singapore's first Catholic school, whose silvery dome rang to the sounds of school bells until 1987. Though extensions have been necessary, many of the original rooms survive, among them the school chapel. There's also an annexe, **8Q**, housing more art in another former Catholic school round the corner at 8 Queen St. The museum focuses on a diverse and challenging range of contemporary art from Singapore and East Asia, and it's likely that this emphasis will continue even after the National Art Gallery opens (see p.34), with the latter showcasing regional art of a slightly older vintage.

### Waterloo Street

Head up Waterloo Street from the Art Museum and almost immediately you encounter one of the area's many places of worship, the peach-coloured **Maghain Aboth Synagogue**, looking for all the world like a colonial mansion except for the Stars of David on the facade. The surrounding area was once something of a Jewish enclave – you'll see another building prominently bearing the Star of David midway along nearby Selegie Road – though the Jewish community, largely of Middle Eastern origin, never numbered more than around a thousand. The synagogue, which dates from the

1870s, can be visited, though this must be arranged in advance by calling ☎6337 2189.

Opposite is the blue-and-white **Church of Sts Peter and Paul**, built around the same time and likewise dwarfed by the hypermodern **National Library** tower a couple of blocks beyond.

A couple of minutes' walk on, at the intersection with Middle Road, is a tiny orange-painted building bearing a striking resemblance to a church, which is no surprise given that it was erected in the 1870s as the Christian Institute. Soon after it became the focal point of Singapore's Methodist missionaries before becoming a Malay-language church, serving the Peranakan community, in 1894. Today it is known as **Sculpture Square**, its grounds and interior featuring modernist works by local artists (Mon–Fri 10am–6pm).

### The Sri Krishnan Temple

152 Waterloo St • ☎ 6337 7957

Just outside the pedestrianized section of Waterloo Street, the **Sri Krishnan Temple** began life in 1870, when it amounted to nothing more than a thatched hut containing a statue of Lord Krishna under a banyan tree. The present-day temple is a fine example of Southeast Asian religious harmony and syncretism in action, with worshippers from the neighbouring Buddhist Kwan Im Temple often seen praying outside.

### The Kwan Im Temple

178 Waterloo St • ☎ 6337 3965

The best-known sight on Waterloo Street is the **Kwan Im Temple**, named for the Buddhist goddess of mercy. The current version dates only to the 1980s – hence its substantial and rather slick appearance – and draws thousands of devotees daily; it can be filled to overflowing during festivals. As you might anticipate, fortune-tellers, religious artefact shops and other traders operate in a little swarm just outside.

## Albert Street

Intersecting Waterloo Street just before it meets Rochor Road is **Albert Street**, which half a century ago was lined with shophouses offering some of Singapore's finest street eating. Now the street is dominated by modern complexes and has been so remodelled it doesn't even appear in its entirety on some maps, though its past is hinted at in the few restaurants trading at ground level. If you do head this way, try to take in the zigzagging glass facades of the **Lasalle College of the Arts** between Albert and McNally streets.

## Bugis Street and Bugis Junction

**Bugis** (pronounced "boogis") **Street**, the southern extension of Albert Street, once crawled with rowdy sailors, prostitutes and ladyboys by night. The notorious street was eventually cleared, partly because it was anathema to the government, and partly so that the Bugis MRT station could be built. In its place today is **Bugis Village**, a claustrophobic bunch of market stalls and snack sellers crammed into two alleyways. While hardly the Bugis Street of old, it does recapture something of the bazaar feel some Singapore markets once had, and amid the T-shirt vendors is at least one outlet selling sex aids – about the only link to the street's seedy past.

Across Victoria Street from here is another throwback to the past, the **Bugis Junction** development, where whole streets of shophouses have been gutted, scrubbed clean and encased under glass roofs as part of a modern shopping mall and hotel, the *Intercontinental*. If you are passing by, be sure to take a quick look at the Gothamesque **Parkway Square** tower just diagonally across on the south side of North Bridge Road. Though this office block is only a decade old, its styling just screams 1930s New York Art Deco.

## Little India

Of all the old districts of Singapore, the most charismatic has to be **Little India**. Though the remaining shophouses are fast being touched up from the same pastel paintbox as that which restored Chinatown to its present cuteness, the results seem to work better in an Indian context.

The original occupants of this convenient downtown niche were Europeans and Eurasians who established country houses here, and for whom a racecourse was built in the 1840s on the site of today's Farrer Park. Many of the roads in Little India started out as private tracks leading to these houses, and their names – Dunlop, Cuff, Desker, Norris – recall these early colonial settlers. Only when Indian-run **brick kilns** began to operate here did a markedly Indian community start to evolve. Indians have featured prominently in the development of Singapore, though not always out of choice: from 1825 onwards, convicts were transported from the subcontinent and by the 1840s there were more than a thousand Indian prisoners labouring on buildings such as St Andrew's Cathedral and the Istana. Today, migrant Tamil and Bengali men labour to build the island's MRT stations, shopping malls and villas, and on weekends they descend on Little India in their thousands, making the place look like downtown Chennai or Calcutta after a major cricket match.

The district's backbone is **Serangoon Road**, dating from 1822 and hence one of the island's oldest roadways. Its southwestern end is a kaleidoscopic of Indian life, packed with restaurants and shops selling everything from nose studs and ankle bracelets to incense sticks and *kumkum* powder (used to make the red dot Hindus wear on their foreheads). Here you might even spot a parrot-wielding **fortune-teller** – you tell the man your name, he passes your name onto his feathered partner, and the bird then picks out a card with your fortune on it. To the southeast, stretching as far as Jalan Besar, is a tight knot of roads that's good for exploration. Parallel to Serangoon Road is **Race Course Road**, at whose far end are a couple of noteworthy temples. Note that **buses** serving Serangoon Road make their return journey along Jalan Besar to the southeast.

### Tekka Market

At the start of Serangoon Rd, on the left (western) side of the road

**Tekka Market** is a must-see, combining many of Little India's commercial elements under one roof. It's best to arrive in the morning when the wet market – as Singaporeans term a traditional market where the floor is periodically cleaned by hosing it down – is at its busiest. More sanitary than it once was thanks to recent renovations, the market is nevertheless hardly sanitized – halal butchers push around trolleys piled high with goats' heads, while at seafood stalls live crabs, their claws tied together, shuffle in buckets. Look out also for a couple of stalls selling nothing but banana leaves, used to serve up delicious curry meals all over Singapore but especially in Little India. The cooked food at the **hawker centre** here is excellent, and though the same can't be said of the mundane outlets upstairs selling Indian fabrics and household items, there are great views over the wet market to be had from here.

### Buffalo Road

**Buffalo Road**, along the northern side of Tekka Market, sports a few provisions stores with sacks of spices and fresh coconut, ground using primitive machines. Its name, and that of neighbouring Kerbau ("buffalo" in Malay) Road, recall the latter half of the nineteenth century when cattle and buffalo yards opened in the area, causing the enclave to grow as more Indians were lured here in search of work. Singapore's largest maternity hospital, nearby on Bukit Timah Road, is called Kandang Kerbau ("buffalo pen").

### Kerbau Road

**Kerbau Road** is noteworthy for its meticulously renovated shophouses and for being, like Waterloo Street 1km to the south, a designated "arts belt", home to theatre companies and other creative organizations. Curiously, the road has been split into two, with a pedestrianized bit of greenery in the middle. Here, at no. 37, you can't miss the gaudily restored **Chinese mansion**, built by one Tan Teng Niah, a confectionery magnate, in 1900 and now used as commercial premises. Look out also for the traditional Indian picture framer's shop at no. 57, packed with images of Hindu deities.

### The Sri Veeramakaliamman Temple
141 Serangoon Rd, just beyond Belilios Lane • ☎ 6295 4538, ⓦ www.sriveeramakaliamman.com

The most prominent shrine on Serangoon Road, the **Sri Veeramakaliamman Temple** has a fanciful *gopuram* that's flanked by lions atop the temple walls. The temple is dedicated to Kali, the Hindu goddess of power or energy, and within the *mandapam* (worship hall) are several depictions of her with ten arms; some have blue skin and fangs, while others show her apparently trampling on her husband Lord Shiva, recalling an episode from the Hindu scriptures.

### Hastings Road to Cuff Road
Across from Tekka Market on the other side of Serangoon Road, the restored block of shophouses comprising **Little India Arcade** is a sort of Little India in microcosm: behind its pastel-coloured walls and green shutters you can purchase textiles and tapestries, bangles, religious statuary, Indian sweets, tapes and CDs, and even Ayurvedic herbal medicines.

The roads nearby are also worth exploring. Exiting the arcade onto Campbell Lane leaves you opposite the riot of colours of **Jothi flower shop** where staff thread jasmine, roses and marigolds into garlands for prayer offerings. A new **Indian Heritage Centre** museum at the corner with Clive Street is due to open in 2014.

#### Dunlop Street
**Dunlop Street** is defined by beautiful **Abdul Gaffoor Mosque** (at no. 41; daily 8.30am–noon & 2.30–4pm), whose green dome and bristling minarets have enjoyed a comprehensive and sympathetic renovation. With cream walls decorated with stars and crescent moons, the mosque features an unusual sundial whose face is ringed by elaborate Arabic script denoting the names of 25 prophets.

One more street along are Dickson Road and, back towards Serangoon Road, **Upper Dickson Road**, where *Khulfi Bar*, an unexpectedly swish little shop and café at no. 15, sells overpriced *kulfi*, Indian ice cream. Next along is **Cuff Road**, home to a tiny, primitive spice grinder's shop at no. 2, open mainly at weekends. At the eastern end of Cuff Road, the simple white **Kampong Kapor Methodist Church** is just one of many fine but unsung examples of Art Deco that you'll see in downtown Singapore. Dwarfed by nearby tower blocks, it grew out of the Waterloo Street church that is now Sculpture Square (see p.49).

### The Thieves' Market
On and around Pitt St • Sat & Sun late morning to dusk

If you're in Little India at the weekend, you can take in a long-established flea market a short walk from Dunlop Street, up Jalan Besar. To the right you'll soon see dozens of traders selling all manner of bric-a-brac. Once upon a time, much of the gear was of dubious provenance – hence the appellation **Thieves' Market** – though these days it's merely of dubious desirability, everything from old slippers to assorted mobile-phone chargers.

### Rowell and Desker roads
Both **Rowell and Desker roads** mark a noticeable shift from the South Indian flavour of much of Little India. Here Bengali features prominently on some shops signs, and at weekends the streets throng with Bengali migrant workers. However, both roads have another claim to fame – or infamy: they have long been synonymous in Singapore with

**2**

---

## DEEPAVALI

Never dull, Little India springs even more gloriously to life over the colourful Hindu festival of **Deepavali** (or Diwali), which falls in October or November. Local Hindus mark the festival by lighting oil lamps (*diyas*) or candles in their homes. And no wonder – this is, after all, the Festival of Lights. The festival marks Lord Krishna's slaying of the demon Narakasura, who ruled the kingdom of Pradyoshapuram by terror, torturing his subjects, and kidnapping the women and imprisoning them in his palace. Lord Krishna destroyed the demon, and Hindus across the world have given praise ever since. More universally, the festival celebrates the triumph of light over darkness, and of good over evil.

For Hindus, Deepavali is a period of great excitement, a time to dress up in colourful new clothes, deck their houses out in multi-hued decorations, prepare festive delicacies, exchange cards and gifts, and pay respects to their elders. On the morning of the festival itself, worshippers bathe themselves in oil, then proceed to the temple to thank the gods for the happiness, knowledge, peace and prosperity they have enjoyed in the year past, and to pray for more of the same in the coming year.

If you visit Little India in the run-up to Deepavali, you may find special **markets** selling decorations, confectionery, garlands and clothes around the Little India Arcade and also in the open areas close to the Angullia Mosque on Serangoon Road.

---

vice, and there's something about the openness of goings-on that's almost radical on this strait-laced island. Between the two roads, running along the backs of the shophouses, is an alleyway whose doorways are illuminated at night. Here gaggles of bored-looking prostitutes sit watching TV, apparently oblivious to the men gathered outside who are mostly more inclined to observe than partake, as though treating the whole thing as some kind of street entertainment.

### Race Course Lane

One striking building stands out on **Race Course Lane**, on the west side of Serangoon Road just before Rowell Road. Here the newly refurbished **Mahatma Gandhi Memorial Building**, at no. 3, bears the great man's image to one side of its mainly brick exterior. Although it looks like it might be a museum, it is in fact the offices of the Singapore Hindi Society, which runs Hindi languages classes here and in schools around the island.

### Syed Alwi Road to Petain Road

Little India takes on a more Islamic feel around **Syed Alwi Road**, across from whose northern end is the **Angullia Mosque**, but the road is better known for being the hub of the shopping phenomenon that is the **Mustafa Centre**. Just "Mustafa" to locals, it's an agglomeration of department store, moneychanger, travel agent, jeweller, fast-food joint and supermarket, much of the place open 24/7. The business started modestly and somehow knew no bounds, growing into the behemoth that occupies several interlinked buildings of its own as well as part of the Serangoon Plaza on the main drag. You'll probably find a visit here much more appealing than Orchard Road, as you rub shoulders with Indian families salivating over confectionery from Delhi, Chinese and Malays seeking pots and pans or luggage, even African businessmen buying consumer goods that are hard to find back home.

Running along the back of the Mustafa Centre is **Sam Leong Road**, worth a detour for its attractive **Peranakan shophouses**, their facades decorated with depictions of stags, lotuses and egrets.

### North of Rangoon and Kitchener roads

Rangoon and Kitchener roads more or less mark the northern boundary of Little India, but it's worth venturing beyond to discover a couple of temples and yet more restored

Peranakan shophouses on **Petain Road**, which are covered with elegant ceramic tiles reminiscent of Portuguese *azulejos*. There's more Peranakan architecture on display on Jalan Besar – turn right at the end of Petain Road.

### The Sri Srinivasa Perumal Temple

397 Serangoon Rd • Daily 6.30am–noon & 6–9pm, though it may be possible to look around at other times • ☎ 6298 5771

On Serangoon Road, opposite the start of Petain Road, is the **Sri Srinivasa Perumal Temple**, dedicated to Lord Perumal (Vishnu), the Preserver of the Universe. Besides a five-tiered *gopuram*, it features a sculpted elephant leg caught in a crocodile's mouth, on the wall to the right of the front gate. But the temple's main claim to fame is that it is the starting point for the gruesome melee of activity at Thaipusam (see p.148), when Hindu devotees don huge metal frames (*kavadis*) that are fastened to their flesh with hooks and prongs. The devotees then leave the temple, stopping only while a coconut is smashed at their feet for good luck, and parade all the way to the Chettiar Temple on Tank Road (see p.44).

### The Sakaya Muni Buddha Gaya Temple

366 Race Course Rd • Daily 8am–4.30pm

Just beyond the Sri Srinivasa temple, a small path leads northwest to Race Course Road, where the **Sakaya Muni Buddha Gaya Temple** (or Temple of the Thousand Lights) is a slightly kitsch affair that betrays a strong Thai influence – not surprising, since it was built by a Thai monk. On the left of the temple as you enter is a huge Buddha's footprint, inlaid with mother-of-pearl, and beyond it a 15m-high Buddha ringed by the thousand electric lights from which the temple takes its alternative name. Twenty-five dioramas depicting scenes from the Buddha's life decorate the pedestal on which he sits. It is possible to walk inside the statue, through a door in its back; inside is yet one more diorama, depicting the Buddha in death. One wall of the temple features a sort of wheel of fortune, decorated with Chinese zodiac signs. To discover your fate, spin it (for a small donation) and take the numbered sheet of paper that corresponds to the number at which the wheel stops.

### The Thekchen Choling Temple

2 Beatty Lane • Daily 24hr • ☎ 6466 3720, ⊛ thekchencholing.org

If you made it as far as Petain Road, it's just a couple of minutes' walk on to the surprisingly gaudy **Thekchen Choling**, one of a handful of Tibetan Buddhist temples in Singapore. The present temple, a modern replacement for one in Bukit Timah that had to make way for redevelopment, boasts an array of impressive gilt statuary, including a multi-armed Chenrezig – the Bodhisattva better known as Avalokiteshvara – as well as its own giant prayer wheel.

## The Arab Street district

Before the arrival of Raffles, the area of Singapore west of the Rochor River housed a Malay village known as **Kampong Glam**, possibly named for a type of tree that used to grow here, though it's also said that a group of resident sea gypsies gave their name to the area. After signing his dubious treaty with the newly installed "Sultan" Hussein Mohammed Shah, Raffles allotted the area to the sultan and designated the land around it as a Muslim settlement. Soon the zone was attracting Malays, Sumatrans and Javanese, as well as traders from what is now eastern Yemen, and the area is now commonly referred to as **ARAB STREET**. Today, Singapore's Arab community, descended from those Yemeni traders, is thought to number around fifteen thousand, though, having intermarried with the rest of Singapore society and being resident in no particular area, they are not distinctive by appearance or locale.

Like Little India, the area remains one of the most atmospheric pockets of old Singapore, despite the fact that its Islamic character has been diluted over the years as gentrification has started to take hold. Now it's the schizophrenia of the place that appeals: rubbing shoulders with the **Sultan Mosque**, traditional fabric stores and old-style curry houses are brash Middle Eastern restaurants and a peppering of alternative boutiques and shops selling crafts and curios.

## Arab Street

While Little India is memorable for its fragrances, it's the vibrant colours of the shops of **Arab Street** and its environs that stick in the memory. Textile stores and outlets selling Persian carpets are the most prominent, but you'll also see leather, perfumes, jewellery and baskets for sale. It's easy to spend a couple of hours weaving in and out of the stores, but don't expect a quiet window-shopping session – some traders are old hands at drawing you into conversation and before you know it, you'll be loaded up with sarongs, baskets and leather bags.

**2**

## Haji and Bali lanes

South of Arab Street, **Haji Lane** and tiny **Bali Lane** – the last of these petering out into the wide walkway next to Ophir Road – have smartened up a fair bit of late. Both have something of London's Brick Lane about them, with traditional shops rubbing up against trendy boutiques; in the evenings and at weekends DJs set up informally on Haji Lane, spinning dance sounds from their computers or record decks. It's one of Singapore's most appealing and organic enclaves, and yet it's not hard to discern that not all is rosy: the local community is having to cope with fast-rising rents while trying, often unsuccessfully, to maintain a semblance of an Islamic character by getting new restaurants to subscribe to a voluntary no-booze policy.

## Sultan Mosque

3 Muscat St • Daily except Fri 9am–noon & 2–4pm, Fri 2.30–4pm • ☎ 6293 4405, ⓦ www.sultanmosque.org.sg

Pause at the Baghdad Street end of pedestrianized Bussorah Street for a good view of the golden onion domes of the **Sultan Mosque** or Masjid Sultan, the beating heart of the Muslim faith in Singapore. An earlier mosque stood on this site, finished in 1825 and constructed with the help of a $3000 donation from the East India Company. The present building was completed a century later to a design by colonial architects Swan and MacLaren. Look carefully at the base of the main dome and you'll see a dark band that looks like tilework, though it actually consists of the bottoms of thousands of glass bottles. The wide foyer has a digital display listing prayer times. Beyond and out of bounds to non-Muslims is the main prayer hall, a large, bare chamber fronted by two more digital clocks.

During the Muslim fasting month of Ramadan, neighbouring **Kandahar Street** is awash with stalls from mid-afternoon onwards, selling *biriyani*, *murtabak*, dates and cakes. Relaxed **Bussorah Street** itself has some good restaurants and souvenir outlets.

## Istana Kampong Glam (The Malay Heritage Centre)

85 Sultan Gate, between Kandahar and Aliwal streets • Tues–Sun 10am–6pm • $4/$2, with free guided tours Thurs–Sun at noon & 3pm • ☎ 6391 0450, ⓦ www.malayheritage.org.sg

Between Kandahar and Aliwal streets, the colonially styled **Istana Kampong Glam** was built as the royal palace of Sultan Ali Iskandar Shah, son of Sultan Hussein who negotiated with Raffles to hand over Singapore to the British. Until just a few years ago the house was still home to the sultan's descendants, though it had fallen into disrepair. Then the government compulsorily acquired it and the similar but smaller dark yellow house in the same grounds. The istana is now the over-smart **Malay Heritage Centre**, a mixed bag of history and culture spanning boats, fishing gear, ceremonial drums and so forth. Traditional artefacts dominate upstairs, where the theme is the history of Kampong Glam; look out here for some examples of jewellery belonging to nobility, as well as a map of the Malay diaspora, showing how seaborne trade has created Malay communities as far afield as Africa. Downstairs, the focus shifts to Singapore as a centre for Malay literary and artistic endeavour, with displays on the local film industry and so forth.

As for the yellow house, **Gedung Kuning**, it used to belong to the descendants of a wealthy merchant but was likewise acquired by the state; it now houses an attempt at an upmarket Malay restaurant, *Mamanda*.

## North of Sultan Mosque

The stretch of **North Bridge Road** between Arab Street and Jalan Sultan has a less touristy feel, and though gentrification is spreading even here, the strip's shops and restaurants tend to be geared more towards locals than tourists. Kazura Aromatics, at no. 705 for instance, sells alcohol-free perfumes, while neighbouring shops stock items such as the *songkok* hats worn by Malay men, and *miswak* sticks – twigs the width of a finger used by some locals to clean their teeth.

Several roads run off the western side of North Bridge Road, including Jalan Kubor (Grave Street) which, across Victoria Street, takes you to an unkempt Muslim **cemetery** where, it is said, Malay royalty are buried. Turn right here up Kallang Road to reach Jalan Sultan and the blue **Malabar Mosque**, built for Muslims from the South Indian state of Kerala and a little cousin of the Sultan Mosque, with more golden domes. Its traditional styling belies its age – the mosque was completed in the early 1960s.

## Beach Road

At the southern boundary of the Arab Quarter, **Beach Road** still has shops that betray its former proximity to the sea – ships' chandlers and fishing tackle specialists – until land reclamation created the Marina Centre area to the southeast. There are no specific sights, though it's worth having a look at two quirky edifices that could not be more different.

### The Gateway

150 & 152 Beach Rd, southwest of Arab St

The two logic-defying office buildings that together comprise **The Gateway** rise magnificently into the air like vast razor blades. Designed by I.M. Pei (who was also behind the *Swissôtel* complex, see p.36), they appear two-dimensional when viewed from certain angles. When **Parkview Square**, the retro Art Deco conceit on North Bridge Road, was built, much care was taken to site it dead between the Gateway's sharp points for good feng shui.

### The Hajjah Fatimah Mosque

4001 Beach Rd, just east of the junction with Jalan Sultan

Not only does the minaret of the **Hajjah Fatimah Mosque** resemble a steeple (perhaps because its architect was European), it also has a visible six-degree tilt; locals call it Singapore's Leaning Tower of Pisa. The mosque is named after a wealthy businesswoman from Malacca who amassed a fortune through her mercantile vessels, and whose family home formerly stood here. After two break-ins and an arson attack on her home, Fatimah decided to move elsewhere, then funded the construction of a mosque on the vacated site.

# Chinatown, Tanjong Pagar and the Financial District

The two square kilometres of Chinatown, west and south of the Singapore River, were never a Chinese enclave in what is, after all, a Chinese-majority country, but they did once represent the focal point of the island's Chinese life and culture. More so than the other old quarters, however, Chinatown has seen large-scale redevelopment and become a bit of a mishmash. Even so, a wander through the surviving nineteenth-century streets still unearths musty and atmospheric temples and clan associations, and you might hear the rattle of a game of mahjong being played.

To the southwest, the adjacent district of **Tanjong Pagar** has yet more old terraces of shophouses and one major museum of Peranakan heritage, the **Baba House**. There's no such subtlety about the skyscrapers of the area to the southeast, Singapore's **Financial District**.

## Chinatown

The area now known as **Chinatown** was first earmarked for Chinese settlement by Raffles, who decided in 1819 that Singapore's communities should be segregated. As immigrants poured in, the land southwest of the river took shape as a place where new arrivals from China, mostly from Fujian (Hokkien) and Guangdong (Canton) provinces and to a lesser extent Hainan Island, would have found temples, shops with familiar products and, most importantly, *kongsi*s – clan associations that helped them find lodgings and work as small traders and coolies.

This was one of the most colourful districts of old Singapore, but after independence the government chose to grapple with its tumbledown slums by embarking upon a redevelopment campaign that saw whole streets razed. Someone with an unimpeachable insight into those times, one Lee Kuan Yew, is quoted thus in the area's Singapore City Gallery: "In our rush to rebuild Singapore, we knocked down many old and quaint buildings. Then we realized that we were destroying a valuable part of our cultural heritage, that we were demolishing what tourists found attractive." Not until the 1980s did the remaining shophouses and other period buildings begin to be conserved (see box, p.65), though restoration has often rendered them improbably perfect. Furthermore, gentrification has seen the clan houses and religious and martial arts associations often replaced by hotels, art galleries, new-media companies and upmarket (or sometimes not so salubrious) bars. Ironically, getting a taste of the old ways of Chinatown now often means heading off the main streets into the concrete municipal housing estates.

Even so, as in Little India, the character of the area has had a bit of a shot in the arm courtesy of recent immigrants. As regards sights, the Thian Hock Keng, Buddha Tooth Relic and Sri Mariamman temples are especially worthwhile, as is the Chinatown Heritage Centre museum, and there's plenty of shophouse architecture to justify a leisurely wander.

### Chinatown Heritage Centre

48 Pagoda St • Daily 9am–8pm, last admission 7pm • $10/$6 • ☎ 6221 9556, ⓦ www.chinatownheritagecentre.sg

One exit from Chinatown MRT brings you up into the thick of the action on Pagoda Street's tacky souvenir stalls, where the **Chinatown Heritage Centre** brings to life the history, culture, labours and pastimes of Singapore's Chinese settlers, with evocative displays and the liberal use of oral history clips.

Early on, the scene is set by a model junk, like those on which the *singkeh* (literally "new guests"), the early migrants, arrived; accounts tell of the privations they endured sailing across the South China Sea. Once ashore at Bullock-Cart Water (the translation of the Chinese name, used to this day, for what would become Chinatown), settlers not only looked for work but also formed or joined clan associations, or the less savoury secret societies or triads. These connections, and every other facet of Chinatown life, are made flesh in displays like the mock-up of the prostitute's shabby boudoir and the pictures and footage of haunted addicts seeking escape through opium.

The museum's climax is a re-creation of the conditions that migrants endured in Chinatown's squalid shophouses, the effect heightened by the absence of air conditioning in this section. Landlords once shoehorned as many as forty tenants into a single floor; if you think it couldn't possibly happen today, spare a thought for the thousands of mainly Indian and Bangladeshi migrant workers who can be seen toiling on building sites all over Singapore. Most live in basic dormitories, and a few years ago a journalist documented 54 workers crammed into triple-decker beds in an 8m-by-6m room.

## Along South Bridge Road

Head down Pagoda Street from the Chinatown Heritage Centre and you come to South Bridge Road, one of Chinatown's main thoroughfares, carrying southbound traffic, with the Pinnacle@Duxton (see p.68) looming over its far end. At no. 218, on the corner of Mosque Street, the pastel-green **Jamae Mosque** (also called the **Chulia Mosque**) was established by South Indian Muslims in the 1820s. Its twin minarets appear to contain miniature windows while above the entrance stands what looks like a tiny doorway, all of which makes the upper part of the facade look strangely like a scale model of a much larger building.

One street northeast, at the junction with Upper Cross Street, the Japanese screened locals for signs of anti-Japanese sentiment in the infamous Sook Ching campaign of World War II (see p.86). That tragic episode is commemorated by a simple, signposted monument in the **Hong Lim Complex**, a housing estate that also happens to boast walkways lined with medical halls, makers of chops (rubber stamps), stores selling dried foodstuffs and so forth – much more representative of the area's original character than more recent arrivals.

To top up your blood-sugar level while wandering the area, try the venerable **Tong Heng** pastry shop (daily 9am–10pm) at no. 285, which sells custard tarts, lotus seed paste biscuits and other Chinese sweet treats.

### The Sri Mariamman Temple

244 South Bridge Rd • Daily 7am–noon & 6–9pm, though it may be possible to look around at other times • Free • ☏ 6223 4064

Singapore's oldest Hindu shrine, the **Sri Mariamman Temple**, boasts a superb entrance *gopuram* bristling with brightly coloured deities. A wood and *atap* hut was first erected here in 1827 on land belonging to Naraina Pillay, a government clerk who arrived on the same ship as Stamford Raffles when he first came ashore at Singapore; the present temple was completed around 1843. Inside, look up at the roof to see splendid friezes depicting a host of Hindu deities, including the three manifestations of the supreme being: Brahma the creator (with three of his four heads showing), Vishnu the preserver, and Shiva the destroyer (holding one of his sons). The main sanctum is devoted to Mariamman, a goddess worshipped for her healing powers. Smaller sanctums dotted about the walkway circumnavigating the temple honour other deities. In the one dedicated to the goddess Periachi Amman, a sculpture portrays her with a queen lying on her lap, whose evil child she has ripped from her womb; it's odd, then, that Periachi Amman is the protector of children, to whom babies are brought when one month old.

Once a year, during the festival of **Thimithi** (Oct or Nov), an unassuming patch of sand to the left of the main sanctum is covered in red-hot coals that male Hindus run across to prove the strength of their faith. The participants, who line up all the way along South Bridge Road waiting for their turn, are supposedly protected from the heat of the coals by the power of prayer.

### The Eu Yan Sang Medical Hall

269A South Bridge Rd • Mon–Sat 8.30am–6pm • ☏ 6225 3211

The beautifully renovated **Eu Yan Sang Medical Hall** is one of the oldest Chinese herbalists in the area. The smell in the store is the first thing you'll notice (a little like a compost heap on a hot day); the second, the weird assortment of ingredients on the shelves, which to the uninitiated look more likely to kill than cure. Besides the usual herbs and roots favoured by the Chinese, there are various dubious remedies derived from exotic and endangered species. Circulation problems and wounds are eased with centipedes and insects, crushed into a "rubbing liquor"; the ground-up gall bladders of

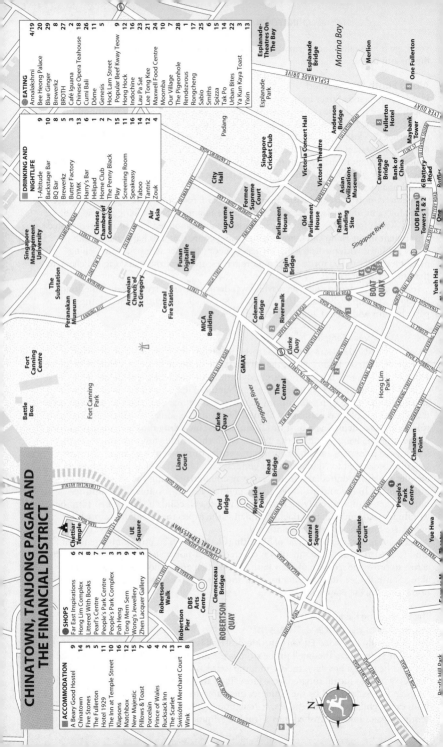

CHINATOWN, TANJONG PAGAR AND THE FINANCIAL DISTRICT

snakes or bears apparently work wonders on pimples; and deer penis is supposed to provide a lift to any sexual problem.

Upstairs, the small but engaging **Birds' Nest Gallery** casts light on this curious Chinese delicacy. The edible nests, made by swiftlets, are a mixture of saliva, moss and grass, and emerged as a prized supplement among China's royal and noble classes during the Ming dynasty. Today they are still valued for their supposed efficacy in boosting the immune system and curing bronchial ailments. The birds live high up in the limestone caves of Southeast Asia, and harvesting them is arduous and sometimes dangerous work, but the nests command such good prices that in Malaysia, town-centre shophouses are being bricked up as "caves" for rearing swiftlets.

### The Buddha Tooth Relic Temple

288 South Bridge Rd, just after Sago St • Daily 7am–7pm • Free • ☎ 6220 0220, ⓦ www.btrts.org.sg • No shorts, vests or non-vegetarian food

Right at the end of South Bridge Road is something of an upstart – the imposing **Buddha Tooth Relic Temple**, the most in-your-face addition to Chinatown's shrines in many a year. The place simply clobbers you with its opulence – even the elevators have brocaded walls – and with its thousands upon thousands of Buddhist figurines lining various interior surfaces. It also boasts its own museum and a gallery of Buddhist art.

The temple has its origins in the discovery, in 1980, of what was thought to be a tooth of Buddha inside a collapsed stupa at a Burmese monastery. The monastery's chief abbot visited Singapore in 2002 and decided the island would make a suitable sanctuary for the relic, to be housed in its own new temple. A prime site in Chinatown was duly secured, and the temple opened in 2007.

#### The main hall

The focus of the **main hall** is **Maitreya**, a Buddha who is yet to appear on Earth. Carved from juniper wood said to be a thousand years old, his statue has a yellow flame-like halo around it. But what really captures the attention are the Buddhas covering the entire side walls. There are a hundred main statuettes, individually crafted, interspersed with thousands more tiny figurines embedded in a vast array of shelving, each with its own serial number displayed. Signage soon makes you aware that many things in the temple are up for "adoption" – figurines and fittings can be the object of sponsorship, presumably winning donors good karma while recouping the $62 million construction bill and helping the temple keep up with its outgoings. Behind the main hall, another large hall centres on the Avalokitesvara Bodhisattva.

The **mezzanine** affords great views over proceedings and chanting ceremonies in the main hall, while **level 2** contains the temple's own teahouse.

#### The Buddhist Culture Museum

Daily 8am–6pm

On **level 3** are some seriously impressive examples of Buddhist statuary in brass, wood and stone, plus other artworks. They're all part of the **Buddhist Culture Museum**, with panels telling the story of Gautama Buddha in the first person. At the back, the relic chamber displays what are said to be the cremated remains of Buddha's nose, brain, liver etc, all looking like fish roe in different colours.

#### Sacred Buddha Tooth Relic Stupa

Daily 9am–noon & 3–6pm

On **level 4** you finally encounter what all the fuss is ultimately about – the **Sacred Buddha Tooth Relic Stupa**. Some 3m in diameter, it sits in its own chamber behind glass panels and can't be inspected close up, though there is an accurate scale model at the front. The Maitreya Buddha is depicted at the front of the stupa, guarded by four lions, with a ring of 35 more Buddhas below; floor tiles around the stupa are said to be made of pure gold.

The roof garden

The temple's lovely **roof garden** has walls lined with twelve thousand tiny figurines of the Amitayus Buddha, but its centrepiece is "the largest cloisonné prayer wheel in the world", around 5m tall. Each rotation (clockwise, in case you have a go) dings a bell and represents the recitation of one sutra.

## West of South Bridge Road

The tight knot of streets between **Pagoda Street** and **Sago Street** were once Chinatown's nucleus, teeming with trishaws and food hawkers, while opium dens and brothels lurked within the shophouses. Now it's Chinatown at its most touristy, packed with souvenir sellers and foreigner-friendly restaurants. More down to earth, though workaday, is the modern **Chinatown Complex** at the western end of Sago Street, housing stalls selling silk, kimonos and household goods.

Until as recently as the 1950s, Sago Street was home to several death houses – rudimentary hospices where skeletal citizens saw out their final hours on rattan camp beds. Trishaw riders collecting the dead would, as one interviewee recounts at the Chinatown Heritage Centre, "put a hat on the corpse, put it onto the trishaw, and cycle all the way back to the coffin shop". The morbid theme survives at one of the few traditional businesses left, Nam's Supplies on 22 Smith St. It churns out paper versions of shirts, watches, mobile phones and laptops, to be burnt at Chinese funerals, all to ensure that the deceased don't lack creature comforts in the next life.

The heart of Chinatown recaptures something of the best of its original atmosphere around Chinese New Year, when streets are crammed with stalls selling festive branches of willow blossom, oranges, sausages and so-called waxed ducks, cooked and dried until they become almost flat.

## The Bukit Pasoh conservation area

In the southernmost corner of Chinatown, west of Kreta Ayer Road and accessible from Outram Park MRT, is an area packed with restored shophouses, worth a look not only for their beautifully painted facades, some in Art Deco style, and tilework, but also because the area is the evolving new Chinatown in microcosm. **Clan houses** were once the claim to fame of **Bukit Pasoh Road**, and they can be found on neighbouring **Keong Saik Road** too, though until recently it had a more unsavoury reputation as a red-light area. But while some clan houses have survived with their character intact, such as the Yee Clan Association at 9 Bukit Pasoh Rd, many more have morphed into boutiques or boutique hotels; the Gan Clan's building at 18/20 Bukit Pasoh Ro now rents out space to a posh restaurant. Other glimpses of the old Chinatown survive, for example, at 13 Keong Saik Rd, where you'll find a shrine that looks slightly too pristine for its own good. Unmissable at the northern end of the same road is the small **Sri Layan Sithi Vinayagar Temple**, with an unusually gaudy *gopuram* and occasional Chinese worshippers; it's managed by the Hindu association that runs the Chettiar Temple (see p.44).

## New Bridge Road and Eu Tong Sen Street

Chinatown's main shopping drag comprises southbound **New Bridge Road** and northbound **Eu Tong Sen Street**, along which are a handful of shopping malls. A number of *bak kwa* (barbecued pork) vendors can be found on New Bridge Road, close to Chinatown MRT. It's worth sampling the thin, flat, red squares of meat, coated with a sweet marinade, which give off a rich, smoky odour as they cook that is pure Chinatown. Chewing on your *bak kwa* provides the chance to contemplate two striking buildings across on Eu Tong Sen Street. On the left is the Art Deco **Majestic Theatre**, built in 1927 as a Chinese opera house by Eu Tong Sen, the wealthy businessman behind the Eu Yan Sang Chinese medicine company; note the five images of figures from Chinese opera on its facade. Today it has been sadly reduced to housing a few shops and a betting agency where punters can put money on horse races at the Turf Club in the north of the island. Just beside it and built a few years later, the **Yue Hwa Chinese Products Emporium** occupies the former *Great Southern Hotel*, once the tallest building here. In its fifth-floor nightclub, wealthy locals would drink liquor, smoke opium and pay to dance with so-called "taxi girls".

## Ann Siang Hill
**Ann Siang Hill** is a lane that leads southeast off South Bridge Road up the hill of the same name, where it forks into Club Street on the left and Ann Siang Road, which veers gently right. Despite being only a few paces removed from the hubbub of the main road, the hill is somehow a different realm, a cosy collection of gentrified shophouses with a villagey feel. Packed with swanky restaurants, cafés and bars, plus the occasional boutique, the area typifies the new Chinatown. At the southern end of the road, a short flight of steps leads up to **Ann Siang Hill Park**, a sliver of greenery whose only attraction is that it offers a short cut to Amoy Street, to which there's no direct road access from here.

## Club Street
The temple-carving shops on Club Street have long since gone, and hardly any of the clan associations and guilds whose presence gave the street its name remain. Most notable of all is the **Chinese Weekly Entertainment Club** at no. 76, on a side street also called Club Street. Flanked by roaring lion heads, this mansion-like building was constructed in 1891 as a venue where Peranakan tycoons could socialize, and still serves as a private club today.

## The Singapore City Gallery
URA Centre, 45 Maxwell Rd • Mon–Sat 9am–5pm • Free • ☎ 6321 8321, ⊕ www.ura.gov.sg/gallery
Town planning may not sound the most fascinating premise for a gallery, but then again, no nation remodels with such ambition as Singapore, with planners constantly erasing roads here and replacing one ultramodern complex with an even more souped-up development there. The latest grand designs for the island are exhibited west of Ann Siang Hill at the surprisingly absorbing **Singapore City Gallery**, within the government's Urban Redevelopment Authority headquarters.

The URA has rightly been criticized in the past for slighting Singapore's architectural heritage, so it is heartening that displays on the first and second floors make reassuring noises about the value of the venerable shophouses and colonial villas that remain. But the gallery's emphasis is more upon the future than the past, amply illustrated by the vast and intricate scale model of downtown Singapore, every row of shophouses, every roof of every building – including some not yet built – fashioned out of plywood. This and other scale models are turned out by a dedicated team whose workshop is sadly not open to the public, though you might catch a glimpse of them at work through the glass. Regular temporary exhibitions, some featuring best practice in international town planning, are another attraction on the ground floor.

## Amoy Street
**Amoy Street**, together with Telok Ayer Street, was designated a Hokkien enclave in the colony's early days (Amoy being the old name of Xiamen city in China's Fujian province). Long terraces of smartly refurbished shophouses flank the street, all featuring characteristic five-foot ways, or covered verandas, so called because they jut five feet out from the house. If you descend here from Ann Siang Hill Park, you'll emerge by the small **Sian Chai Kang Temple** at no. 66. With the customary dragons on the roof, it's dominated by huge urns, full to the brim with ash from untold numbers of burned incense sticks. Two carved stone lions guard the temple; the fancy red ribbons around their necks are said to attract prosperity.

## SHOPHOUSES

Though Singapore has no shortage of striking modern buildings, it's the island's rows of traditional **shophouses** that are its most distinctive architectural feature. Once often cramped and unsanitary, many were demolished in the years following independence, but since the 1980s whole streets of them have been declared conservation areas and handsomely restored.

As the name suggests, shophouses were originally a combination of shop and home, with the former occupying the ground floor of a two- or three-storey building; eventually many came to be built purely as townhouses, but the original name stuck. Unusually, the facade is always recessed at ground level, leaving a space here that, combined with adjoining spaces in a row of shophouses, would form a sheltered walkway at the front (the **"five-foot way"**, so named because of its minimum width) – hence the lack of pavements on Singapore's older streets. Another notable feature is that shophouses were built narrow and surprisingly deep. Behind the ground-floor shop or reception hall there might be a small courtyard, open to the sky, then yet another room; this layout can be seen at the Baba House (see p.68) and the Katong Antiques House (see p.94). Also, shophouses were usually built back to back, with tiny **alleyways** separating the rear sections of adjoining rows; it's down one such alleyway that the brothels of Desker Road (see p.52) are tucked away.

Shophouses began to be built from the mid-nineteenth century. The oldest ones are no longer standing, but slightly later examples, which still exist on and around Telok Ayer and Arab streets, for example, feature the characteristic shuttered windows and tiled roofs that continued to be used for several decades. Otherwise, their **decoration** was limited, say, to simple stuccowork, but by the turn of the last century, the shophouse had blossomed into a dizzy melange of Western and Eastern styles, which both European and local architects enjoyed blending. So-called Neoclassical, Chinese Baroque and Rococo shophouses featured decorative Corinthian columns, mini-pediments, fanlights, a riot of multicoloured tilework and stucco, even curvy gables. Local ornamentations included wooden trelliswork and eaves overhung with a row of fretted fascia boards, both often seen in Malay palaces; Peranakan *pintu pagar*, half-height swing doors like those in Wild West bars; and Chinese touches such as floral and animal motifs. You can see fine wedding-cake-like rows of shophouses in these styles around Joo Chiat Road in Katong (see p.94) and on Sam Leong and Petain roads at the northern edge of Little India (see p.52).

By the 1930s, global recession and prevailing artistic trends had caused a swing towards more sober Art Deco and modernist buildings, with simpler, geometrical facades often topped by a central flagpole. Shophouses with so-called Tropical Deco stylings continued to be built in Singapore after World War II, even though Art Deco had become old hat elsewhere, and there are quite a few examples in Chinatown, on South Bridge Road for example.

Boxy 1960s shophouses were the form's last hurrah. By the 1980s, shophouses had pretty much fallen out of favour as they were just too small to make efficient use of scarce land, though a semblance of the five-foot way lived on in some concrete shopping developments of the time.

As with heritage buildings the world over, today's surviving shophouses are often but a handsomely restored shell concealing insides that have been totally gutted and rejigged. Many no longer serve as shops, homes or clan houses, functioning instead as bars, beauty salons or offices.

### Telok Ayer Street

One street removed from Amoy Street is Telok Ayer Street, whose southern end starts near Tanjong Pagar MRT. The name, meaning "Watery Bay" in Malay, recalls the mid-nineteenth century when the street would have run along the shoreline. Nowadays, thanks to land reclamation, it's no closer to a beach than is Beach Road, but some of Singapore's oldest buildings cling on between the modern towers – temples and mosques where newly arrived immigrants and sailors thanked their god(s) for their safe passage.

The first building of note you come to if you walk up from the station is the square 1889 **Chinese Methodist Church**, whose design – portholes and windows adorned with white crosses and capped by a Chinese-temple-style roof – is a pleasing blend of East and West. Just beyond McCallum Street, the blue-and-white **Al-Abrar Mosque** is built on the spot where South Indian worshippers set up a makeshift thatched mosque in 1827.

## Thian Hock Keng Temple

158 Telok Ayer St • Daily 7.30am–5.30pm • Free • ☎ 6423 4616, ⓦ www.thianhockkeng.com.sg

From across the street, the immaculately restored **Thian Hock Keng Temple** looks spectacular: dragons stalk its broad roofs, while the entrance to the compound bristles with ceramic flowers, foliage and figures. Construction began in 1839 using materials imported from China, on the site of a small joss house where immigrants made offerings to Ma Zu, the queen of heaven. A statue of the goddess, shipped in from southern China in time for the temple's completion in 1842, stands in the centre of the main hall, flanked by the martial figure of Guan Yu on the right and physician Bao Sheng on the left.

Against the left wall, look out for an altar containing the curious figures of General Fan and General Xie. The two are said to have arranged to meet by a river bridge, but Xie was delayed; Fan waited doggedly in the appointed spot and drowned in a flash flood, which supposedly accounts for his black skin and the grimace on his face. When Xie finally arrived, he was filled with guilt and hanged himself – hence his depiction, with his tongue hanging down to his chest.

The temple stands in marked contrast to the ostentatious glass tower opposite, belonging to the Hokkien clan association, which manages it, but the gulf between the tower and the association's old headquarters is even more stark – it's the understated white building just to the left of the temple, with blue-shuttered windows and the year 1913 at the top of the facade.

## Nagore Durgha Shrine

**Museum** Daily 10am–6pm • Free

It's a testament to Singapore's multicultural nature that Thian Hock Keng's next-door neighbour is the charming brown-and-white **Nagore Durgha Shrine** to the Muslim ascetic, Shahul Hamid of Nagore. It was built by South Indian Muslims, as was the Jamae Mosque (see p.59), so it's no surprise that the buildings appear cut from the same cloth, so to speak; more significantly, the shrine is one of the oldest buildings in Singapore, having been finished in the late 1820s.

Part of the shrine now houses an excellent small **museum** of the history of Telok Ayer Street. The few simple artefacts and photographs also do a good job of unpacking the nuances of Muslim Indian identity in Singapore, a place where Hindu members of the Indian community are referred to by the part of India they emigrated from, whereas their Muslim counterparts have been lumped together under the banner of their faith.

## Ying Fo Fui Kun

98 Telok Ayer St • Daily 10am–10pm • Free

Beyond the junction with Cross Street, the **Ying Fo Fui Kun** is one of the smartest of Chinatown's surviving clan houses. Established in 1822 by Hakkas from Guangdong province, the place has narrowly avoided being swallowed up by the adjacent Far East Square complex. In its present orderly state, with an immaculate altar boasting gilt calligraphy and carvings, it's hard to imagine it having been the social hub of an entire community. The clan association that runs it has been undertaking membership drives to stop itself decaying into a senior citizens' club, a real danger in a country where provincial dialects – traditionally used as a marker of identity among the Chinese – have been on the decline since the 1970s after an often aggressive state campaign to standardize on Mandarin.

## Far East Square

**Far East Square** is a sort of heritage development that absorbs the northernmost section of Amoy Street into what is otherwise a rather mundane collection of shops, restaurants and offices on Cross Street. Also co-opted into the complex is the **Fuk Tak Chi Street**

**Museum**, 76 Telok Ayer St (daily 10am–10pm; free). This was once Singapore's oldest surviving temple, having been established by the Hakka and Cantonese communities in 1824; today it's a mere "street museum", its altar holding a model junk crewed by sailors in blue shorts. A diorama depicts Telok Ayer Street in its waterfront heyday, with pigtailed labourers taking part in a procession to the temple, depicted with a stage set up in front where opera performers are getting ready to strut their stuff.

### Hong Lim Park

North of Upper Pickering St and sandwiched between New Bridge Rd and South Bridge Rd

A few minutes' walk southwest from the Singapore River, **Hong Lim Park** amounts to not much more than a field ringed by trees, but it's of symbolic significance as the home of **Speakers' Corner**, at the park's New Bridge Road end. Since the site's designation in 2000, citizens have, in theory, been able to speak their minds here, just as people do at its famous exemplar in central London. This being Singapore, the reality is one of regulations that require you to register your intention to speak and that ban discussing religion or anything that could be deemed to provoke racial discontent. Despite this, the site's libertarian leanings have rubbed off on the park itself, which has regained some of its historic role as a site for rallies and demonstrations – a much-needed channel for public expression after the suffocation of the 1970s and 1980s.

### Boat Quay

The pedestrianized row of waterfront shophouses known as **Boat Quay**, almost at the old mouth of the Singapore River, is one of the island's notable urban regeneration successes. Derelict in the early 1990s, it's since become a thriving hangout, sporting a huge collection of restaurants and bars. The area's historical significance may be easier to appreciate through its street names – Synagogue Street nearby, for example, was indeed the site of Singapore's first synagogue.

### The Yueh Hai Ching Temple

30B Philip St

South of Boat Quay, the twin-shrined **Yueh Hai Ching Temple** (also called **Wak Hai Ching Bio**) nestles delightfully amid the towers where Chinatown shades into the Financial District. Built in the 1850s, it's yet another of Chinatown's former waterfront temples, and its name (Hai Ching means "calm sea") made it a logical target for early migrants who had arrived safely; an effigy of Tian Hou or Mazu, the queen of heaven and protector of seafarers, is housed in the right-hand shrine. The ornate roof is crammed with tiny depictions of Chinese village scenes.

---

**TAKING CHINESE TEA**

At two Tanjong Pagar teahouses, visitors can glean something of the intricacies of the deep Chinese connection with tea by taking part in a tea workshop lasting up to an hour. Participants are introduced to different varieties of tea and talked through the history of tea cultivation and the rituals of brewing and appreciating the drink. The water, for example, has to reach an optimum temperature that depends on which type of tea is being prepared; experts can tell its heat by the size of the rising bubbles, described variously as "sand eyes", "prawn eyes", "fish eyes", etc. Both venues also stock an extensive range of tea-related accoutrements such as tall "sniffer" cups used to savour the aroma of the brew before it is poured into squat teacups for drinking.

**Tea Chapter** 9–11 Neil Rd ☎6226 1175, 🌐tea -chapter.com.sg. Tea workshops for $20–30 per head, or around $10 per person for a quick tea-making demonstration and sampling session.

**Yixing Yuan Teahouse** 30–32 Tanjong Pagar Rd ☎6224 6961, 🌐yixingxuan-teahouse.com. Workshops from $20 per head for a group of at least five.

## Tanjong Pagar

The district of **Tanjong Pagar,** fanning out south of Chinatown between Neil and Maxwell roads, was once a veritable sewer of brothels and opium dens. Then it was earmarked for regeneration as a conservation area, following which dozens of shophouses were painstakingly restored and converted into bars, restaurants and shops, notably on Neil Road and Duxton Hill just south of it. A grander example of the area's architecture can be found right where South Bridge Road flows into Neil and Tanjong Pagar roads: here you'll easily spot the arches and bricked facade of the **Jinrikisha Building**, constructed at the turn of the last century as a terminus for rickshaws. They were superseded by trishaws after World War II, and today the building serves as office space – with a celebrity landlord, the Hong Kong actor Jackie Chan.

Tanjong Pagar's main sight is the **Baba House**, though as an architectural attention-grabber it's rivalled by the seven interlinked towers of the **Pinnacle@Duxton**, a showpiece public housing development that offers fine views over much of Singapore. One more attraction is worth a look: the **Red Dot Design Museum**, celebrating the best in product design and advertising.

### The Baba House

157 Neil Rd • Compulsory tours (4 weekly) – book at least a week in advance • Free • ☎ 6227 5731, Ⓦ nus.edu.sg/museum/baba • Outram Park MRT (Cantonment Rd exit), or bus #174 from Orchard Rd or Bras Basah Rd

The **Baba House** is one of Singapore's most impressive museums, because it is and isn't a museum: what you see is a Peranakan house from the turn of the last century, meticulously restored to its appearance in the late 1920s, a particularly prosperous time in its history.

The house is easily spotted as it's painted a vivid blue. Note the phoenixes and peonies on the eaves above the entrance, signifying longevity and wealth and, together, marital bliss. Even more eye-catching is the *pintu pagar*, the pair of swing doors with beautiful gilt and mother-of-pearl inlays.

#### The ground floor

Yet more exquisite inlay work is in evidence on the antique chairs in the **main hall**, used for entertaining guests. The altar here, among the last of its kind in Singapore, is backed by an exquisitely carved wood screen behind which the women of the household could eavesdrop on proceedings. Behind is the **family hall**, with an air well, open to the sky, in its midst. Note the original tilework depicting roses and tulips, indicating a European influence, and the gilt bats on the walls; the Mandarin term for bats is *bianfu*, and *fu* also happens to be the pronunciation of the Chinese character meaning "good fortune".

#### The upper floors

Upstairs at the front end of the house, the centrepiece of the **main bedroom** is an ornate wooden four-poster bed with gilt and red lacquer decorations, and bearing carved motifs such as musical instruments and yet more bats. Your guide will almost certainly open up the peephole in the floor, exposing a small shaft down to the main hall. The third storey, a later addition, is used for temporary exhibitions.

### The Pinnacle@Duxton

1 Cantonment Rd • Skybridge (50th floor) daily 9am–10pm but limited to 200 visitors per day • Call ☎ 6225 8842 or check Ⓦ pinnacleduxton.com.sg to find out if they have hit their daily quota • $5 (EZ-Link card required for payment) at the management office on the ground floor of Block 1g, the southernmost tower • Outram Park MRT or bus #167 from Orchard Rd/the Colonial District to the Maritime House bus stop

It's hard to believe that the **Pinnacle @ Duxton**, comprising seven slab-like towers that form a sickle when viewed from the air, is actually a state housing project – the result of

**OPPOSITE** SKYSCRAPERS AT RAFFLES PLACE >

an international design contest and, at fifty storeys high, the tallest in the country. The towers' facades boast an intricate arrangement of windows and balconies that gives them the appearance of a console packed with sliding controls and buttons. Two continuous decks called **Skybridges** link all seven towers; the upper Skybridge, right at the top of the structure, offers fascinating perspectives northeast over Chinatown – a serried collection of red-roofed shophouse terraces, viewed from this high up – and the Financial District; southwest to the port at Keppel, with Sentosa Island beyond; west to the Southern Ridges and Jurong; and northwest to Bukit Timah.

### The Red Dot Design Museum

28 Maxwell Rd • Mon, Tues & Fri 11am–6pm, Sat & Sun 11am–8pm, plus crafts market until midnight one Fri every month • ☎ 6327 8027, ⓦ red-dot.sg • $8/$4, though free during crafts market

Housed in a rather grand bright red building, the **Red Dot Design Museum** focuses on international product design and the creative use of illustration and multimedia, following the process from conceptualization all the way through to the realized work, be it a sports car or art installation. It's at its best during the monthly crafts market, **MAAD**, when local artists and designers set up stall to showcase their work, and local bands play in the bar area.

## The Financial District

The area south of the mouth of the Singapore River was swamp until land reclamation in the mid-1820s rendered it fit for building. Within just a few years, Commercial Square here had become the colony's busiest business address, boasting the banks, ships' chandlers and warehouses of a burgeoning trading port. The square was later Singapore's main shopping area until superseded by Orchard Road in the late 1960s; today the square, now called Raffles Place, forms the nucleus of Singapore's **Financial District** (also referred to as the **CBD**, or Central Business District). Until recently, if the area figured in the popular imagination at all, it would have been because of the rogue trader Nick Leeson, whose antics here brought about the **Barings Bank collapse** of 1995, though his transgressions seem like small beer when set against the global financial improprieties of recent years. East of here, the southern jaw of Marina Bay, Marina South, is home to yet more banks and features risk-taking in a different vein as the site of the striking *Marina Bay Sands* hotel and casino.

### Raffles Place

**Raffles Place** makes a good prelude to a stroll along the south bank of the river to Boat Quay (see p.67) or across Cavenagh Bridge to the Colonial District (see p.32), but the main reason to visit the Financial District itself is to feel like an ant in a canyon of skyscrapers. To see what things look like from the top of that canyon, the best place to head is One Raffles Place, the complex to the west of the square, with truly stunning views from its rooftop bar, *1-Altitude* (see p.140). The three roads that run southwest from Raffles Place – Cecil Street, Robinson Road and Shenton Way – are all chock-a-block with more high-rise banks and financial houses.

### Battery Road

Heading towards the river from Raffles Place, you come to Battery Road, whose name recalls the days when Fort Fullerton (named after Robert Fullerton, first governor of the Straits Settlements) and its attendant battery of guns used to stand to the east on the site of what is now the Fullerton Building. From here, Cavenagh Bridge (see p.35) is only a couple of minutes' walk away.

The main attraction here, Boat Quay aside, is the elegant **Fullerton Building**, worth viewing from Collyer Quay to the east for its facade fronted by sturdy pillars. This was one of Singapore's tallest buildings when it was constructed in 1928 as the headquarters for the General Post Office (a role it fulfilled until the mid-1990s). These days, the building is the luxury *Fullerton* hotel, whose atrium is worth a peek if only to admire the enormous columns within; the lighthouse that used to flash up on the roof is now a swanky Italian restaurant.

## Collyer Quay

**Collyer Quay** runs south along from what was the mouth of the Singapore River along the western shore of Marina Bay, linking the Colonial District with Raffles Quay and Shenton Way further south, both of which mark the former line of the seafront. Just east of Collyer Quay are the **One Fullerton** complex of bars and restaurants, run by the company behind the *Fullerton* hotel, and the **Merlion Park**, home to a cement statue of Singapore's national symbol, the **Merlion**. Half-lion, half-fish and wholly ugly, the creature reflects the island's maritime connections and the old tale concerning the derivation of its present name, derived from the Sanskrit "Singapura", meaning "Lion City".

### Clifford Pier and Customs House
Clifford Pier 80 Collyer Quay • Customs House 70 Collyer Quay

The Art Deco **Clifford Pier** building, long the departure point for boat trips out to Singapore's southern islands, was rendered defunct by the barrage that seals Marina Bay off from the sea. Now both it and the nearby **Customs House** building have been transformed into restaurant and leisure complexes, also run by the company that owns the *Fullerton* hotel; part of Clifford Pier forms the entrance to the hotel's even-pricier new sibling, the *Fullerton Bay*.

Incidentally, the curious low tower in front of the *Fullerton Bay*, topped by what looks like a giant slide-projector carousel, is a refurbished 1970s project that is now part of a substantial new office development, **OUE Bayfront**. Almost predictably, the tower houses a couple of restaurants.

### Lau Pa Sat
18 Raffles Quay • Daily 24hr

Arguably the best place for refreshments in the Financial District is the charmingly old-world **Lau Pa Sat**, literally "old market" – it was built in 1894 as a produce market, and was soon joined by a second market (which became the "new market") on the site of the present *Swissôtel Merchant Court* hotel, facing Clarke Quay. Also known by its original name, **Telok Ayer Market**, Lau Pa Sat has served as a hawker centre since the 1970s, except for an interregnum in the 1980s when tunnelling for the MRT required the octagonal cast-iron structure to be dismantled, then reassembled piece by piece. Aficionados of satay should turn up in the evening, when vendors set up in a row outside on Boon Tat Street.

GARDENS BY THE BAY, WITH MARINA BAY SANDS BEHIND

# Marina Bay

It's hard not to be awed by the audacity of Marina Bay, the project that has transformed downtown Singapore's seafront over two generations. An exorbitantly ambitious piece of civil engineering, it entailed the creation of three massive expanses of reclaimed land and a barrage to seal off the basins of the Singapore and Kallang rivers from the sea. The result is a seaside freshwater reservoir with a crucial role in reducing Singapore's dependence on Malaysian water supplies. The Marina Bay Sands casino resort dominates the area, with its museum and rooftop restaurants, and it is inevitably the focus of any visit to the bay, along with the extravagant new Gardens by the Bay next door. Close to the Padang, the Theatres on the Bay arts complex is worth a detour for its skyline views, with more of the same available from the oversized Ferris wheel that is the Singapore Flyer.

# Marina Centre

The large triangle of reclaimed land east of the Padang and the *Raffles Hotel*, robbing Beach Road of its beach, is officially called **Marina Centre**, though locals invariably invoke the names of the **Marina Square** or **Suntec City** malls when referring to it. Cross into it, and you immediately notice the jarring transition from the historical neighbourhoods to the west: ordinary amenities such as places of worship and schools are totally absent, and instead the area is dominated by the Suntec Convention Centre, plush offices and hotels, and the aforementioned malls. At the heart of the Suntec development is one minor sight – the huge, circular **Fountain of Wealth**, where there are free sound-and-light shows nightly between 8 and 9pm or so. The best reason to come, though, is to enjoy **views** of the Singapore cityscape from either the southern end of Marina Centre or the Singapore Flyer – or both.

## Esplanade – Theatres on the Bay

1 Esplanade Drive • Daily 10am till late, self-guided tours daily 10am–6pm • $10/$8 for tours, otherwise free • ☏ 6828 8377, Ⓦ www.esplanade.com

Opinion is split as to whether the two huge, spiked shells that roof the **Esplanade – Theatres on the Bay** project, just east of the Padang and the Esplanade Park, are peerless modernistic architecture or indulgent kitsch. They have variously been compared to kitchen sieves, hedgehogs, even durians (the preferred description among locals), though two giant insect eyes is perhaps the best comparison.

The venue boasts a concert hall, theatres, gallery space and, on the third floor, library@esplanade, with a wide range of arts-related books and other resources. It's possible to take a self-guided **iTour** of the building based around audiovisual content stored on a hand-held gizmo, but what lures most casual visitors are the views, particularly fine at dusk, across the bay to the Financial District and Marina Bay Sands.

**4**

## The Singapore Flyer

30 Raffles Ave, 10min east of Theatres on the Bay • Daily 8.30am–10.30pm; 30min • $29.50/$21 • ☏ 6333 3311, Ⓦ www.singaporeflyer.com

Standing a lofty 165m tall – the same elevation as the summit of Bukit Timah, the island's highest point, and about 30m taller than the London Eye – the **Singapore Flyer** falls slightly flat as an attraction, because it's simply not in the right place. From here the most atmospheric areas of old Singapore, including the remaining rows of shophouses in Chinatown and Little India, are largely obscured by a forest of somewhat interchangeable towers; better views can be had more cheaply from the Pinnacle@Duxton (see p.68), or from the rooftop bars such as *1-Altitude* (see p.140).

### The flight

The dollar-a-minute ride – billed as a **flight** – initially has you looking east over the Kallang district, where the grand new Sports Hub stadium complex is due to be completed in 2014. In the distance beyond the shipping lanes, Indonesia's Riau archipelago is so close yet much less connected to Singapore than Malaysia, thanks to the 1824 Anglo-Dutch treaty under which the British let the islands south of Singapore slip into the Dutch sphere of influence. Looking north, it's much more exciting to pick out the golden domes of the Sultan Mosque and the shophouses of Arab Street beyond the twin Gateway buildings on Beach Road. As your capsule reaches maximum height, you might just make out the low hump of Bukit Timah, topped with a couple of radio masts, on the horizon beyond Theatres on the Bay.

The descent affords good views of Marina Bay Sands and the Financial District. Originally the latter could be seen on the ascent, but *feng shui* concerns meant the wheel's direction had to be reversed (apparently having the capsules ascend pointing towards the banks' towers was channelling good luck up and away from the area).

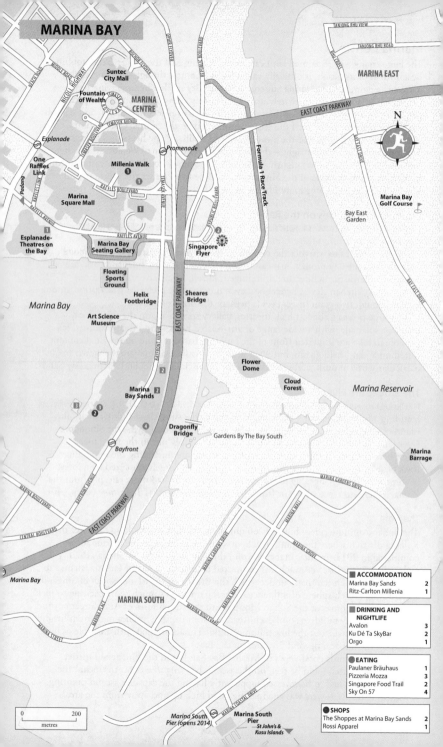

# Marina South

Unlike Marina Centre, which began to open for business in the 1990s, **Marina South** seemed to take years to get going. It had its own MRT station, yet few amenities except the so-so Marina City Park, and its main purpose was to serve as a conduit for part of the East Coast Parkway highway. Then came the bombshell of allowing casinos to set up in Singapore, which ultimately led to the building of **Marina Bay Sands**. Marina South is also the site of what's being billed as a new financial centre, which so far feels more like a spillover from the existing banking district than a separate entity.

## Marina Bay Sands

10 Bayfront Ave • ☎ 6688 8868, box office ☎ 6688 8826, ⓦ www.marinabaysands.com • Bayfront MRT, or bus #106 from Orchard Rd/Bras Basah Rd or #133 from Victoria St

Rarely does a building become an icon quite as instantly as the *Marina Bay Sands* hotel and casino, its three 55-floor towers topped and connected by a vast, curved-surfboard-like deck, the **SkyPark**. The most ambitious undertaking yet by its owners, Las Vegas Sands, it opened in April 2010 and quickly replaced the Merlion as the Singapore image of choice in the travel brochures, summing up the country's glitzy fascination with mammon. Even if you have no interest in the casino – open, naturally, 24/7 – the complex, which includes a convention centre, a shopping mall, two concert venues, numerous restaurants and its own museum, is well worth exploring. The hotel atrium, often so busy with people gawping that it feels like a busy train station concourse, is especially striking, the sides of the building sloping into each other overhead to give the impression of being inside a narrow glassy pyramid.

In the evening, a free laser show, **Wonder Full** (daily 8pm & 9.30pm, Fri & Sat extra show at 11pm; 15min), splays multicoloured beams from atop the hotel's towers onto Marina Bay, with fountains shooting up from below. Visible from around the bay, the display only looks at all interesting if you're at the hotel itself.

**4**

---

## THE MARINA BAY PROJECT

**Marina Bay** can be viewed as yet another triumph, perhaps the most impressive, of Singapore's long-term urban planning. Yet there is an alternative view, namely that the project has proceeded in a slightly haphazard manner. The original idea had been to create a new downtown area for the tiny island. To that end, **Marina Centre** became the first zone to be reclaimed from the sea, in the 1970s and 1980s. Its malls and hotels were already beginning to open in the early 1990s, and development there was crowned by the opening of Esplanade – Theatres by the Bay in 2002.

But back in 1987, Lee Kuan Yew, fed up with constant bickering over the pricing of water supplies that Malaysia was piping to Singapore via the Causeway, had floated another idea: what if land reclamation, combined with a dam, could create an enormous coastal **reservoir**? The scheme, together with smaller counterparts elsewhere, would reduce or end this potentially crippling dependency. Still, it wasn't until seventeen years later that the government would invite companies to tender to build the **Marina Barrage**. One year after that came the announcement that casinos were going to be licensed in Singapore. With the successful launch of *Marina Bay Sands*, **Marina South** finally seemed to have found its *raison d'être*.

The last piece of the jigsaw was the sheer amount of green space built into the area, in the form of gardens, plus a golf course at **Marina East**. On the face of it, this offers a poor return on the huge amount of taxpayers' money pumped into creating Marina Bay, unless you regard the greenery as an environmentally worthwhile gesture. The reality may, as is usually the case in Singapore, be one of pragmatism: the vision of a new downtown had to be radically scaled back because the reservoir's arrival curtailed the density of the surrounding buildings – cleanliness of the waters being now the paramount issue.

### The SkyPark

Observation deck Mon–Thurs 9.30am–10pm, Fri–Sun 9.30am–11pm • $20/$14, tickets and access from box office on basement 1 of tower 3, at the northern end of the complex

From what would have been an impossible vantage point, high above the sea before the creation of Marina Bay, the observation deck of the **SkyPark** affords superb views over Singapore's Colonial District on one side and the conservatories of the new Gardens by the Bay project on the other. Unfortunately tickets are overpriced, and you only get up close to one of the SkyPark's iconic features, its 150m infinity pool, if you buy a ticket to coincide with a guided tour (daily at 10am, 2pm & 9pm; 15min). However, if you treat yourself to a meal or a drink at any SkyPark restaurant or bar, you don't need a ticket, and prices aren't always as sky high as you might assume (see p.140).

### The ArtScience Museum

At the northern end of the complex, close to the helix footbridge that links the area with the Singapore Flyer and Marina Centre • Daily 10am–10pm, last admission 9pm • Prices vary, generally $15 for one exhibition or $28 for all areas

The **ArtScience Museum**, perhaps meant to temper the relentless obsession with consumption everywhere else in the complex, is easily spotted: its shape is meant to represent a stylized lotus blossom, though from certain angles it looks more like a stubby-fingered hand in concrete. The museum's remit is to decode the connections between art and science, but its permanent gallery is so tiny and full of waffle as to be almost laughable. In practice it majors on world-class travelling exhibitions, sometimes only tenuously linked to the museum's supposed theme – crowd-pullers have included artefacts salvaged from the *Titanic*, a collection of works by Salvador Dalí and the self-explanatory Harry Potter: The Exhibition.

## Gardens by the Bay South

18 Marina Gardens Drive • ☎ 6420 6848, ⓦ www.gardensbythebay.org.sg • Daily 5am–2am; conservatories 9am–9pm • Free admission; OCBC Skyway $5/$3; conservatories $28/$15; last ticket sales at 8pm • Bayfront MRT(enter via the Dragonfly Bridge from Marina Bay Sands) or bus #400 (3 hourly) from Marina Bay MRT to the front entrance

From afar, two vast conservatories, roofs arched like the backs of foraging dinosaurs, announce the southern section of **Gardens by the Bay**. Touted as a second botanic garden for Singapore, it is split into three chunks around Marina Bay; the southern area, next to *Marina Bay Sands*, is the largest and very much the centrepiece.

One conservatory houses Mediterranean and African flora, the highlight being the stands of small, bizarrely shaped **baobab** trees; less impressive are the collections of flowering plants, so tidy that they look like a formal display in a well-kept European park. The neighbouring conservatory nurtures **cloud forest** of the kind found on Southeast Asia's highest peaks, and includes a 35m "mountain" covered in ferns, rhododendrons and insect-eating sundews and butterworts.

The gardens' other big draw is the **Supertree Grove**, an array of towers resembling gigantic golf tees and sheathed in a sort of red trelliswork. Their sides are planted with climbers, ferns and orchids, which poke out from the gaps in the trellis. The towers don't look so alluring from close up; more exciting is to walk the long, slightly wobbly **OCBC Skyway**, arcing between the tallest two supertrees high up and providing good views over the gardens and around Marina Bay. At night the supertrees are lit up using power from their own solar cells, and take centre stage in free **light shows** at 7.45pm and 8.45pm.

## The Marina Barrage

8 Marina Gardens Drive • ☎ 6514 5959, ⓦ www.pub.gov.sg/Marina/ • Unrestricted access to barrage and grounds; Singapore Sustainability Gallery daily except Tues 9am–9pm • Free • Bus #400 (3 hourly) from Marina Bay MRT

As a feat of engineering, the **barrage** at the southeastern corner of Marina Bay is undoubtedly impressive, but it's underwhelming to walk along the top of the dam, a straight, 330m-long concrete structure. The barrage's modus operandi is simple: it only allows water to flow seaward, driven either by pumps or, when the tide is low or Marina Bay is swollen by rains, using the force of gravity. As a result, the salinity of Marina Bay fell inexorably once the dam commenced operations in 2008, to the point that it is now a freshwater reservoir.

West of the dam is the barrage's control complex, whose enormous **green roof** – carpeted with grass and surrounding an oval-shaped central atrium – is the key attraction for many locals. It's popular as a spot to picnic and fly kites in the cool of the evening, with great vistas back towards the Singapore Flyer and the glittering skyline of the Financial District and Marina Centre.

### The Singapore Sustainability Gallery

Also here is the **Singapore Sustainability Gallery**, an interactive museum emphasizing the island's eco-friendly credentials. Perhaps the best bit of the museum is the model of the barrage and its sluice gates, describing its role in the government's much-vaunted (but also much-criticized – see p.165) flood management system. Otherwise, some of the museum's claims have the ring of green-wash – this is, after all, a tropical island that hardly uses solar power, relying instead on fossil fuels to drive its generators.

## Marina East: Bay East Garden

Western shore of Marina East • Daily 24hr (but south entrance from Marina Barrage 7am–7pm) • Bus #158 southbound from Aljunied or Mountbatten MRT to the north gate at Rhu Cross, or walk from Marina Barrage to the south gate

The sole attraction in **Marina East** – the third "jaw" of Marina Bay – is **Bay East Garden**, the east wing of Gardens by the Bay, and a plain Jane compared to its southern neighbour. There are plans to put in themed gardens, including one that will feature food crops, but at the time of writing no dates had been set for work to begin; for now, come here to chill out, stroll and enjoy more views of the jagged skyline.

**4**

BOTANIC GARDENS

# Orchard Road and the Botanic Gardens

It would be hard to conjure an image more at odds with the present reality of Orchard Road than historian Mary Turnbull's depiction of a colonial-era "country lane lined with bamboo hedges and shrubbery, with trees meeting overhead". A hundred years ago, merchants here for their daily constitutionals would have strolled past rows of nutmeg trees, followed at a discreet distance by their manservants. Today, Orchard Road is lined with symbols of consumption: huge, glitzy shopping malls (see p.151) and worthwhile restaurants and bars, either in the malls themselves or housed in a number of top-flight hotels. The bucolic allure of the plantation avenue of old survives 1500m west of its start, where you'll find the area's one true sight, Singapore's excellent Botanic Gardens.

Orchard Road channels eastbound traffic from Tanglin Road all the way to Bras Basah and Selegie roads, 3km away near the Colonial District; all **buses** along Orchard Road return west along Penang Road, Somerset Road, Grange Road and Orchard Boulevard.

# Orchard Road

Although the parade of designer names on **Orchard Road** – often with multiple outlets for each brand – is dazzling, it's noteworthy that the area has not been totally untouched by the malaise afflicting city-centre shopping precincts the world over, losing trade to malls elsewhere in the downtown area and all over the island. Perhaps with this in mind, Singapore's planners have put Orchard Road through a costly makeover in recent years, revamping walkways and adding three new malls. The most striking, **Ion Orchard**, right above Orchard MRT, has a bulgy glass frontage vaguely reminiscent of Theatres on the Bay, and is topped by a tower of luxury apartments. Just about the only building of significant age left on Orchard Road itself can be glimpsed west of Scotts Road, where the **Thai embassy** has its origins in the purchase of a mansion here by the Siamese king in the late nineteenth century. Today the embassy cuts a distinguished but lonely figure, dwarfed by the modern architecture around it.

## Dhoby Ghaut

The **Dhoby Ghaut** area, at the eastern tip of Orchard Road, is where Indian *dhobies* (laundrymen) used to wash clothes in the Stamford Canal, which once ran along Orchard and Stamford roads.

### Cathay building

2 Handy Rd

While the days of the *dhobies* are long gone, something of the past survives in the **Cathay building** (ⓦwww.cathay.org.sg), home to the company behind one of Singapore's oldest cinema chains. The building houses a multiplex cinema and boasts a 1939 Art Deco facade that looks better than ever after a recent remodelling which saw the tower behind demolished and, unusually, replaced by a smaller construction.

### The Cathay Gallery

Level 2, the Cathay building • Mon–Sat 11am–7pm • Free • ☏ 6732 7332, ⓦ www.thecathaygallery.com.sg

The Cathay Gallery offers a window into the past by displaying memorabilia of the Cathay Organization's eight decades in the movie business, including its heyday in the 1950s and 1960s, when the company made its own Chinese- and Malay-language films.

## The Istana

A three-minute walk west along Orchard Road from Dhoby Ghaut MRT takes you past the Plaza Singapura mall, beyond which stern-looking soldiers guard the main gate of Singapore's **Istana** (Malay for "palace"), built in 1869. With ornate cornices, elegant louvred shutters and a high mansard roof, the building was the official residence of Singapore's British governors; now it's home to Singapore's president, a ceremonial role for which elections are nonetheless contested. The first Sunday of the month (except in July and August) sees a changing-of-the-guard ceremony at the main gate at 5.45pm. Visitors can only enter the grounds five days a year ($1, or $2 with access to part of the Istana buildings); details on ⓦwww.istana.gov.sg.

## The Tan Yeok Nee Mansion

101 Penang Rd • Not open to the public

Across Orchard Road from the Istana is a little architectural curiosity, the **Tan Yeok Nee Mansion**, built in the 1880s in traditional South Chinese style for a wealthy Teochew merchant who dealt in pepper and gambier (a resin used in tanning). Featuring ornate

**5**

roofs and massive granite pillars, this courtyard house served as headquarters to the Singapore Salvation Army from 1940 until 1991, and is now home to the Singapore offshoot of the University of Chicago's business school.

## Emerald Hill

Not ten minutes' walk west of the Istana, a number of architecturally notable houses have survived the bulldozers at **Emerald Hill**, behind the Centrepoint mall. The hill was granted to Englishman William Cuppage in 1845 and was for some years afterwards the site of a large nutmeg plantation. After his death in 1872, the land was subdivided and sold off, much of it to members of the Peranakan community. Walk up Emerald Hill Road today and you'll see exquisite houses from the era, in the so-called Chinese Baroque style, typified by the use of coloured ceramic tiles, carved swing doors, shuttered windows and pastel-shaded walls with fine plaster mouldings. Unsurprisingly, quite a few now host trendy restaurants and bars, with a few more in a tastelessly jazzed-up row of shophouses called Cuppage Terrace, close to the Centrepoint mall.

## The Goodwood Park Hotel
22 Scotts Rd

Malls line the initial stretch of Scotts Road, leading north from Orchard MRT towards Newton Circus, before giving way to the impressive **Goodwood Park Hotel**, with gleaming walls and a distinctive squat, steeple-like tower. Having started life in 1900 as the Teutonia Club for German expats, it was commandeered by the British Custodian

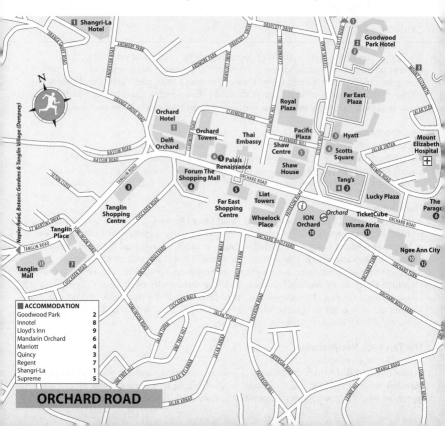

| ■ ACCOMMODATION | |
|---|---|
| Goodwood Park | 2 |
| Innotel | 8 |
| Lloyd's Inn | 9 |
| Mandarin Orchard | 6 |
| Marriott | 4 |
| Quincy | 3 |
| Regent | 7 |
| Shangri-La | 1 |
| Supreme | 5 |

**ORCHARD ROAD**

of Enemy Property with the outbreak of war across Europe in 1914, and didn't open again until 1918, after which it served for several years as a function hall. In 1929, it became a hotel, though by 1942 it and the *Raffles* (designed by the same architect, incidentally) were lodging Japanese officers; perhaps fittingly, the *Goodwood Park* was later used for war-crimes trials. Today the hotel remains one of the classiest in town and is a well-regarded venue for a British-style tea.

## The Botanic Gardens

1 Cluny Rd • Daily 5am–midnight • Free; website lists weekend tours of some sections plus concerts, also free • ☎ 6471 7138, ⓦ sbg.org .sg • Tanglin gate: bus #7 from Arab St area or #174 from Chinatown, both via Penang Rd/Somerset Rd. Bukit Timah Rd entrance: Botanic Gardens MRT or bus #66 or #170 from Little India, or #171 from Somerset Rd

Singapore has long made green space an integral part of the island's landscape, but none of its parks comes close to matching the refinement of the **Singapore Botanic Gardens**. Founded in 1859, the gardens were where the Brazilian seeds that gave rise to the great rubber plantations of Malaya were first nurtured in 1877. Henry Ridley, named the gardens' director the following year, recognized the financial potential of rubber and spent the next twenty years persuading Malayan plantation-owners to convert to this new crop, an obsession that earned him the nickname "Mad" Ridley. In later years the gardens became a centre for the breeding of new orchid hybrids.

Recent additions have extended the park all the way north to Bukit Timah Road, where the Botanic Gardens MRT station (a long journey from downtown on the Circle

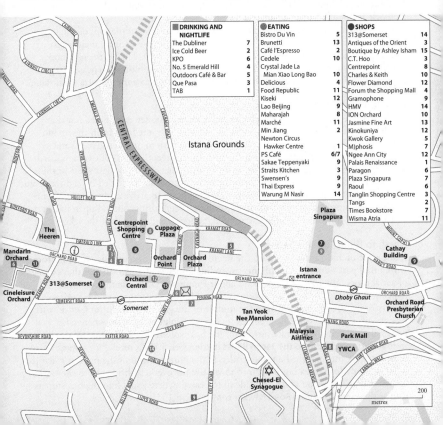

| ■ DRINKING AND NIGHTLIFE | | ● EATING | | ● SHOPS | |
|---|---|---|---|---|---|
| The Dubliner | 7 | Bistro Du Vin | 5 | 313@Somerset | 14 |
| Ice Cold Beer | 2 | Brunetti | 13 | Antiques of the Orient | 3 |
| KPO | 6 | Café l'Espresso | 2 | Boutique by Ashley Isham | 15 |
| No. 5 Emerald Hill | 4 | Cedele | 10 | C.T. Hoo | 3 |
| Outdoors Café & Bar | 5 | Crystal Jade La | | Centrepoint | 8 |
| Que Pasa | 3 | Mian Xiao Long Bao | 10 | Charles & Keith | 10 |
| TAB | 1 | Delicious | 4 | Flower Diamond | 12 |
| | | Food Republic | 11 | Forum the Shopping Mall | 4 |
| | | Kiseki | 12 | Gramophone | 9 |
| | | Lao Beijing | 9 | HMV | 14 |
| | | Maharajah | 8 | ION Orchard | 10 |
| | | Marché | 11 | Jasmine Fine Art | 13 |
| | | Min Jiang | 2 | Kinokuniya | 12 |
| | | Newton Circus | | Kwok Gallery | 5 |
| | | Hawker Centre | 1 | M)phosis | 7 |
| | | PS Café | 6/7 | Ngee Ann City | 12 |
| | | Sakae Teppenyaki | 9 | Palais Renaissance | 1 |
| | | Straits Kitchen | 3 | Paragon | 6 |
| | | Swensen's | 9 | Plaza Singapura | 7 |
| | | Thai Express | 9 | Raoul | 6 |
| | | Warung M Nasir | 14 | Tanglin Shopping Centre | 3 |
| | | | | Tangs | 2 |
| | | | | Times Bookstore | 7 |
| | | | | Wisma Atria | 11 |

**5**

Line) offers a route to the least interesting part of the gardens; the itinerary that follows assumes the classic approach up Tanglin and Napier roads to the **Tanglin gate** at the start of Cluny Road. Note that if you're feeling peckish while visiting, there are plenty of restaurants and cafés in the gardens itself or nearby at **Tanglin village** (see p.132).

### Into the gardens

Once through the Tanglin gate, you can take a sharp right up the slope to the **Botany Centre** just ahead, a large building containing an information desk with free garden maps. Alternatively, continue straight down the path from the gate, lined with frangipanis, casuarinas and the odd majestic banyan tree, for five minutes to reach the tranquil main lake, nearly as old as the gardens themselves. At the lake's far end, paths run through a small tract of surviving rainforest to the **ginger garden**, packed with flowering gingers as exotic and gaudy as anything you could hope to see in the tropics.

### The National Orchid Garden

Daily 8.30am–7pm, last admission 6pm • $5/$1

A feast of blooms of almost every hue are on show at the National Orchid Garden. Most orchids anchor themselves on trees in the wild, so it's initially odd to see them thriving here at ground level in specially adapted beds. There's an entire section of orchids named after dignitaries and celebrities who have visited; *Dendrobium Margaret Thatcher* turns out to be a severe pink with two of its petals looking like twisted ribbons, while *Vandaenopsis Nelson Mandela* is a reassuring warm yellowy-brown. Looking slightly out of place is a colonial-era house, **Burkill Hall**, with more than a hint of mock Tudor about it; the gardens' director once lived here.

Be sure to visit the superb **cool house**, mimicking conditions at the tops of equatorial mountains; through its mists you'll spot some stunning slipper orchids, their petals forming a pouch below, as well as insectivorous pitcher plants. Finally, the gift shop stocks an incredible range of orchid paraphernalia, including blossoms encased in glass paperweights or plated with 24-carat gold (or even silvery rhodium for extra snob value).

### Back to Tanglin gate

By now you've seen the best of what the gardens have to offer, and there's not that much to be gained by continuing north. An alternative route back from the orchid garden involves proceeding up the Maranta Avenue path to one of the park's most stunning trees, a 47m *jelawai*; this and several other exceptionally tall trees are fitted with lightning conductors. Close by, to the right, is one of the loveliest spots in the gardens, a grassy area with a 1930s bandstand in the middle, encircled by eighteen rain trees for shade. From here you can either go straight on to arrive at the Botany Centre, passing Holttum Hall, where a **museum** of the gardens' history should open in late 2013, or head downhill through the sundial garden to end up back at the lake.

### North to Bukit Timah Road

Exiting the orchid garden, head up the boardwalk to enter a second patch of rainforest with a trail past numbered highlights, including a spectacular banyan tree that's a mass of aerial roots. The trail and forest end above **Symphony Lake**, where occasional concerts are staged. Nearby are another colonial house, once home to the gardens' deputy director, and, marooned in the middle of the gardens, the **Visitor Centre**, with its own gift shop and café. Next comes the dreary **Evolution Garden**, where fake petrified trees help to illustrate how plant life has evolved over millennia. With children in tow, you could head to the **Jacob Ballas garden** (see p.157), or else it's several minutes' walk through the bamboo garden at the northern end of the park to reach the MRT station. To catch a bus back into town, use the overhead bridge from the station across to Dunearn Road on the far side of the canal, where you'll find the bus stop as well as the excellent **Adam Road hawker centre** (see p.133).

SUNGEI BULOH WETLAND RESERVE

# Northern Singapore

North of the downtown area, it's still possible to glimpse Singapore's wilder side. True, this sector is as packed with satellite new towns as elsewhere and suburbs shadow the major thoroughfares, but the island's core remains dominated by thirty square kilometres of rainforest and reservoirs, forming a central nature reserve. Jungle hikes are perfectly feasible and not too taxing, and there are many other points of interest, too, such as Memories at Old Ford Factory, a museum housed in the building where the British surrendered to the Japanese, and Bukit Brown, one of Singapore's last remaining historic cemeteries. Up in the far north of the island is the area's main lure, Singapore's highly regarded zoo (and its Night Safari spin-off), as well as the Sungei Buloh wetland reserve.

# Bukit Timah

Making up the western fringes of the central nature reserve, **Bukit Timah** is Singapore's highest hill and the ideal place to tackle Singapore's last remaining pocket of primary rainforest. It's most easily reached from downtown by catching a bus from Little India up Bukit Timah Road, which traverses leafy suburbs en route to Johor Bahru (it was the main road to the Causeway until superseded by the Bukit Timah Expressway). Some 9km on from Little India, the road becomes Upper Bukit Timah Road and soon arrives at the hill itself.

Incidentally, Bukit Timah is Malay for "hill [of] tin]", though why it has this name is a mystery as its only mineral resource is granite, as two quarry lakes within this part of the reserve attest. Locals often refer to the peak as "Bukit Timah Hill", a deliberate tautology to distinguish it from the surrounding district, also known as Bukit Timah.

## The hill

Hindhede Drive • Visitor Centre exhibition 8.30am–5pm; access to the hill is unrestricted, though walkers are strongly discouraged from entering after dark • ⓦ nparks.gov.sg • Free • Bus #171 from Somerset and Scotts roads, or #67 or #170 from opposite Little India MRT (follow signs for bus stop 1/Exit A); ask to be let off opposite Bukit Timah Shopping Centre, from where you use the overhead footbridge to the shopping centre, then curl around to the far side of the building to another bridge over Jalan Anak Bukit, and finally head left to Hindhede Drive; buses back to town use the stop on Jalan Anak Bukit

The nature reserve at Bukit Timah was established in 1883 by Nathaniel Cantley, then superintendent of the Botanic Gardens. Wildlife abounded in this part of Singapore in the mid-nineteenth century, when the natural historian **Alfred Russel Wallace** came here to do fieldwork; he later observed that "in all my subsequent travels in the East I rarely if ever met with so productive a spot". Wallace also noted the presence of tiger traps, but by the 1930s Singapore's tigers had met their end (the Visitor Centre displays a photo of the last specimen to be shot on the island).

**Long-tailed macaques** remain easy to spot, though that does not necessarily mean they are thriving. The central nature reserve has been dissected by highways, degrading its habitat, and when wild fruits are not in season, the macaques may emerge to scavenge around the houses at the base of the hill, peeking in bins for discarded food.

Otherwise, what really impresses is the dipterocarp forest itself, with its towering **emergents** – trees that have reached the top of the jungle canopy as a result of a lucky break, a fallen tree allowing enough light through to the forest floor to nurture saplings to maturity.

### Exploring the reserve

Four colour-coded **trails** head uphill from the Visitor Centre (the information counter has maps, also downloadable from the "nature reserves" section of ⓦnparks.gov.sg). All require only a moderate level of fitness, though three share a very steep start up a sealed road (the exception, the green trail, meanders along the side of the hill before rejoining the others). Most people tackle the red trail (30min), which is the road up to the summit at a paltry 164m; a flight of narrow steps halfway along – the Summit Path – offers a short cut to the top. Note that it's also possible to access the forest from Dairy Farm Nature Park (see p.86).

# Memories at Old Ford Factory

351 Upper Bukit Timah Rd, 1km northwest of Bukit Timah • Mon–Sat 9am–5.30pm, Sun noon–5.30pm • $3 • ⓦ moff.nas.sg • Bus #171 from Somerset and Scotts roads, or #67 or #170 from opposite Little India MRT; get off beyond the Hillside apartment complex, four stops on from Bukit Timah Shopping Centre

The old Ford car factory was the first plant of its type in Southeast Asia when it opened in Bukit Timah in October 1941. But by February 1942 the Japanese had arrived, and on February 15 Lt Gen Percival, head of the Allied forces in Singapore, surrendered to Japan's General Yamashita in the factory's boardroom. Today the Art Deco building

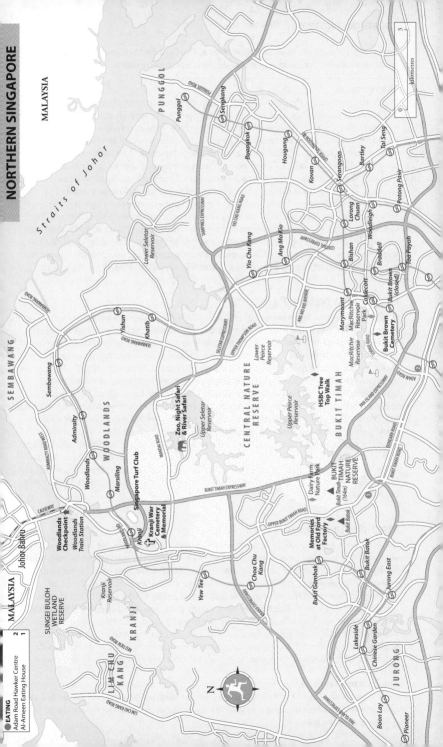

# NORTHERN SINGAPORE

**MALAYSIA**

Straits of Johor

MALAYSIA

Johor Bahru

SUNGEI BULOH WETLAND RESERVE

LIM CHU KANG

KRANJI

Kranji Reservoir

CAUSEWAY

Woodlands Checkpoint
Woodlands Train Station

SEMBAWANG

Sembawang

Admiralty

WOODLANDS

Woodlands

Marsiling

Yishun

Khatib

Singapore Turf Club

Kranji War Cemetery & Memorial

Kranji

Yew Tee

Choa Chu Kang

Bukit Gombak

Bukit Batok

Lower Seletar Reservoir

Zoo, Night Safari & River Safari

Upper Seletar Reservoir

CENTRAL NATURE RESERVE

Lower Peirce Reservoir

Upper Peirce Reservoir

HSBC Tree Top Walk

BUKIT TIMAH

Dairy Farm Nature Park

BUKIT TIMAH NATURE RESERVE

Bukit Timah (164m)

Memories at Old Ford Factory

Jurong East

Chinese Garden

Lakeside

Boon Lay

Pioneer

JURONG

Yio Chu Kang

Ang Mo Kio

Bishan

Marymount

MacRitchie Reservoir Park

MacRitchie Reservoir

Caldecott

Bukit Brown Cemetery

Bukit Brown (closed)

Braddell

Toa Payoh

Lorong Chuan

Woodleigh

Serangoon

Kovan

Hougang

Buangkok

Sengkang

Punggol

PUNGGOL

Potong Pasir

Tai Seng

Bartley

0  1  2  3
kilometres

N

houses a little wartime museum, **Memories at Old Ford Factory**, making good use of military artefacts, period newspapers and oral history recordings.

### The museum

While the surrenders that bookended the Japanese occupation obviously get some attention, as do the lives of British POWs (see p.95), it's with its coverage of the civilian experience of the war that the museum really scores. Predictably, the occupiers mounted cultural indoctrination campaigns, and displays recall how locals were urged to celebrate Japanese imperial birthdays, and how Japanese shows were put on at Victoria Memorial Hall. This was not a benign intellectual sort of occupation, however. Stung by local Chinese efforts to raise funds for China's defence against Japan, the Japanese launched **Sook Ching**, a brutal purge of thousands (the exact number is unknown) of Singapore Chinese thought to hold anti-Japanese sentiments. These violent events are illustrated by, among other items, some moving sketches by Chia Chew Soo, who witnessed members of his own family being killed in 1942. Not least among the privations of occupation were food shortages, as recalled by displays on wartime crops – speak to any Singaporean above a certain age today, and chances are they can tell you of having to survive on stuff like tapioca during those dark years.

## Dairy Farm Nature Park

Free • ⓦ nparks.gov.sg • Bus #171 from Somerset and Scotts roads, or #67 or #170 from opposite Little India MRT (on any of these, get off after Bukit Panjang Methodist Church, then take a 5min walk north for Dairy Farm Road, and another 10min walk east to reach the Wallace Education Centre) or #700/#700A from Orchard or Newton MRT to the start of Petir Rd, opposite the Wallace Education Centre

**Dairy Farm Nature Park** is a grand name for what is simply the northern fringe of the Bukit Timah nature reserve. The main reason to come is to tackle a slightly longer alternative route up Bukit Timah, the **Dairy Farm loop**, beginning at a long, low building called the **Wallace Education Centre** along Dairy Farm Road. As displays explain, the centre was once a cowshed at, bizarrely, the area's now defunct dairy farm, one of very few – if not the only one – in the tropics that wasn't up a mountainside.

Steps close to the building are the start of the loop, which forks after just a few minutes; both branches eventually join the yellow trail marked on Bukit Timah maps and will get you to the summit in 30 to 45 minutes. If you turn right where the trail forks, you can later ascend via a separate branch trail called the **Seraya loop**, which can boast good views over a quarry lake if the vegetation at the vantage point has recently been hacked back.

## MacRitchie Reservoir Park

Main entrance at the eastern end of Lornie Rd • No formal hours • Free • ☎ 6468 5736, ⓦ nparks.gov.sg • Caldecott MRT, then a 5min walk west along Toa Payoh Rise and up Thomson Rd to reach entrance, or bus #166 from opposite Little India MRT, or bus #167 from Newton MRT

In the southeastern corner of the central reserve, **MacRitchie Reservoir** is one of the oldest of Singapore's reservoirs – it was created in the 1860s – and the closest to downtown, Marina Bay excepted. The manicured gardens surrounding the entrance on Lornie Road don't set the right note for a nature park, but it's easy enough to get away from them on flattish trails that skirt the glassy waters and then take you into the jungle (allow half a day for the longest loop). Much more relaxed are the water's-edge boardwalks a short walk to the west and east of the car park. A map of the trails can be downloaded from ⓦ nparks.gov.sg, which also lists details of monthly guided walks.

### The Treetop Walk

Close to the western end of Island Club Rd • Daily 9am–5pm (Sat & Sun from 8.30am) • Free • To hike there, turn right from the entrance and use the trails that begin at the eastern edge of the water (1hr 30min one-way); alternatively catch bus #166 or #167 to the start of Island Club Rd, then walk in (45min)

In the jungle on the far side of the reservoir, some 2.5km from the Lornie Road entrance as the crow flies, is the **Treetop Walk**, a 250m circular trail suspended above ground, giving a monkey's-eye view of the forest. It is a bit of a hassle to reach, but as long as there are no noisy school parties bustling across, you've a decent chance of spotting some birdlife.

### Kayaking

Tues–Sun 9am–6pm • Contact Paddle Lodge ☎ 6258 0057 • $15 per kayak for 1hr

You can get out on MacRitchie's waters in a **kayak**, but the experience is a bit of a mixed bag. With a locally recognized kayaking certificate, people can venture along half the reservoir's length, but only using monotonous, straight lanes; unqualified kayakers are restricted to a small area at the reservoir's eastern end. To find out more, talk to Paddle Lodge in the green building a short walk east of the entrance and car park.

## The Bukit Brown cemetery

Main entrance opposite the golf course at the western end of Lornie Rd; walk in via Kheam Hock Rd and then left down Lorong Halwa • Any westbound bus from Lornie Rd opposite the MacRitchie Reservoir entrance, or #157 from Toa Payoh MRT

Only 2km west of the entrance to MacRitchie Reservoir Park, the Chinese cemetery at **Bukit Brown** is imbued with a sense of history, of how Singapore society and customs have changed and are still changing. The site, threatened with redevelopment, has been the focus of a concerted campaign to save it, one by-product of which is that volunteers sometimes lead free half-day walking **tours** that anyone can turn up for (search the web for the latest, or try ⓦ bukitbrown.com). Even if you don't come on a tour, the cemetery is well worth wandering for an hour or more: the grounds are lush, there's the chance to spot wildlife and the tombs are fascinating for their architecture. On a practical note, be sure to bring sunscreen and mosquito repellent.

### The site

The cemetery gates are just five minutes' walk in from Lornie Road, beyond which the graves are clustered across many low mounds. Much of the cemetery is wooded, with some majestic, mature trees covered in ferns, and it's not uncommon to see kingfishers flitting about and, of course, long-tailed macaques. One of the few times of year when Bukit Brown gets busy is during April's **Qing Ming** festival, when people leave offerings of food and paper money at the tombs of their ancestors.

---

### BIRTH AND DEATH OF A CEMETERY

Bukit Brown is named after **G.H. Brown**, a British businessman who lived in the vicinity in the mid-nineteenth century. The land was subsequently bought by three Hokkien businessmen, and then in the 1910s, the colonial government acquired part of it to create a sort of official cemetery open to all Chinese subgroups. That section, launched in the 1920s, has become the Bukit Brown cemetery of today. In the 1970s the cemetery was deemed full, since when it has been more or less abandoned (and since when **cremation** has become largely standard practice in Singapore, given the lack of land).

Bukit Brown's significance today stems not merely from the importance of some personages buried there, but also from its sheer size – it stretches 2km east to Thomson Road – and location fairly close to downtown. Despite the huge potential of the site, it remained untouched while other old cemeteries were uprooted for redevelopment without a great deal of outcry. But with Singaporeans seemingly becoming much less compliant, a campaign of online petitions, Facebook groups and the like has greeted the government's recent plans to push a highway through the middle of the cemetery.

At the time of writing, exhumation of graves in the path of the planned road was ongoing, and the road itself may be built by the time you read this. It's hard to say if the rest of the cemetery will ultimately give way to new housing estates or other projects.

There is a pecking order to the layout: the wealthier someone was, the more likely they are to be buried higher up the slopes. Most tombs have a bench-like gravestone, flanked by figurines that may, depending on the tomb, depict protective deities or lions or mythological characters; a handful even have statues of turbaned Sikh sentinels (burly Sikhs were much in demand among wealthy Chinese as security guards for their homes). Other eye-grabbing decorative features include carvings of bats (representing luck) and lovely majolica **tiles**.

Among the tombs, the most striking kind slope upwards from front to back, with a horseshoe-shaped wall behind and a groove cut into the ground inside the wall for drainage. Most of these tombs are no more than a couple of metres in length, but the largest, that of the tycoon **Ong Sam Leong** (after whom Sam Leong Road, next to Mustafa's in Little India, is named), takes up an entire slope and has its own semicircular forecourt that two dozen people could comfortably mingle on.

## Singapore Zoo

80 Mandai Lake Rd • ☎ 6269 3411, ⓦ www.zoo.com.sg • Buses: #138 from Ang Mo Kio MRT, #927 from Choa Chu Kang MRT or Woodlands Rd, or privately run service from downtown with BusHub ($4.50/$2; ☎ 6753 0506, ⓦ www.bushub.com.sg), with useful return departures from the Night Safari (every 15–30min 9.30–11.30pm)

Both the **zoo** and its **Night Safari** offshoot, on a promontory jutting into Seletar Reservoir, are highly popular, which is partly down to their "open" philosophy: many animals are confined in spacious, naturalistic enclosures behind moats, though creatures such as big cats still have to be caged. It's a thoughtful, humane approach that may well please even those who don't generally care for zoos.

By the time you read this another spin-off may be open – the **River Safari**, (ⓦ riversafari.com.sg) presenting the animals (including **pandas**) and fish of rivers as diverse as the Ganges and the Mississippi.

### The zoo

Daily 8.30am–6pm • $20/$13, $42/$28 with Night Safari, $58/$38 with Night Safari and Bird Park • Theme-park-style trams $5/$3

Home to more than 300 species, the zoo could easily occupy you for half a day if not longer. A tram ($5/$3) does a one-way circuit of the grounds, but as it won't always be going your way, be prepared for a lot of legwork.

Highlights include the **Fragile Forest** biodome, a magical zone where you can actually walk among ring-tailed lemurs, sloths and fruit bats. The **white tigers** are a big draw too. The animals aren't actually white, but resemble Siamese cats in the colour of their hair and eyes; at feeding time (2.20pm) great hunks of meat are thrown for them to catch in their mouths.

**Primates** are something of a strong point: orang-utans swing through the trees overhead close to the entrance, and at the Great Rift Valley zone you can see the communal life of a hundred Hamadryas baboons, including some rather unchivalrous behaviour on the part of males, who bite females to rein them in.

Animal shows and feeding shows run throughout the day, including the excellent **Splash Safari**, featuring penguins, manatees and sea lions. There are also elephant ($8) and pony ($6) rides, plus a popular water play area called **Rainforest Kidzwalk** (from 9.30am; bring your children's swimming gear).

### The Night Safari

Daily 7.30pm–midnight, with shops/restaurants from 6pm and last admission at 11pm • $32/$21, or $42/$28 with zoo or Bird Park, or $58/$38 with both

Many animals are nocturnal, so why not present an opportunity to see them at night? The **Night Safari** section of the zoo addresses this question so convincingly that you

wonder why similar establishments aren't more common. The vaguely Borneo-tinged tribal show at the entrance is admittedly somewhat tacky, and there can be lengthy queues for the tram rides, with commentary, around the complex (included in the ticket price), but these are just niggles.

You can forgo the trams altogether and simply walk around the leafy grounds, an atmospheric experience in the muted lighting, but that way you miss out on several zones, notably those for large mammals such as elephants and hippos. Areas you can visit on foot include the **Fishing Cat Trail**, featuring the Indian gharial – a kind of crocodile, disarmingly log-like in the water, and the binturong, sometimes called the bearcat (you'll understand why when you see it); and the **Leopard Trail**, where your eyes will strain to spot the clouded leopard and slow loris.

It's worth catching the **Creatures of the Night** show (hourly 7.30–9.30pm, plus Fri & Sat 10.30pm, included in ticket), an educational affair touching on the importance of conservation and recycling, and starring otters, racoons, owls and wolves, among others.

## Kranji and Sungei Buloh

Close to the Causeway, the district of **Kranji** still has a relatively open feel compared to most suburbs of Singapore, though thickets of state housing and light industry are never far away and the roads are sometimes clogged with traffic heading up to Malaysia. For visitors, two attractions make it worth considering coming this far from town: the **Kranji War Memorial** and, 4km to the west, the wetland reserve at **Sungei Buloh**.

### The Kranji War Memorial and Cemetery

9 Woodlands Rd, across from the Turf Club • Daily 7am–6pm • Free • Kranji MRT, then a 10min walk west and south, or bus #170 from opposite Little India MRT, or #927 from the zoo to the junction of Woodlands and Mandai Rd, then a 15min walk north

The **Kranji War Memorial and Cemetery** is the resting place of the many Allied troops who died in the defence of Singapore. Row upon row of uniform headstones slope up the manicured hill, some identified only as "known unto God". Beyond the simple stone cross that stands over the cemetery is the memorial, around which are recorded the names of more than twenty thousand soldiers (including personnel from Britain, Canada, Australia, New Zealand, Malaya and South Asia) who died in this region during World War II. Two unassuming tombs stand on the wide lawns below the cemetery, belonging to Yusof bin Ishak and Dr B.H. Sheares, independent Singapore's first two presidents.

### Sungei Buloh Wetland Reserve

301 Neo Tiew Crescent • Mon–Sat 7.30am–7pm, Sun 7am–7pm; guided tours Sat 9.30am, video shows Mon–Sat 9am, 11am, 1pm, 3pm & 5pm, Sun hourly 9am–5pm • Sat & Sun $1, otherwise free • ☎ 6794 1401, ⓦ www.sbwr.org.sg • Bus #925 from Kranji or Choa Chu Kang MRT to the Kranji reservoir car park, then a 15min walk; on Sun the bus becomes #925C and makes a detour to the reserve

The western arm of Kranji is dominated by a coastal reservoir, beyond which is one of Singapore's most rural corners, where something of the island's agricultural past clings on by way of the odd prawn farm or hydroponic vegetable garden. This is also the site of the **Sungei Buloh Wetland Reserve**, the island's only wetland nature park. Beyond its Visitor Centre, embanked trails and walkways lead through expanses of mangrove and mud flats, with views across the strait to the southern Malaysian city of Johor Bahru.

The vegetation rapidly gets monotonous, but then **birdlife** is the main reason to come. You've a reasonable chance of spotting sandpipers, egrets and kingfishers, and between September and March, migratory birds from around Asia roost and feed here, especially in the early morning. Several hides dot the landscape, and you can get an elevated view over the reserve from the tallest of them, the oversized-treehouse-like **Aerie**. It's worth gazing down at the creeks and mud flats, too, harbouring mudskippers, banded archerfish – which clobber insect prey by squirting water at them with their mouths – and even the occasional saltwater crocodile.

# Eastern Singapore

In the 1970s, eastern Singapore still had a rural feel, its ribbons of middle-class suburbs interspersed with Malay kampongs (villages). Inevitably, the area hasn't escaped the mushrooming of high-rise new towns, and much of the southeast coast has been radically altered by land reclamation to create the East Coast Park, a long strip of leisure and watersports facilities. For visitors, the points of interest mainly lie along or close to where the coast once was. Closest to downtown is the suburb of Geylang, which has retained some of its old Malay identity; neighbouring Katong likewise has traces of its historical Peranakan character. At the eastern end of the island, Changi is where the Japanese interned Allied troops and civilians during World War II, commemorated at the thought-provoking Changi Museum. The rustic Singapore of old clings on at Pulau Ubin, an island visitable by boat from Changi.

## Geylang and Katong

Beyond the Kallang River, marking the eastern edge of downtown, Malay culture has held sway in and around the adjoining suburbs of Geylang and Katong since the mid-nineteenth century, when Malays and Indonesians arrived to work first in the local *copra* (dried coconut kernel) processing factory and later on its *serai* (lemon grass) farms. Parts of **Geylang** retain quite a strong Malay feel today, and although Singaporeans now regard the district as rather seedy, at its best its shophouses exude something of the street life of the Chinatown of old. As for **Katong**, the wealthy, including many of Peranakan descent, built their villas here in prewar times, when it was a still beachfront district. Thankfully, the area's Peranakan heritage lives on to some degree in what is now a middle-class neighbourhood, and provides the main lure for visitors.

### Geylang Road

Kallang, Aljunied or Paya Lebar MRT, or bus #2 or #51 (from Chinatown) and #7 (from the Botanic Gardens and Orchard Rd) and #51, all of which pass through Victoria St, close to Arab St, en route to Sims Ave

Geylang's main thoroughfare is **Geylang Road**, carrying westbound traffic into town (eastbound cars use Sims Avenue to the north). Lined by shophouses, the 2.5km road is punctuated by more than three dozen numbered *lorongs* (lanes; odd numbers to the north), each packed with more shophouses, a few now serving as brothels. Thankfully, the overall feel of the district is one of a thriving, multicultural neighbourhood, well worth a wander for its *kopitiams* and little shops. There are no specific sights, though you may want to check out **Lorong 24A** (south of Aljunied MRT), where eight 1920s shophouses have been handsomely restored (ⓦ thelor24ashophouseseries.com).

### Geylang Serai

Paya Lebar MRT, then a short walk south and east, or bus #2 or #51 (from Chinatown) and #7 (from the Botanic Gardens and Orchard Rd) and #51

At Geylang's eastern edge is the **Geylang Serai** district, its newly rebuilt market very much the focus of the area's Malay life. A large, two-storey complex, it's easily spotted on the north side of Sims Avenue, with sloping roofs reminiscent of certain styles of a kampong house. The stalls are predominantly Malay, selling textiles, *kuih* (sweetmeats) and snacks such as *rempeyek*, delicious fried flour rounds encrusted with spices and peanuts.

Just to the west, a collection of incongruous kampong houses, genuine in style but not substance, comprise the so-called **Malay Village**, set up by the government in the 1980s as a sort of right-on folk museum, and now practically defunct. Despite a half-hearted campaign to save what should probably never have been attempted in the first place, at the time of writing it looked as though the complex would be sold for redevelopment – an unhappy fate for the few examples of kampong architecture left on Singapore's main island.

### The Joo Chiat Complex

Geylang Road becomes Changi Road at the northern end of Joo Chiat Road, opposite the Geylang Serai market. The **Joo Chiat Complex** here is worth a look, though it appears to be a drab suburban mall. Inside it feels more like a market, again with a notable Malay/Islamic feel; shops sell batik, *jamu* – herbal remedies – and Malay music CDs, and you can occasionally watch people doing the old-fangled *joget* dance at a stage behind.

### Joo Chiat Road

Bus #33 from Bugis, Lavender or Kallang MRT to Tembeling Rd, one street away, or walk from Paya Lebar MRT

Laidback **Joo Chiat Road** is where Geylang shades into Katong, the latter now a middle-class residential area, though a little of the former's seediness spills over here after dark. The 1.5km stroll south into Katong proper at East Coast Road is hardly a chore thanks to several distractions, including some traditional businesses amid the

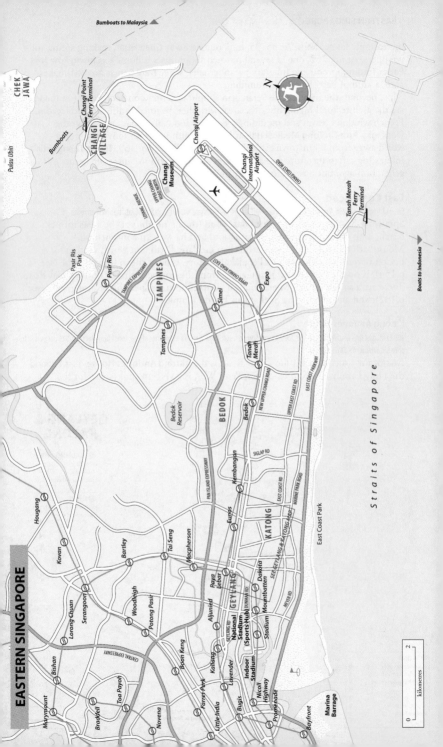

increasingly fancy shops. At no. 95, look out for **Kway Guan Huat**, making spring-roll wrappers. At no. 252, one of several restored shophouses is home to **Chiang Pow Joss Paper Trading**, producing funerary paraphernalia, while **Nam San** at no. 261 makes *otah*, a kind of flattish seafood dumpling.

Just beyond, the immaculate Peranakan shophouses on **Koon Seng Road** (on the left) are the architectural highlight of the area, with their restored multicoloured facades, French windows, eaves and mouldings. Back on Joo Chiat Road, peek in at the workaday **Ann Tin Tong Medical Hall** at no. 320, with its 1960s louvred windows, a world away from Chinatown's slick herbalists. Finally, at no. 369, **Teong Theng** sells interesting rattan furniture and accessories, popular items in Singapore homes a generation ago, but now almost totally out of favour.

## East Coast Road

Bus #12 from Chinatown, Victoria St and Lavender MRT, or #14 from Orchard Rd; both call at Mountbatten MRT en route

Sprawling Katong centres on **East Coast Road** (the name hints at the area's former beach, long obliterated by land reclamation) and its western continuation, Mountbatten Road. It's less colourful than Geylang Road, but worth visiting for a pocket of outlets celebrating its Peranakan history. One of these, Rumah Bebe (see p.154), is on the right (west) if you arrive from the northern stretch of Joo Chiat Road. There are also restaurants where you can sample the area's speciality, Katong *laksa* (see p.132), and an entertaining Sri Lankan Hindu temple.

### Katong Antiques House

208 East Coast Rd • Usually daily except Mon 11am–5pm, though it's best to call in advance of your visit • Optional tours $15 per person by prior arrangement • ☏ 6345 8544

East of the junction with Joo Chiat Road is the **Katong Antiques House**, just beyond the Holy Family Church. Its owner, Peter Wee, is a veteran spokesman for the

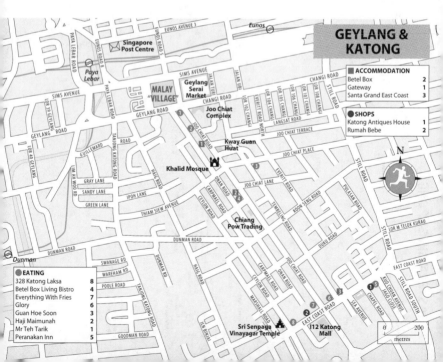

**GEYLANG & KATONG**

| ■ ACCOMMODATION | |
|---|---|
| Betel Box | 2 |
| Gateway | 1 |
| Santa Grand East Coast | 3 |

| ● SHOPS | |
|---|---|
| Katong Antiques House | 1 |
| Rumah Bebe | 2 |

| ● EATING | |
|---|---|
| 328 Katong Laksa | 8 |
| Betel Box Living Bistro | 4 |
| Everything With Fries | 7 |
| Glory | 6 |
| Guan Hoe Soon | 3 |
| Haji Maimunah | 2 |
| Mr Teh Tarik | 1 |
| Peranakan Inn | 5 |

Peranakan community and has amassed a treasure-trove of artefacts, from wedding costumes to vintage furniture and, more prosaically, old books in Baba Malay, a blend of Malay and Hokkien Chinese. He can give you a formal tour of the traditionally decorated shophouse, which is a much bigger building than you might assume from its facade.

### The Sri Senpaga Vinayagar Temple

19 Ceylon Rd • Daily 5.30am–10.30pm • ☎ 6345 8176, ⓦ senpaga.org.sg

In the mid-nineteenth century, a statue of Vinayagar (Lord Ganesh) was apparently unearthed in this area, leading to the building of a temple here by the Ceylonese Tamil community. The present-day **Sri Senpaga Vinayagar Temple**, one street west of Joo Chiat Road, has several unusual features, beginning with the *gopuram* – not the multicoloured affair you may have seen elsewhere, but in off-white, the deities picked out in a curry-powder yellow.

Inside, the four main columns feature eight sculptures each, depicting all 32 forms of Ganesh, and all murals and deities are conveniently labelled in English – for the younger generation of worshippers – as well as Tamil. Most prominent is the striking flagpole-shaped mast, plated in gold and representing the connection between man and the divine. Gold also features at the top of a tower built over the main sanctuary; you'll get a clear view if you head to the open space at the back of the temple.

**7**

# Changi

Tanah Merah MRT, then bus #2 from exit B; alternatively (much slower), pick up the bus from Chinatown or elsewhere downtown

In Singaporean popular consciousness, the **Changi** district has long embodied a beachside idyll, and indeed the beach at Changi Point remains popular today, though it's no great shakes. Most tourists who head this far east come to see the wartime Changi Museum, which is a little way before Changi Point.

## Changi Museum

1000 Upper Changi Rd North • Daily 9.30am–5pm • Free, audio guides or guided tours $8 • ☎ 6214 2451, ⓦ changimuseum.sg • Tanah Merah MRT, then a 20min ride on bus #2

The infamous Changi Prison was the site of a World War II POW camp in which Japanese jailers subjected Allied prisoners, both military and civilian, to the harshest of treatment. Those brutalities are movingly remembered in the **Changi Museum**. Formerly housed within the prison itself, which is still in use – drug offenders are periodically executed here – the museum was moved wholesale just up the road when the prison was extended a few years ago.

Novelist James Clavell drew on his experience of Changi in writing *King Rat*, never forgetting that in the cells "the stench was nauseating… stench from a generation of confined human bodies". No museum could possibly bring home the horrors of internment, though this one does a reasonable job of picking over the facts of the Japanese occupation and the conditions prisoners endured. Memorable exhibits include artworks by internees, with pride of place given to reproductions of Stanley Warren's so-called **Changi Murals**, depicting New Testament scenes (the originals are housed within an army camp nearby where Warren was interned). A final section features a re-creation of an improvised theatre where internees put on entertainments to amuse fellow inmates, though here there's only a TV screen showing wartime footage.

In the museum courtyard is a simple wooden **chapel**, typical of those erected in Singapore's wartime camps; the brass cross on its altar was crafted from spent ammunition casings. The messages on its board of remembrance are often touching and worth a read (ask staff for pen and notepaper to add your own).

## Changi Point and the beach

Tanah Merah MRT, then a 30min ride on bus #2

Beyond Changi Prison, the tower blocks thin out and the landscape becomes a patchwork of fields, often a relic of colonial-era military bases still used by Singapore's forces. Ten minutes on via the #2 bus is the coast at **Changi Point**, with a cluster of eating places and shops called **Changi Village** mainly serving the beach-going public.

To reach the **beach** from the bus terminus, head on past the market and food court and bear left to the *Ubin First Stop* seafood restaurant, where you'll see a canalized inlet from the sea. The footbridge here leads to a stretch of manicured grass and trees, the prelude to a narrow strip of brownish sand fronting greenish-blue water – actually not uninviting, and the sight of aircraft rumbling in low every couple of minutes on the Changi flight path soon ceases to be a distraction. Facilities include showers and a couple of **bike rental** outlets (from $7/hr; you may have to leave your passport as a deposit). For **food**, there's ample choice in Changi Village itself – the food court isn't at all bad and the restaurants on the main road offer everything from steak to *murtabak*.

**7**

# Pulau Ubin

Bumboats leave from the Changi Point ferry terminal, left of the footbridge to Changi beach (daily roughly 5.30am–9pm; $2.50, plus $2 for a bicycle; boats leave when full) • ☎ 6542 4108, ⓦ nparks.gov.sg

Few of Singapore's offshore islands are of any significant size, and those that exist tend to be confined to industrial or military use (Sentosa being the extravagant exception). Not so **PULAU UBIN**. Covering an area of ten square kilometres, it's a pleasant anachronism offering a taste of what rural Singapore was like half a century ago, and is managed as a national park. The island warrants a half-day visit for its wetland site, **Chek Jawa**, and for its scattering of quaint wooden bungalows – though the scenery may underwhelm if you've been to kampongs in Malaysia or Indonesia.

## Ubin village

Bumboats like those used for Singapore River trips, only pleasingly basic, make the 2km crossing from Changi and dock at a jetty more or less in the centre of Ubin's southern shore. Here you'll find a cluster of houses that passes for a **village**, home to simple restaurants specializing in seafood, a bright red temple to the Tua Pek Kong deity, a stage where evening Chinese opera performances are put on during the Hungry Ghost festival (see p.148), and a handful of small outlets renting **bikes** in various states of repair (from $5 for the day). At the right-hand edge of the village is a **nature gallery** with displays on the island's flora and fauna, while at the other end of the village is the so-called **volunteer hub** that serves as an informal information point.

## Around the island

Vehicles are scarce on Ubin, and while you'll encounter a van owner or two in the village advertising a "taxi" service, cycling is by far the best option for getting around on the island; the areas that can be visited stretch some 3km west, north and east of the jetty. Roads are mostly sealed, though there are some undulating stony tracks (occasionally steep; heed signs to dismount).

Ubin's landscape is defined by a scattering of old wooden **houses**, some built on stilts, surrounded by tidy gardens of allamanda, hibiscus and bougainvillea. It's a classic formula, still common in rural Malaysia and one that can arouse feelings of nostalgia among Singaporeans of a certain age (mostly the over-50s). Otherwise, the island is dotted with several **quarry lakes** (*ubin* is Malay for "granite") that can offer pleasant views, though swimming isn't allowed. As for wildlife, this is one of the best places in Singapore to try to spot a distinctive Southeast Asian bird, the **oriental pied hornbill**, with black-and-white plumage and a projection called a casque on its upper beak.

## COOKING CLASSES

One of the more unusual things you can do on Pulau Ubin is a **cooking class** in one of the island's old houses. Run by self-styled "food sorceress", the friendly and articulate Ruqxana Vasanwala ($130 for a half-day), they focus on a wide range of local dishes, some quite unusual. If your visit doesn't coincide with one of her Ubin sessions (currently on the last Saturday of the month; book places at least a couple of weeks in advance), you can take advantage of regular classes at her home in Siglap, east of Katong. For schedules, a list of dishes covered in each session and to book, go to Ⓦcookerymagic.com.

### Chek Jawa
Daily 8.30am–6pm

In terms of natural interest, the best spot is undoubtedly **Chek Jawa**, at the eastern end of the island. You're required to leave bikes just a short way from the site and proceed on foot to an information kiosk and more nature exhibits, the latter inside the recently restored **House no. 1**. Built in the 1930s, it resembles a bizarre cross between a Tudor cottage and a Swiss chalet, complete with fireplace.

Chek Jawa's claim to fame is its intertidal habitat. **Sea grasses** are revealed when the tide is out (Ⓦnparks.gov.sg publishes tide tables), and there are extended boardwalks for you to scrutinize them and the coastal **mangroves**; if you're lucky, you might spot horseshoe crabs or mudskippers. There's also a 20m-high observation tower where **wild pigs** can sometimes be seen rooting around in the mud beneath, and offering vistas north to low peaks in Malaysia.

7

JURONG BIRD PARK

# Western Singapore

Hilly and green, the western part of the island is home to the country's premier university, the National University of Singapore at Kent Ridge. It lies at the start of a nine-kilometre series of ridges and peaks now collectively labelled the Southern Ridges, stretching southeast to Mount Faber near Tanjong Pagar downtown. Several minor attractions nestle along the route, but a major part of the ridges' appeal is the chance to do a couple of hours' walk from one lush hill to another using a network of interconnecting bridges. Further west is the industrial new town of Jurong, where, true to form, Singapore's planners have woven several sights and leisure facilities into the fabric of the area, the pick of them being the Jurong Bird Park. In between these areas and downtown is the suburb of Holland Village, boasting a string of restaurants and bars popular with foreigners.

# The Southern Ridges and Pasir Panjang

Along the southwest coast of Singapore is **Pasir Panjang**, a district whose name means "long sands" in Malay, though any significant beach has long gone – as have the sleepy villages that used to dominate what is becoming an increasingly urbanized area. It's home to one worthy sight, the delightful Buddhist theme park that is **Haw Par Villa**, which makes a reasonable starting point for an exploration of the **Southern Ridges** just inland, where you can take in the wartime museum **Reflections at Bukit Chandu** and views from **Mount Faber**.

The account below takes the Southern Ridges walk in an easterly direction, ending at HarbourFront MRT beneath Mount Faber – a sensible choice as this avoids a steep climb up the hill and allows you to finish at the massive **VivoCity** mall, where you can assuage any appetite and thirst worked up along the way (or even continue to Sentosa). Haw Par Villa, the sight furthest west, is really an optional extra as far as the walk is concerned. One more practical point: the links between parks on the walk often offer little shade, so be assiduous about **sun protection** and bring a reasonable supply of water.

## Haw Par Villa

262 Pasir Panjang Rd • Daily 9am–7pm • Free • ☎ 6872 2780 • Haw Par Villa MRT or bus #200 from Buona Vista MRT or #51 from Chinatown

Delightfully unmodernized, **Haw Par Villa** is an unexpected star among Singapore's lesser-known sights. Featuring a gaudy parade of hundreds of statues of people and creatures from Chinese myth and legend, it was once the estate of the Aw brothers, Boon Haw and Boon Par, who made a fortune early last century selling Tiger Balm – a cure-all ointment created by their father. Within the grounds were their villa and private zoo, but when the British began licensing the ownership of large animals, the brothers replaced the zoo with statuary; subsequently the park acquired a new appellation, a mishmash of the brothers' names.

The main path through the grounds curls up and around a hill past one hilariously kitsch tableau after another. One of the best shows titanic combat as the **Eight Immortals** of Taoist mythology attack the Dragon King's undersea palace. Elsewhere, look out for a pool of Chinese-faced mermaids and a curious folk-tale scene in which a deer and a goat, the latter talking into a bakelite telephone, take tea with a rabbit and a rat, who are newlyweds.

A vacant area at the highest point of the site is where the Aw brothers' **villa** once stood. Within a few years of its completion, the Japanese troops arrived, causing one of the brothers to flee. He died before the British returned, and his surviving brother had the house – by now in a bad state – demolished.

### The Ten Courts of Hell

Closes 6pm

Haw Par Villa's centrepiece is the **Ten Courts of Hell**, a concrete tunnel housing gory depictions of punishments meted out to deceased sinners. Prostitutes are drowned in the "filthy blood pool", tax dodgers and late rent payers "pounded with a stone mallet", to name two; in one tableau someone appears to be being gored to death by a giant brush. Finally, the dead have their memories wiped by drinking a cup of "magic tea" prior to reincarnation.

## Reflections at Bukit Chandu

31K Pepys Rd • Tues–Sun 9am–5.30pm • $2, or $4 with Memories at Old Ford Factory • Ⓦ www.1942.org.sg • Pasir Panjang MRT, then a 10min walk north uphill

The Malay Regiment's defence of Pasir Panjang during World War II is remembered at the tiny **Reflections at Bukit Chandu** museum. Near the midpoint of the Southern Ridges trail, it's a ten-minute walk up from Pasir Panjang MRT: head north up Pepys Road until you see the lone surviving colonial house at no. 31k, built as officers' accommodation though it became a munitions store during the war. It was here that "C" company of the Malay Regiment's 2nd Battalion made a brave stand against the

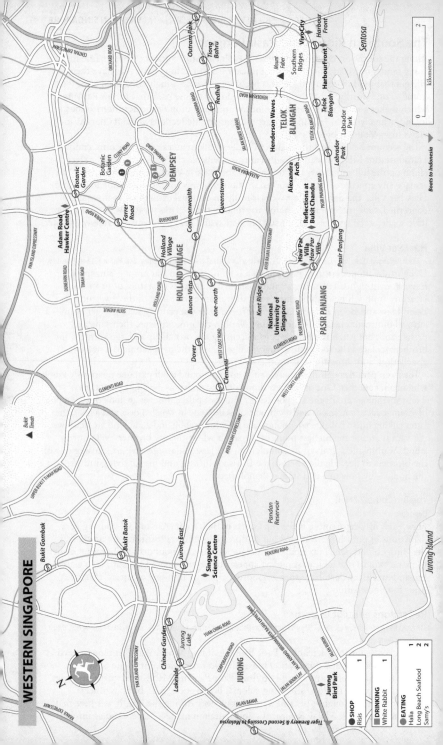

Japanese on February 13, 1942 – two days before the British capitulation – and sustained heavy casualties in the process.

There's nothing special about the museum's small collection of artefacts, and indeed you can glean a lot of the salient information by perusing the museum's website. The displays do, however, get across the human toll of the conflict as well as highlighting British ambivalence about working with the Malays. The Malay Regiment was only begun as an experiment in what is now Malaysia to see "how the Malays would react to military discipline", and it was only when they began to prove themselves that members of the regiment were sent to Singapore for further training. This supposed slighting of the Malay community is still cited in Malaysia today as one reason for maintaining its controversial positive discrimination policies in favour of Malays.

### The canopy walk and Hort Park

Leaving the museum, bear left along the ridge for your first taste of the Southern Ridges trail – and a wonderful introduction it is too, for this is where the elevated **canopy walk** begins. Soaring above the actual trail, the walkway takes you east through the treetops, with signage pointing out common Singapore trees such as cinnamon and *tembusu*, and views north across rolling grassy landscapes, the odd mansion poking out from within clumps of mature trees. After just a few minutes, the walkway rejoins the trail leading downhill to some mundane nurseries and the west gate of **Hort Park** (daily 6am–10pm; free). A hybrid of garden and gardening resource centre, it's sadly dull, and you'll probably want to exit promptly to Alexandra Road via the east gate.

### Alexandra Arch to Mount Faber

For Alexandra Arch, bus #166 from HarbourFront MRT or Dover MRT, or #51 from Chinatown

It's possible to start a Southern Ridges walk at the Alexandra Road end of Hort Park, very close to one of the huge, purpose-built footbridges on the trail, the white **Alexandra Arch**. Meant to resemble a leaf, it looks more like the Singapore River's Elgin Bridge on steroids.

On the east side of Alexandra Arch, a long, elevated metal walkway zigzags off into the distance; it's called the **forest walk** though it passes through nothing denser than mature woodland on its kilometre-long journey east. The walkway zigzags even more severely as it rises steeply to the top of **Telok Blangah Hill** (you can save a bit of time by using a flight of steps that begins before the last few bends), whose park offers views of the usual public housing tower blocks to the north and east, and of Mount Faber and Sentosa to the southeast.

Proceed downhill and east, following signage for **Henderson Waves**, and after 700m or so you come to a vast footbridge of wooden slats over metal. Way up in the air over wide Henderson Road, the bridge has high undulating parapets – Henderson Waves indeed – featuring built-in shelters against the sun and rain.

### Mount Faber

Mount Faber Rd • Free • Ⓦ mountfaber.com.sg • Bus #409 from HarbourFront MRT (Sat & Sun noon–9pm; 2 hourly)

On the far (east) side of the Henderson Waves Bridge is the road to the top of leafy **Mount Faber**, named in 1845 after government engineer Captain Charles Edward

**8**

---

#### MOUNT FABER'S CABLE CARS

Undoubtedly the classiest way to arrive at Sentosa is by **cable car**. State-of-the-art eight-seater cable cars, each with glittering lighting inside and out, leave from the top of Mount Faber for the island (daily 8.45am–10pm; $29/$18 return). They call in at the HarbourFront Centre en route, and you can choose to start the ride here or at Sentosa, if you wish. The best time for views is at dusk, when you see Singapore lighting up from Jurong in the west to the Financial District closer by, to the northeast.

Faber. In bygone years this was a favourite recreation spot for its superb views over downtown, but these days you'll have to look out for breaks in the dense foliage for vistas over Bukit Merah new town to Chinatown and the Financial District, or head to the **Jewel Box**, a complex of pricey bars and restaurants at the very apex of the summit.

To descend from Mount Faber, follow signs for the **Marang Trail**, which eventually leads down a flight of steps on the south side of the hill to VivoCity. If you do want to try the hike up from VivoCity, note that it only takes ten minutes but is steep in places.

### VivoCity and HarbourFront Centre

Telok Blangah Rd • HarbourFront MRT

The most interesting thing at the foot of Mount Faber is the **VivoCity** mall, with a curious fretted white facade that looks like it was cut out of a set of giant false teeth, and housing three good food courts (in particular *Food Republic* on level 3), a slew of restaurants, a cinema and other amenities; it's also the main gateway to Sentosa. The red-brick box of a building with the huge chimney east (on the left if you're descending the hill) of the mall, and connected to it by an elevated walkway, is **St James Power Station**, a bevy of clubs and bars housed in, surprise surprise, a converted power plant.

In the other direction on Telok Blangah Road is the **HarbourFront Centre**, a glorified ferry terminal from where boats set off for Indonesia's Riau archipelago, as well as being the departure point for cable cars heading to Mount Faber and Sentosa Island.

## Holland Village

**8**

Holland Village MRT or bus #7 or #77 from Orchard Rd or the Botanic Gardens (#77 also comes here from Bukit Timah), or #165 from MacRitchie Reservoir

Only a short bus ride from Orchard Road and the Botanic Gardens, **Holland Village** is one of the few suburbs that draws visitors. This residential district housed some of the British troops based in Singapore a few decades ago, and today foreigners still hone in on its restaurants and bars. At the heart of the area is the **Holland Village Shopping Centre**, a good place to find stores selling antiques and novel home furnishings. The relevant listings chapters cover these places in more detail.

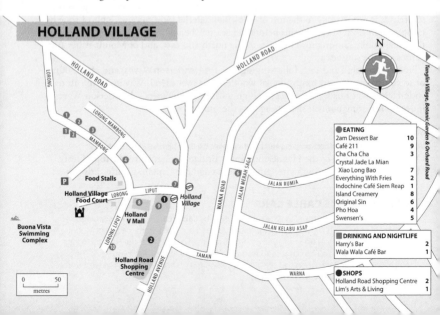

HOLLAND VILLAGE

● EATING
| 2am Dessert Bar | 10 |
| Café 211 | 9 |
| Cha Cha Cha | 3 |
| Crystal Jade La Mian Xiao Long Bao | 7 |
| Everything With Fries | 2 |
| Indochine Café Siem Reap | 1 |
| Island Creamery | 8 |
| Original Sin | 6 |
| Pho Hoa | 4 |
| Swensen's | 5 |

■ DRINKING AND NIGHTLIFE
| Harry's Bar | 2 |
| Wala Wala Café Bar | 1 |

● SHOPS
| Holland Road Shopping Centre | 2 |
| Lim's Arts & Living | 1 |

# Jurong and Tuas

The new town of **Jurong** was created out of swampy terrain in the 1960s, amid great scepticism about its chances of success. Today it and neighbouring **Tuas** boast a diverse portfolio of industries, including pharmaceuticals and oil refining – in which Singapore is a world leader despite having nary a drop of black gold of its own – and Jurong's centre is being remodelled with new leisure facilities in mind. As far as sights are concerned, Jurong's **Bird Park** is presently the only must-see, though the **Singapore Science Centre** is ahead of the curve as far as science museums go, and is not to be missed if you've got kids to entertain. More pertinent to grown-ups are tours of the **Tiger Brewery**, though note that these have to be booked in advance.

## Jurong Bird Park

2 Jurong Hill • Daily 8.30am–6pm • $18/$12, $32/$21 with zoo, $42/$28 with Night Safari, $58/$38 all three • ☎ 6265 0022, ⓦ www .birdpark.com.sg • Boon Lay MRT, then bus #194 or #251 (heading back, you can pick up the #194 from the stop where you arrived, while for the #251 you should cross to the other side of the road)

Lining Jalan Ahmad Ibrahim, the **Jurong Bird Park** is home to one of the world's biggest bird collections, with nearly four hundred species. You'll need at least a couple of hours to have a good look around the grounds, though you can save a little time using the park's tram rides ($5/$3).

Besides the four huge walk-in aviaries, described below, the park also has a number of worthwhile smaller enclosures, such as the hugely popular **Penguin Coast** (feeding times 10.30am & 3.30pm). Just inside the entrance, it juxtaposes half a dozen penguin species against the backdrop of a mock Portuguese galleon, meant to evoke the sighting of penguins by explorers such as Vasco da Gama. Utterly different is **World of Darkness**, a fascinating owl showcase that uses special lighting to swap day for night.

The park also puts on various bird shows, the most exciting of which is **Kings of the Skies** (daily 10am & 4pm), in which eagles, hawks, falcons and owls show off their predatory skills. You can get even more intimate with the falcons by signing up for the pricey **falconry** taster session (daily 2pm; 30min; $100; book before 12.30pm).

### The walk-in aviaries

The **Southeast Asian Birds** section, while not the most impressive of the major aviaries, has a special impact as it showcases some birds you may have fleetingly glimpsed around Singapore, as well as some you'd count yourself lucky to see after days in the wilds of Borneo. Here fairy bluebirds, black-naped orioles and other small but delightful creatures feast on fruit slices, with a simulated thunderstorm to liven things up at noon. Close by are **Jungle Jewels**, featuring South American birdlife in "forest" surroundings, and the **Lory Loft**, a giant aviary under netting, its foliage meant to simulate the Australian bush. Its denizens are dozens of multicoloured, chattering lories and lorikeets, which have no qualms about perching at the viewing balcony or perhaps even on your arm, hoping for a bit of food (suitable feed is on sale).

At the far end of the park from the main entrance is the **African Waterfall Aviary**, long the park's pride. It boasts a 30m-high waterfall and 1500 winged denizens, including carmine bee-eaters and South African crowned cranes.

## Singapore Science Centre

15 Science Centre Rd • Daily 10am–6pm • $9/$5 • ☎ 6425 2500, ⓦ www.science.edu.sg • Jurong East MRT, then a 10min walk west or bus #66 or #335, or ride the #66 all the way from Little India

Interactivity is the watchword at the **Science Centre**, on the eastern edge of the parkland around the artificial Jurong Lake. Galleries here hold hundreds of hands-on displays focusing on genetics, space science, marine ecology and other disciplines, allowing you to calculate your carbon footprint, test your ability to hear high-pitched sounds and be befuddled by weird optical illusions. The material goes down well with the seemingly hyperactive schoolkids who sweep around the place in deafening waves.

**8**

If you're visiting with kids in tow, you might want to extend your visit to the winter-themed Snow City (see p.157) or stick with science at the Omni-Theatre.

### Omni-Theatre

21 Jurong Town Hall Rd • Mon–Fri 10am–6pm, Sat & Sun 10am–8pm; Observatory Fri 7.50–10pm • $10 or $16 joint ticket with Science Centre; observatory free • Ⓦ www.omnitheatre.com.sg

Just north of the Science Centre, the **Omni-Theatre** shows hourly IMAX movies about the natural world. It also houses an observatory that does free **stargazing** sessions on Fridays. Being almost on the equator, Singapore enjoys views of both the northern and southern skies, though light pollution and clouds put a big dampener on things.

## Tiger Brewery

459 Jalan Ahmad Ibrahim • Tours Mon–Fri 10am, 11am, 1pm, 2pm, 4pm & 5pm • $16/$12; book on ☎ 6860 3005, Ⓦ tigerbrewerytour .com.sg • Boon Lay MRT, then bus #182 (20min)

**Tiger** is undoubtedly one of Singapore's best-known brands internationally. The beer has been brewed here since 1931, when its home was on Alexandra Road at Malayan Breweries, a joint venture between Heineken and a local drinks manufacturer. The German giants Beck's soon set up a brewery to produce a rival, Anchor, but Malayan Breweries then acquired the upstart. In 1990 the company became Asia Pacific Breweries and moved into its present plant in Tuas, where it makes Tiger, Anchor as well as Guinness and several other brands. Recognizing the success of Tiger, in particular, Heineken renewed its commitment to the company by taking a controlling stake in 2012.

Tours of the brewery take in a mini-museum and let you see the space-age brewing, canning and bottling halls, before you indulge in some free quaffing in the sizeable bar, done out like an old-fashioned pub.

8

# Sentosa and the southern isles

Though only just off the south coast of the main island of Singapore and linked to it by a bridge, Sentosa still has something of an out-of-town feel to it, and locals treat it as a kind of resort for full-day trips or weekend breaks. Don't expect a quiet, unspoilt deserted isle, though – this is effectively one giant theme park, as epitomized by Universal Studios, and its three beaches are decidedly ordinary. That said, if you have kids in tow you'll find plenty to keep them entertained for hours. Other, much smaller, islands lie further south within Singapore's territorial waters, including St John's and Kusu. They're easy enough to reach by ferry, and while not blighted by development, they are hardly unspoilt either, having become somewhat manicured in true Singapore style.

**9**

# Sentosa

Nominal $1 admission fee • ☎ 1 800 7368672, ⓦ sentosa.com.sg • HarbourFront MRT, then a 10min walk using the Sentosa Boardwalk footbridge from the VivoCity mall

Thirty years of rampant development have transformed **Sentosa** into the most developed of Singapore's southern islands (with the possible exception of one or two that are home to petrochemical installations), so it's ironic that its name means "tranquil" in Malay. Sentosa has come a long way since colonial times, when it had the charming name Pulau Blakang Mati, or the "Island of Death Behind", and was home to a British military base. Contrived but enjoyable in parts, the Sentosa of today is promoted for its rides, passable beaches, hotels and massive new casino resort on the northern shore. Besides the mandatory casino and much-hyped Universal Studios theme park, *Resorts World Sentosa* has half a dozen hotels, a maritime museum and a Marine Life Park.

If you do visit Sentosa, it's best to come on a weekday (and not during the school holidays either; see p.30) unless you don't mind the place being positively overrun. For details on **transport** to and around the island, see p.110.

## Resorts World Sentosa

Close to Waterfront station on the island's north shore • ☎ 6577 8888, ⓦ rwsentosa.com

The *Resorts World* development is visually plastic, like something out of a Silicon Valley corporate headquarters, but it does boast some of Sentosa's biggest attractions.

### Universal Studios Singapore

Resorts World Sentosa • Daily 10am–7pm • $68/$50, plus a $6/$4 surcharge at weekends; many rides have minimum height requirements and may not be suitable for young children • ☎ 6577 8899

The ersatz character of *Resorts World* becomes rather entertaining at the **Universal Studios** theme park, where fairy-tale castles and American cityscapes rear bizarrely into view in the sultry heat. The park is divided into seven themed zones, encompassing everything from ancient Egypt – the least convincing of the lot – to DreamWorks' animated hit *Madagascar*. Standard tickets offer unlimited rides, but there's much more to do than get flung around on cutting-edge roller coasters or, in the case of the *Jurassic Park* Rapids Adventure, on a circular yellow raft: museum-type exhibits unwrap the world of film production, and you can watch musical spectaculars in a recreation of Hollywood's Pantages theatre.

Early booking on the *Resorts World* website is recommended – tickets can sell out days or weeks in advance – and be prepared for long queues in the sun for the rides, in any case.

### The Maritime Experiential Museum

Turn right from the Sentosa Boardwalk where it reaches the island • Mon–Thurs 10am–7pm, Fri–Sun 10am–9pm • $5/$2, plus $6/$4 for the Typhoon Theatre • ☎ 6577 8899

Highlighting the historical sea trade between China and India and the Middle East, the **Maritime Experiential Museum** might seem a touch too intellectual for a casino development. In the event, it does stoop to some rather tacky audiovisual trickery to try to entertain. The centrepiece is a massive replica of the bow of a ship used by the Ming-dynasty emissary Cheng Ho (also known as Zheng He), which has a lion's head figurehead whose eyes flare red as it exhales smoke. It's a preamble to the **Typhoon Theatre**, where videos show Chinese actors with American accents enacting the events leading up to a shipwreck – evoked with thunder and lightning, sprays of water across the audience and a final catastrophic capsize that does something unusual to the entire room.

The most impressive exhibit is sadly marooned on pillars up near the ceiling: the **Jewel of Muscat**, a recreation of a ninth-century Arab dhow. Built without nails – coconut fibre binds the timbers – it was a gift to Singapore from the Omani government in 2010. Delivery took 68 days, under sail, of course.

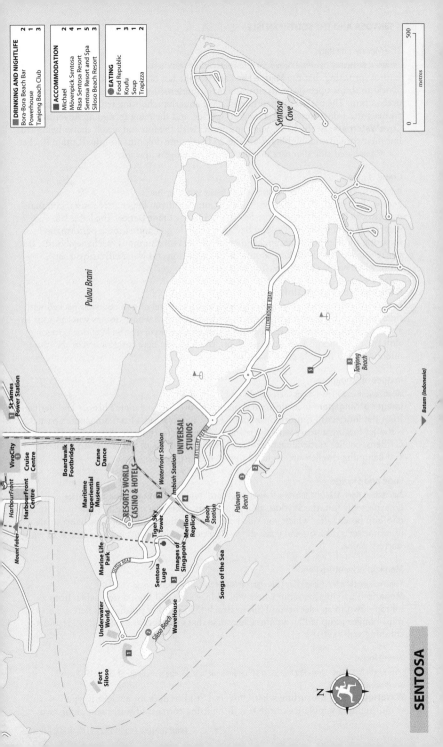

**SENTOSA**

| ■ DRINKING AND NIGHTLIFE | |
|---|---|
| Bora-Bora Beach Bar | 2 |
| Powerhouse | 1 |
| Tanjong Beach Club | 3 |

| ■ ACCOMMODATION | |
|---|---|
| Michael | 2 |
| Mövenpick Sentosa | 4 |
| Rasa Sentosa Resort | 1 |
| Sentosa Resort and Spa | 5 |
| Siloso Beach Resort | 3 |

| ● EATING | |
|---|---|
| Food Republic | 1 |
| Koufu | 3 |
| Soup | 1 |
| Trapizza | 2 |

Pulau Brani

Sentosa Cove

St-James Power Station

VivoCity
HarbourFront Centre
HarbourFront
Mount Faber

Cruise Centre

Boardwalk Footbridge

Maritime Experiential Museum

Crane Dance

RESORTS WORLD CASINO & HOTELS

Waterfront Station

Imbiah Station

UNIVERSAL STUDIOS

ARTILLERY AVENUE

ALLENBROOKE ROAD

Tiger Sky Tower

Marine Life Park

Merlion Replica

Beach Station

Sentosa Luge

Images of Singapore

SILOSO ROAD

Songs of the Sea

Underwater World

WaveHouse

Siloso Beach

Fort Siloso

Pulawan Beach

Tanjong Beach

▶ Batam (Indonesia)

N

0        500
metres

**9**

The Marine Life Park

Just west of the Maritime Experiential Museum. See 🐦 rwsentosa.com for times and prices

It's not surprising that the **Marine Life Park** was the last of the key attractions at Resorts World to throw open its doors: it was a major undertaking, touted as the world's largest oceanarium. The park is divided into a lavish **aquarium**, housing tens of thousands of animals and fish representing some 800 species, and the more intriguing **Adventure Cove Waterpark**. At the latter, you can snorkel with the fish and watch sharks being fed, but the two signature highlights are the 25 bottlenose dolphins and the Riptide Rocket – a water-based ride that uses magnets to lift passengers upwards.

Crane Dance

Close to the Maritime Museum and Waterfront station • Mon & Fri–Sun 9pm; 10min • Free

Sentosa isn't much of a night-time destination, but if you linger after sunset, you may want to catch either Songs of the Sea (see p.110) or **Crane Dance**. The latter was commissioned by *Resorts World* to be "the world's largest animatronic performance", featuring the computer-manipulated courtship of two enormous mechanical birds. If you're not sure about sticking around for the lighting and water effects, you can preview the whole shebang on YouTube.

## Other Sentosa attractions

Just about every patch of Sentosa that isn't a beach, hotel or golf course is packed with rides or other diversions, ranging from a Merlion replica whose insides you can tour to a vertical wind tunnel that replicates the sensation of skydiving by keeping a person aloft on a continuous upward blast of air. The selection here covers a few of the more interesting and sensibly priced offerings.

Images of Singapore

Imbiah Lookout, west of Imbiah station • Daily 9am–7pm • $10/$7

**Images of Singapore** uses life-sized dioramas to present Singapore's history and heritage from the fourteenth century through to 1945. Iconic images from Singapore's past – Raffles forging a treaty with the island's Malay rulers, rubber tappers at the Botanic Gardens, coolies at the Singapore River – spring to life, and actors dressed as labourers and kampung dwellers are on hand to provide further insight.

Luge and Skyride

Daily 10am–9.30pm • $12.50 ($8.50 for Skyride alone) • ☎ 6274 0472 • Beach Station for Skyride, Imbiah station for Luge

Unexpectedly fun, the **Skyride**, akin to a ski lift, takes you up a leafy slope at the start of Siloso beach, after which you ride your **Luge** (rhymes with "huge") – like a small unmotorized go-kart – and coast down either of two long, curving tracks back to your starting point.

Megazip Adventure Park

A 5min walk west of Imbiah station • Daily 11am–7pm • ☎ 6884 5602, 🐦 www.megazip.com.sg

**Megazip** is a flying-fox setup where you slide, suspended from a steel cable, from a hilltop down to an islet beyond Siloso Beach ($35). Other possibilities here are a mini-bungee jump ($15), an obstacle course that's all ropes and netting ($35) and a climbing wall ($20).

WaveHouse

Siloso Beach • Daily 11am–11pm • First hour $35 or $45 depending on "ride", $5 more at weekends • ☎ 6377 3133, 🐦 www
.wavehousesentosa.com

**WaveHouse** does for surfing what Universal Studios does for ancient Egypt, conjuring up a semblance of the real thing using torrents of water sent along two

**9**

contoured blue slopes. One generates a continuous 2m curling wave; the other is flat and suitable for beginners.

## Fort Siloso

At the northwest tip of the island, beyond Siloso Beach • Daily 10am–6pm, free tours Fri–Sun 12.40pm & 3.40pm • $8/$5

**Fort Siloso**, a cluster of buildings and gun emplacements above a series of tunnels bored into the island, guarded Singapore's western approaches from the 1880s until 1956, but its obsolescence was revealed when the Japanese marched in from Malaya. Today, the recorded voice of one Battery Sergeant Major Cooper talks you through a mock-up of a nineteenth-century barracks, complete with living quarters, guard room, laundry and assault course. Be sure to check out the **Surrender Chambers**, where life-sized figures re-enact the British and Japanese surrenders of 1942 and 1945, respectively. After that you can explore the complex's hefty gun emplacements and tunnels.

## Underwater World

80 Siloso Rd, on the northwest shore • Daily 9am–9pm, "Meet the Dolphins" 11am, 2pm, 4pm & 5.45pm • $26/$18 • ☎ 6275 0030, ⓦ underwaterworld.com.sg

It remains to be seen if **Underwater World** can hold its own after the Marine Life Park at *Resorts World* opens, but the site does excite kids with its moving walkway inside a hundred-metre tunnel, taking visitors through two large tanks of sharks, stingrays and shoals of gaily coloured fish. Another highlight is the **dolphin lagoon**, where the marine acrobatics of Indo-Pacific humpback dolphins (and some seals) can be seen during the "Meet the Dolphins" sessions.

## Songs of the Sea

Close to Beach station • Daily 7.40pm & 8.40pm, Sat also 9.40pm; 25min • $10

Many visitors leave Sentosa by dusk; those who hang around into the evening are either heading to one of the beach bars (such as *Bora-Bora*; see p.141) or to Songs of the Sea, a lavish, 25-minute sound-and-light show whose canvas is not ancient monuments but screens of water. Seating is right at the seafront just off Beach Station.

## Beaches

The best that can be said about Sentosa's three **beaches**, created with vast quantities of imported beige sand, is that they're decent enough, with bluey-green waters, the odd lagoon and facilities for renting canoes, surfboards and aqua bikes. For tranquillity, however, you'd probably do better at Changi Beach (see p.96), because at Sentosa you have to deal with not only crowds but also the view of one of the world's busiest shipping lanes – expect a parade of container ships and other vessels all day.

**Siloso Beach**, which extends 1500m northwest of Beach Station, is the busiest of the three, with well-established resorts and facilities, including good restaurants. **Palawan Beach**, just southeast of Beach Station, is meant to be the most family-oriented and boasts a children's play area centred on a mock galleon (see p.157). It also features a suspension bridge leading out to an islet billed as the "Southernmost Point of Continental Asia" – though a sign concedes that this is so only by virtue of three man-made links, namely the suspension bridge itself, the bridge from HarbourFront to Sentosa, and the Causeway. Beyond Palawan, **Tanjong Beach** tends to be slightly quieter than the other two as it starts a full kilometre from Beach Station.

## ARRIVAL AND DEPARTURE                                                                     SENTOSA

The most sensible way to get to Sentosa is on foot: from HarbourFront MRT, head up through the VivoCity mall and out along the Sentosa Boardwalk (10min), where you pay the $1 admission fee as you reach the island.

**By light rail** The Sentosa Express (daily 7am–midnight; $3.50 including Sentosa admission) leaves from level 3 of the VivoCity mall. See opposite for details of stops on the island.

**By cable car** The most stylish way to reach Sentosa is via the recently revamped cable-car system from Mount Faber (see p.101).

**By bus** *Resorts World* operates free buses to Universal Studios, calling at a few hotels on Orchard Road and in the Colonial District, plus *Marina Bay Sands* (daily 9am–10pm or so; 2 hourly; details on ⓦ rwsentosa.com). There's also the #RWS8 service from HarbourFront/VivoCity to *Resorts World* ($2 return) and the weekend night buses #NR1 and #NR6 between downtown and Sentosa (Fri & Sat 11.30pm–4.30am; $4.50); details of all these on ⓦ smrt .com.sg.

**By taxi** It's straightforward to get a taxi to the island, though note that trips incur a surcharge of several dollars.

## GETTING AROUND

Transport services within Sentosa are free.

**By light rail** Sentosa Express trains call at Waterfront station on Sentosa's northern shore for Resorts World, then at the central Imbiah Station (close to the Merlion replica), and finally at Beach Station on the southern shore (for the beaches). Note that you do not need a ticket to ride the train back to VivoCity.

**By bus** The island has three colour-coded internal buses that run on loop routes, plus a so-called beach tram running the length of the southern beaches; all routes are explained on the comprehensive map available at the Sentosa Express terminal and at the information point at the southern end of the Sentosa Boardwalk.

**By bike** You can rent a bicycle from Gogreen on Siloso Beach for a hefty $12/hr.

# Kusu and St John's islands

ⓦ sentosa.com.sg/en/nature/southern-islands • At least 2 boats daily to each island from the Marina South Pier (see p.26) • $15/$12 for either island • Timetables at ⓦ islandcruise.com.sg

**St John's** and **Kusu** islands, 6km south of the "mainland", offer some respite from the hubbub of the city state, though both are a little manicured. The more interesting of the two is Kusu, also known as **Turtle Island**. Singaporean legend tells of a Chinese and a Malay sailor who were saved from drowning by a turtle that transformed itself into an island; today the island is home to a major **temple**, complete with turtle statues, and three Malay *keramat*s (shrines). Once a year during the ninth lunar month (mid-Oct to mid-Nov or thereabouts), tens of thousands of Singaporean pilgrims descend upon Kusu's temple to pray for prosperity.

It's not permitted to **stay** overnight on Kusu, although St John's has a "holiday bungalow" that sleeps up to ten and has its own kitchen ($54 per night on weekdays, double that at weekends and quadruple that at weekends during school breaks). For bookings, call ☏ 6736 8672.

INFINITY POOL AT MARINA BAY SANDS

# Accommodation

While prices may disappoint, the range of accommodation in Singapore will not. The island has a plethora of luxury hotels – including a handful that exude colonial splendour, notably the Raffles and the Fullerton – plus competently run, if unexciting, no-frills and mid-range establishments. The best of the upstart boutique hotels have an unorthodox or ultra-luxurious design aesthetic, though some of the more affordable places tend simply to boast a smattering of antique furniture. There are also numerous hostels and guesthouses (the distinction between them is blurry), offering affordable dorm beds and some private rooms. A few of these places are spartan, but most are housed in nicely refurbished shophouses and offer air conditioning, wi-fi, a comfy communal lounge and breakfast, included in the rate; the very slickest have bespoke bunk beds and free toiletries to boot.

## ESSENTIALS

**Breakfast** Hostels and guesthouses almost always provide a simple, self-service breakfast of toast plus coffee and tea, possibly with cereal and fruit as well. Cheaper hotels may well include breakfast in the rate if they have a café; at expensive hotels it's almost always a paid extra unless you're staying on a package deal that includes it.

**Check-in/check-out** The earliest time you can check into a hotel room is usually 2pm, while you have to be out of your room by noon or pay for another day's stay.

**Children's beds** The majority of mid-range and upmarket hotels in Singapore make no charge for children under 12, and beds may well be large enough that kids can easily snuggle up beside parents. If you do need to have an extra bed put in the room, it may incur a surcharge of $50 or so.

**Costs** If there's one thing that might frustrate you in Singapore, it's the cost of accommodation. Room rates – the steepest in the region – have been rising steadily for years, and not many downtown mid-range hotels now charge less than $150 a night for a double. At least soaring hotel rates have been tempered by the corresponding growth in guesthouses and backpacker hostels, where dorms start at around $20 a night and private rooms with shared facilities at $50 a night, though you can pay double these prices to stay at the fanciest places. For further information on rates, see box below.

**Hourly rates** If a hotel has hourly or "transit" rates, it often means that locals use them for discreet hanky-panky, which may involve prostitution. Normally only cheap hotels offer such rates, though even the well-run, and ubiquitous, budget hotel chains *81* and *Fragrance* have been tainted by this in the past. All establishments reviewed here should be free of this.

**Internet access** Free wi-fi is de rigueur at hostels and guesthouses, but hotels often charge for internet access, whether it's cabled or wireless. If there is a rule, it's that the pricey hotels charge, whereas boutique hotels and some mid-range places use free wi-fi as a selling point, and the cheapest hotels have no internet provision at all.

**Reservations** It's a good idea to book, especially if you're considering one of the more popular guesthouses, and not just for peace of mind, either: many of the best hotel rates are only available online. Besides contacting establishments directly, you can try ⓦagoda.com for a good selection of hotel deals, while ⓦhostelworld.com lists most guesthouses in town.

10

## THE COLONIAL DISTRICT

The area immediately north and east of the Singapore River only has a few places to stay, all hotels.

**Fort Canning** 11 Canning Walk, northern side of Fort Canning Hill ☎ 6559 6770, ⓦ hfcsingapore.com; see map p.34. Hotel facades don't come much more imposing than that of the former British military HQ that houses this plush boutique hotel. Little colonial atmosphere survives inside, however, and it's a bit of a trek down flights of steps to reach Dhoby Ghaut MRT and Orchard Rd. Rooms are spacious, immaculately decorated, and boast a bathtub that's curiously often either smack in the middle of the room or out towards the window, with blinds for privacy. Pools on two levels and lush gardens, too. $̶4̶5̶0̶

**Novotel Clarke Quay** 177a River Valley Rd ☎ 6338 3333, ⓦ novotel.com; see map p.34. This dull tower block might seem like just another bland business-oriented hotel, but the wood-panelled lobby and tasteful contemporary furnishings make clear this is all about giving the boutique hotels a run for their money. Comes with the usual four-star amenities, including pool and jacuzzi. $̶3̶4̶0̶

**Peninsula Excelsior** 5 Coleman St ☎ 6337 2200,

---

## ACCOMMODATION PRICES

One quirk of Singapore hotels is that their published tariffs are often somewhat meaningless: many inexpensive and mid-range hotels have **promotional deals** almost year-round that can slash ten to twenty percent off their official rates, while all the more upmarket hotels continually adjust their room prices based on demand. High season, when good deals are much harder to come by, covers Christmas and New Year, the Formula 1 Grand Prix (in the third week of September, or thereabouts) and, to a lesser extent, June to the end of August.

The rates quoted in our reviews represent the minimum that you can reasonably hope to pay for an establishment's cheapest double rooms or dorms during high season if you book early, and include the 10 percent service charge (levied by most accommodation except budget places and the cheaper mid-range establishments) plus 7 percent **GST on top**; it's worth reading the fine print on any deals you come across to check if these surcharges have been included. Outside of high season, where a promotional rate does not apply, prices often fall by 10 to 20 percent in any case.

**10**

ⓦytchotels.com.sg; see map p.34. Really two hotels merged together – as hinted at by the presence of two swimming pools at either end, one of which abuts the current lobby – and nicely modernized, unlike the 1970s shopping arcades below. Decent value, with weekend discounts too. §235

**Raffles** 1 Beach Rd ☏6337 1886, ⓦraffleshotel.com; see map p.34. Though the modern extension is a mixed bag, *Raffles* remains refreshingly low-rise and still has colonial-era charm in spades, especially evident in the opulent lobby and the courtyards fringed by frangipani trees and palms. Amenities include a dozen restaurants and bars, a rooftop pool and a spa. All rooms are suites, and you'll need deep pockets to stay, of course. §800

**Robertson Quay Hotel** 15 Merbau Rd ☏6735 3333, ⓦrobertsonquayhotel.com.sg; see map p.34. A circular riverside tower with great views of the river, a cute round pool and a gym. Rooms are on the small side and the place can be a little disorganized, but at their prices, which include breakfast, you can probably put up with all that. §180

**Swissôtel The Stamford** 2 Stamford Rd ☏6338 8585, ⓦsingapore-stamford.swissotel.com; see map p.34. Upper-floor rooms – and the restaurants and bars on the 70th to 72nd floors – aren't for those with vertigo, though the views are as splendid as you'd expect from one of the tallest hotels in the world, with over a thousand rooms. Perhaps even more impressive is having an MRT station (City Hall) in the basement. §680

## BRAS BASAH ROAD TO ROCHOR ROAD

The grid of streets between Bras Basah Road and Rochor Road (and a bit beyond, uphill from Selegie Road) has been rendered a bit sterile by redevelopment, which has also eliminated most of the cheap accommodation that once packed Bencoolen Street. What remains are mostly modern mid-range hotels. The area remains a good choice if you can afford it, as it's within walking distance of the Singapore River, Little India and the eastern end of Orchard Road.

### HOSTELS AND GUESTHOUSES

★**G4 Station** 11 Mackenzie Rd ☏6334 5644, ⓦg4station.com; see map pp.46–47. Short on atmosphere but impeccably run, with dorms of various sizes plus double rooms, all with a/c, plenty of modern fittings (including chunky lockers). There's a communal Wii, too. Dorms §28, doubles §80

★**Hangout @ Mount Emily** 10A Upper Wilkie Rd ☏6438 5588, ⓦhangouthotels.com; see map pp.46–47. Owned by the company behind the historic Cathay cinema at the foot of Mount Emily, the *Hangout* is an impressive designer guesthouse with a breezy rooftop terrace that's great for chilling out in the evening. The only drawback is that it's 10min walk uphill from Selegie Rd. Book online, both because the place is popular, and because you can get much lower prices that way. Dorms §60, doubles §120

★**Tree In Lodge** 2 Tan Quee Lan St ☏6844 5512, ⓦwww.treeinlodge.com; see map pp.46–47. This guesthouse puts its green credentials in the spotlight – they recycle, use eco cleaning products and avoid plastic – but just as importantly it's well kept, the dorms (of six to twelve beds) complemented by plenty of toilets and showers. The friendly management are full of suggestions for visits to unusual nooks and crannies of the island, and sometimes organize trips. Dorms §28

### HOTELS

**Carlton** 76 Bras Basah Rd ☏6338 8333, ⓦcarltonhotel.sg; see map pp.46–47. Boasting a grand new extension and a redesigned lobby dominated by a spidery glass artwork suspended from the ceiling, this towering four-star hotel has elegant rooms, a pool and gym – and keen rates for what's on offer. §430

★**Ibis** 170 Bencoolen St ☏6593 2888, ⓦibishotel.com; see map pp.46–47. If you've stayed in other hotels run by this no-frills chain, you'd probably describe them as functional and modern – a perfect match for Singapore, then. This vast new establishment is well insulated from traffic noise and has wi-fi throughout. The 7-Eleven shop right in the lobby feels totally apt. §225

**Intercontinental** 80 Middle Rd ☏6338 7600, ⓦintercontinental.com; see map pp.46–47. Like the adjoining Bugis Junction mall, the *Intercontinental* incorporates some of the area's original shophouses, here converted into so-called "shophouse rooms" with supposedly Peranakan decor, though this merely amounts to Oriental-looking vases and paintings of tropical fruit. Still, the hotel is luxurious and has all the amenities you could want, and rates can fall by a quarter at weekends. §520

**Marrison** 103 Beach Rd ☏6333 9928, ⓦmarrisonhotel.com; see map pp.46–47. This new hotel is surprisingly comfortable, the rooms done out in neutral hues, with the bonus of a DVD player and free wi-fi. A good deal, given the location. §160

**Naumi** 41 Seah St ☏6403 6000, ⓦnaumihotel.com; see map pp.46–47. The slate-grey exterior, on which what look like vines crawling up behind netting, doesn't inspire, but inside is a stunning boutique hotel where every room is kitted out like a luxury apartment and boasts an iPod dock and a kitchenette. Rooms on one floor are reserved for women only, and there's a rooftop pool. §425

★**South East Asia** 190 Waterloo St ☏6338 2394, ⓦseahotel.com.sg; see map pp.46–47. Behind the yellow and white 1950s facade is a reasonable hotel with functional if slightly tired doubles, featuring the usual mod cons. It's practically next door to the lively Kwan Im temple, to boot. Substantially cheaper than anything else in the area. **$100**

**Strand** 25 Bencoolen St ☎ 6338 1866, ⓦ strandhotel .com.sg; see map pp.46–47. Rooms here are modern, nondescript and more than serviceable, and surprisingly affordable – perhaps because of ongoing work on the Downtown MRT line outside. If you're lucky, you'll get breakfast included in their promotional rate. **$150**

## LITTLE INDIA, ARAB STREET AND LAVENDER STREET

Accommodation in **Little India** tends to be slightly cheaper than elsewhere. The hotels can be uninspired, but there's a good selection of guesthouses in Little India proper and beyond, in the zone extending up to **Lavender Street**, reachable via Farrer Park or Lavender stations, and with an excellent public swimming pool close by (see p.30). The area around **Arab Street** also has a few good places to stay.

**10**

### HOSTELS AND GUESTHOUSES

**Backpackers@SG** 1st floor, 111J King George's Ave ☎ 6683 2924; see map pp.46–47. Exceptionally plain but homelier for it, this is a simple hostel occupying part of a low-rise residential block. Unlike some of its competitors, it doesn't have mega-sized dorms – the largest has eight beds, though that may change when their new extension opens. A reasonable choice if you want a quiet stay and aren't fussed about a buzzy vibe. Dorms **$20**

★ **Bunc@Radius** 15 Upper Weld Rd ☎ 6262 2862, ⓦ bunchostel.com; see map pp.46–47. *Bunc* is a sprawling place, its size matching the scale of its ambition to be one of a handful of "flashpacker" hostels taking the concept of comfort on a budget to new heights. Beyond the expansive, sleek lobby is a warren of dorms with individual lighting fixtures and sockets for each bed; incredibly, some of the beds are even built for two. There's a ladies-only floor and a dedicated gaming room as well. The sole private room has disabled facilities, though anyone can reserve it. Dorms **$40** (double beds **$75**), private room **$140**

**Drop Inn** 253 Lavender St ☎ 6299 3817, ⓦ www .dropinnhostel.com; see map pp.46–47. Not the most exciting place to stay, but it's a decent option and the lounge has a wide central platform for lolling about on. There's a range of doubles in addition to the dorms, too. Dorms **$22**, doubles **$54**

**The Hive** 624 Serangoon Rd (corner of Lavender St) ☎ 6341 5041, ⓦ thehivebackpackers.com; see map pp.46–47. A large hostel where every room is named after a flower and the exterior is done out in black and yellow. Putting the bee metaphors aside, the place is well managed, with a/c in all rooms and dorms. Dorms **$22**, doubles **$55**

★ **The InnCrowd** 73 Dunlop St ☎ 6296 9169, ⓦ the -inncrowd.com; see map pp.46–47. Endearing, recently renovated hostel with dorms plus a range of rooms with TV and a/c. Shared showers and toilets are kept spotless, and there's a comfy lounge, cheap beer and free internet access. Dorms **$20**, doubles **$60**

**The Little Red Dot** 125 Lavender St ☎ 6294 7098, ⓦ atthelittlereddot.com; see map pp.46–47. A competently run, cosy hostel where you can take your pick from ordinary dorm beds or capsule-style ones, though the latter cost quite a bit more. There's a pleasant first-floor communal terrace and Xbox 360s to while away downtime. Dorms **$18**, capsule beds **$50**

**The Mitraa** 427 Race Course Rd ☎ 6396 3925, ⓦ www .mitraa.com.sg; see map pp.46–47. It bills itself as "the friendliest backpacker hostel", and friendly it usually is, as well as organized. If they're full they may be able to put you up at their *Mitraa Inn* offshoot nearby. Dorms **$25**

**Prince of Wales** 101 Dunlop St ☎ 6299 0130, ⓦ pow .com.sg; see map pp.46–47. Justifiably popular place done out in primary colours, with a/c dorms, a couple of double rooms and cheap beer, either from their drinks machines or from their very own bar/beer garden. Dorm beds **$22**, doubles **$60**

**Sleepy Kiwi** 55 Bussorah St No phone, ⓦ sleepykiwi .com.sg; see map pp.46–47. The best thing about this hostel (still sometimes known by its original name, *Sleepy Sam's*) is its superb location in the heart of the Arab St area, just a few steps down from the Sultan Mosque. Besides mixed and women-only dorms, there's a shared triple room plus a single and a double. Amenities include a kitchen and a small café. Dorm beds **$25**, doubles **$89**

### HOTELS

**Aqueen** 139 Lavender St ☎ 6395 7788, ⓦ www .aqueenhotels.com; see map pp.46–47. The bizarre name is of greater interest than the modern, functional fittings at this nondescript hotel. It's always keenly priced, perhaps because it's inauspiciously placed next to a funeral parlour. Rates include breakfast. **$150**

**Broadway** 195 Serangoon Rd ☎ 6292 4661, ⓔ broadway@pacific.net.sg; see map pp.46–47. One of several hotels in the area popular with visitors from India, the *Broadway* has simply furnished, slightly worn rooms. Traffic noise might be a problem, but it's still not a bad deal for the price. **$120**

**Fragrance Imperial** 28 Penhas Rd ☎ 6297 8888, ⓦ fragrancehotel.com; see map pp.46–47. Despite the drab yellow exterior, this is a cut above fellow members of the budget chain, with slick if smallish rooms, a café and rooftop swimming pool. Rates include breakfast. **$150**

**Haising** 37 Jalan Besar ☎ 6298 1223, ⓦ haising.com .sg; see map pp.46–47. Friendly, secure Chinese-run cheapie offering simple, a/c en-suite rooms with TV, rather boxy but not bad for the price. Small surcharges apply at the weekend. **$65**

**10**

**Kam Leng** 383 Jalan Besar ☎6239 9399, ⓦkamleng .com; see map pp.46–47. The nicely renovated Art Deco exterior makes clear that the *Kam Leng* is all about recreating the feel of a distinguished prewar Chinese hotel. Perhaps the prewar focus also explains why it's rather lacklustre inside – there are a few oldish objects in the rather threadbare lobby, and rooms are nothing fancy, with tiled or plain cement floors, though the bathrooms are unapologetically modern. Still, good value. $130

**Landmark Village** 390 Victoria St (main entrance on Arab St) ☎6297 2828, ⓦstayvillage.com; see map pp.46–47. Beyond the dated shopping centre downstairs is a modern hotel, recently partly refurbished, with its own pool, gym and restaurants. $300

**Madras** 28–32 Madras Rd ☎6392 7889, ⓦmadras singapore.com; see map pp.46–47. Smallish, slightly tatty rooms with the standard mod cons and breakfast included in the rate. $140

★ **Mayo Inn** 9 Jalan Besar ☎6295 6631, ⓦwww .mayoinn.com; see map pp.46–47. A partial refurbishment has given a new lease of life to the two dozen rooms at this simple, good-value hotel, which now feature modern bathrooms and, in some cases, a neat Japanese-style "bed" – a wooden dais with a mattress on top. $110

★ **Moon** 23 Dickson Rd ☎6827 6666, ⓦwww.moon .com.sg; map pp.46–47. Aiming to offer a boutique-hotel experience without straining your wallet, the *Moon* has stylishly kitted-out rooms with snazzy wallpaper, iPod docks and strategically placed drapes – to help take your mind off the fact that many are actually windowless. Rates include breakfast. $200

**Parkroyal** 181 Kitchener Rd ☎6428 3000, ⓦparkroyal hotels.com; see map pp.46–47. The classiest place to stay in the area, with a marbled lobby, spacious and tasteful rooms, some recently upgraded, and a pool. If you're heading here by taxi rather than via the nearby Farrer Park MRT, be sure to mention the address as there's a sister hotel of the same name on Beach Rd. $280

**Perak** 12 Perak Rd ☎6299 7733, ⓦperaklodge.net; see map pp.46–47. Set within a nicely restored shophouse and somewhat sedate – probably not a bad thing given the hullaballoo of Little India. Rooms are comfy, if unremarkable, and there's a pleasant residents-only rest area. $150, including breakfast

★ **Santa Grand Bugis** 8 Jalan Kubor ☎6298 8638, ⓦsanta.com.sg; see map pp.46–47. This functional, modern hotel has decent rooms, wi-fi and a pool, but what really edges it ahead of the competition are the family and deluxe rooms in a nicely restored old house next door. Rates include breakfast. $160

**The Sultan** 101 Jalan Sultan ☎6723 7101, ⓦthesultan.com.sg; see map pp.46–47. A pleasant, relatively low-key boutique hotel in a refurbished shophouse, with a variety of rooms, including a handful of cosy singles plus so-called attic rooms on the top floor, which are a little quieter than the rest. Breakfast included if you book online. Singles $190, doubles $260

**Wanderlust** 2 Dickson Rd ☎6396 3622, ⓦwander lusthotel.com; see map pp.46–47. As at its more established boutique sibling, Chinatown's *New Majestic*, there's a touch of modern-art wackiness at *Wanderlust*: the "industrial glam" lobby includes barber's chairs and many rooms are colour-themed, some even equipped with multicoloured lighting whose hues you can control. Facilities include a jacuzzi and French restaurant. Rates include breakfast. $260

## CHINATOWN, TANJONG PAGAR AND BOAT QUAY

When it comes to guesthouses, Little India's main competitor is **Chinatown**, which also boasts a good selection of boutique hotels. To the south, **Tanjong Pagar** has a couple of hotels of its own and is a lot quieter than Chinatown, though it's easily walkable from there. **Boat Quay**, on the south bank of the Singapore River, is dominated by restaurants and bars, but has two worthwhile places to stay, one of which is the splendid *Fullerton* hotel.

### HOSTELS AND GUESTHOUSES

**A Beary Good Hostel** 66A/B Pagoda St ☎6222 4955, ⓦabearygoodhostel.com; see map pp.60–61. A spick-and-span hostel with ten- to fifteen-bed mixed dorms and Wii consoles. The website has details of a couple of offshoots elsewhere in Chinatown, one with women-only dorms. Dorms $27

**Five Stones** Level 2, 61 South Bridge Rd ☎6535 5607, ⓦfivestoneshostel.com; see map pp.60–61. "Five stones" is what locals call the game of jackstones, so it's no big surprise that each room at this hostel has murals illustrating a different childhood game (inexplicably, though, the female dorm breaks style and is pink in tribute to Singapore's national flower). Each bunk bed has its own reading lamp, and the lounge feels unusually cosy; there are two doubles too, though note they don't accept under-16s. Dorms $30, doubles $105

**Matchbox** 39 Ann Siang Rd ☎6423 0237, ⓦmatchbox .sg; see map pp.60–61. One of two sleek designer hostels in the area at the time of writing, *Matchbox* revels in a good location on the ever so slightly chichi Ann Siang Hill. The pod-style beds, built into the wall, are the standout feature, each with an orthopedic mattress, reading light, headboard and power socket. There's also a splendid loft space packed with multicoloured pouffes and with old-school board games to play. Dorm beds $45, doubles (a two-bed dorm taken as a whole) $110

**Pillows & Toast** 40 Mosque St ☎6220 4653,

ⓦ www.pillowsntoast.com; see map pp.60–61. A friendly place with a chilled-out loft lounge and a variety of female or mixed dorms, all with at least eight beds. Not a bad choice. Dorms $\overline{\$26}$

**Prince of Wales Backpackers** 51 Boat Quay ☏6536 9697, ⓦ www.pow.com.sg; see map pp.60–61. Just like the Little India original, this hostel has a downstairs bar – and that's where the similarity ends; things are a lot less laid-back here given the location in the thick of the Singapore River's nightlife. There are a couple of mixed dorms, each with its own facilities and great river views, plus two private rooms, which share a bathroom. Dorms $\overline{\$25}$, rooms $\overline{\$70}$

**Rucksack Inn** 38a Hongkong St ☏6532 4990, ⓦ rucksackinn.com; see map pp.60–61. This hostel has friendly and informed staff and offers a mixed dorm, a female dorm and a handful of private rooms in various sizes. If they're full, they may well send you to their branch nearby on Temple St. Dorm beds $\overline{\$30}$, doubles $\overline{\$100}$

★ **Wink** 8a Mosque St ☏6222 2940, ⓦ winkhostel .com; see map pp.60–61. Alongside *Bunc* in Little India, this is the best designer hostel in town, with hi-tech capsule beds (including some doubles), each with flower-themed rooms with colour-coded lighting to match. Facilities include an upstairs kitchen and lounge, a spacious landing where you can watch DVDs, and free use of a tablet computer for every guest. Dorms $\overline{\$50}$ (double beds $\overline{\$90}$)

**HOTELS**

**Chinatown** 12–16 Teck Lim Rd ☏6225 5166, ⓦ chinatownhotel.com; see map pp.60–61. Not bad for the price and location, the *Chinatown* has serviceable rooms done out in the usual neutral tones. The bathrooms can be a bit poky, but at least a basic breakfast is included in the rate – though you have to serve yourself. $\overline{\$150}$

**The Fullerton** 1 Fullerton Square ☏6733 8388, ⓦ fullertonhotel.com; see map pp.60–61. Nearly as impressive as the *Raffles*, with a stunning atrium propped up on massive columns like an Egyptian temple. Rooms and bathrooms are spacious and feature contemporary styling rather than the Art Deco touches of the original building. Amenities include a gym, spa and pool. $\overline{\$550}$

★ **Hotel 1929** 50 Keong Saik Rd ☏6347 1929, ⓦ hotel1929.com; see map pp.60–61. Less pricey than its sibling, the *New Majestic*, this shophouse hotel looks genuinely 1929 on the outside, but the interior has been renovated to look like a twenty-first-century version of the early 1960s, all very retro chic. Rates include breakfast. $\overline{\$225}$

**The Inn at Temple Street** 36 Temple St ☏6221 5333, ⓦ theinn.com.sg; see map pp.60–61. Packed with old-fangled furniture for that period feel, but the rooms are boxy and there's no breakfast. Still, you can't argue with their prices. $\overline{\$150}$

★ **Klapsons** 15 Hoe Chiang Rd ☏6521 9030, ⓦ klapsons.com; see map pp.60–61. What sort of hotel would house its reception within a metal sphere that reflects sound such that guests at the counter hear themselves chirruping like aliens? That's just one of the quirks of this designer establishment, partly compensating for the less-than-ideal location at the southern edge of Tanjong Pagar. There are just seventeen rooms, each with different decor, though they all feature an iPod dock and free wi-fi; the suites boast a jacuzzi for good measure. $\overline{\$330}$

★ **New Majestic** 31–37 Bukit Pasoh Rd ☏6511 4700, ⓦ newmajestichotel.com; see map pp.60–61. If money is no object, this is the boutique hotel to make a beeline for. In a country whose buildings aspire to arctic levels of a/c, its open-air lobby and shabby ceiling (highlighting the vintage status of the building) offer the first of many surprises. Every room has been eccentrically decorated by local designers – one has arty seaweed simulations growing out of the wall, for example. Other quirks include a pool with floor portholes that allow you to look down into the restaurant – just as diners can look up at you swimming by. Rates include breakfast. $\overline{\$320}$

**Porcelain** 48 Mosque St ☏6645 3131, ⓦ porcelainhotel .com; see map pp.60–61. Browns and beiges are the default colours of most Singapore hotels, but *Porcelain* bucks the trend: Ming pottery motifs in blue and white are much in evidence, giving the otherwise unremarkable, smallish rooms of this new hotel a calming quality. $\overline{\$150}$

**The Scarlet** 33 Erskine Rd ☏6511 3333, ⓦ thescarlet hotel.com; see map pp.60–61. Housed in an impressive shophouse refurbishment, this boutique hotel has an exceptionally extravagant lobby, though here and in the rooms the opulence lacks a unifying theme and the dark hues feel oppressive after a while. $\overline{\$240}$

**Swissôtel Merchant Court** 20 Merchant Rd ☏6337 2288, ⓦ swissotel.com/singapore-merchantcourt; see map pp.60–61. One of downtown's best located hotels, well placed for Clarke and Boat quays and with part of its *Ellenborough Market Café* encroaching on the riverside promenade itself. Rooms have everything the travelling executive could want, and there's a lovely freeform pool, too. $\overline{\$350}$

## MARINA BAY

Marina Bay accommodation is synonymous with modern four- and five-star affairs, all located at the rather bland Marina Centre district next to Beach Road, with the obvious exception of *Marina Bay Sands*.

**Marina Bay Sands** 10 Bayfront Ave, Marina South ☏6688 8868, ⓦ marinabaysands.com; see map p.74.

At a stroke *Marina Bay Sands* has become the largest hotel in Singapore, with an astonishing 2500 rooms. Frankly

10

they're no better than those in most of the other five-star hotels, unless you shell out for, say, one of the Straits suites, with two en-suite bedrooms, a baby grand piano and butler service – for at least $5000 a night. Otherwise, stay here for the architecture and that infinity pool. **$550**

**Ritz-Carlton Millenia** 7 Raffles Ave ☎6337 8888, ☯ritz-carlton.com; see map p.74. Arguably king of the pricey hotels in Marina Centre, with magnificent views across to the Financial District, even from the bathrooms, where butlers will fill the bath for you. **$550**

## ORCHARD ROAD

**10**

Sumptuous hotels abound on and around **Orchard Road**, and though you generally pay a premium to stay here, the area has a couple of more reasonably priced options.

**Goodwood Park** 22 Scotts Rd ☎6737 7411, ☯goodwoodparkhotel.com; see map pp.80–81. Set on a leafy hillock, designed by the architect responsible for the *Raffles*, and likewise a genuine landmark in a cityscape characterized by transience. It still oozes the refinements of a bygone era, too, and boasts a variety of rooms and suites, plus several highly rated restaurants and two pools. Not as pricey as you might think. **$380**

**Innotel** 11 Penang Lane ☎6327 2727, ☯innotelhotel .com.sg; see map pp.80–81. Styling itself the "jewel of Penang Lane", this new business-oriented hotel is hardly a gem but does offer stripped-down, cosy modern rooms. **$250**

**Lloyd's Inn** 2 Lloyd Rd ☎6737 7309, ☯lloydinn.com; see map pp.80–81. Less than 10min walk from Orchard Rd, this motel-like building has large if rather bland and dated rooms; rates are a steal. **$90**

**Mandarin Orchard** 333 Orchard Rd ☎6737 4411, ☯meritus-hotels.com; see map pp.80–81. Female staff at this old favourite wear kitsch quasi-oriental uniforms, but don't let that put you off; the hotel is still at the top of its game, luxurious to a fault, well placed right in the middle of Orchard Rd, and it has its own high-end mini-mall, too. **$400**

**Marriott** 320 Orchard Rd ☎6735 5800, ☯marriott .com; see map pp.80–81. One of the plushest hotels on Orchard Rd, occupying a pagoda-style tower rising above Tangs department store, and featuring a hot tub in every room plus the obligatory pool, spa and gym and plenty of restaurants. **$550**

★ **The Quincy** 22 Mount Elizabeth ☎6738 5888, ☯stayfareast.com; see map pp.80–81. One of the more endearing boutique hotels, melding contemporary aesthetics with comfort. Rooms come with a jumbo-sized flat-screen TV, an iPod dock and a glass-walled bathroom, and there's a pool near the top of the building. The only thing that might put some off is that it's a 10min, slightly uphill walk from Orchard Rd. Rate includes breakfast. **$320.**

**Regent** 1 Cuscaden Rd ☎6733 8888, ☯regenthotels .com; see map pp.80–81. Top-flight hotel with an impressive pyramidal atrium above the lobby and beautifully styled rooms, plus a pool, gym and spa. **$470**

**Shangri-La** 22 Orange Grove Rd ☎6737 3644, ☯shangri-la.com; see map pp.80–81. A 10min walk west of Orchard Rd, this old faithful still epitomizes elegance, with 750 rooms set in oodles of landscaped greenery. Facilities include pitch-and-putt golf, tennis courts and a spa. **$600**

**Supreme** 15 Kramat Rd ☎6737 8333, ☯supremeh .com.sg; see map pp.80–81. This 1970s concrete box has predictably dated rooms, though they're not too cramped; rates include breakfast. **$150**

## GEYLANG AND KATONG

With such a huge range of accommodation available downtown, there are few compelling reasons to stay in the suburbs except to save a little money. **Katong**, with its Peranakan heritage and good restaurants, is as good as place to do this as any, though note that some of neighbouring **Geylang**'s seediness can spill over into Joo Chiat Road after dark.

★ **Betel Box** 200 Joo Chiat Rd ☎6247 7340, ☯betelbox.com; see map p.94. Singapore's socially committed hostel, *Betel Box* tries to highlight the island's cultural heritage by taking guests on trips to interesting districts, has its own little resource library and even runs a retro-themed restaurant below (see p.133). Accommodation comprises mixed and female-only dorms of various sizes, plus some private rooms. A 15min walk from Paya Lebar MRT, or bus #33 from Bedok or Kallang MRT. Dorms **$20**, doubles **$80**

**Gateway** 60 Joo Chiat Rd ☎6342 0988, ☯gatewayhotel.com.sg; see map p.94. They dare to call themselves a boutique hotel, but this is really a rather stodgy place with bland modern rooms, most with a bathtub, at keen prices. 10min walk from Paya Lebar MRT. **$110**

**Santa Grand East Coast** 171 East Coast Rd ☎6344 6866, ☯santagrandhotels.com; see map p.94. One of the nicer offerings from this mid-priced chain, partly housed in a conservation building. Rooms are more than adequate, and the secluded rooftop pool is a bonus. Rates include breakfast. **$170**

## SENTOSA

Staying "offshore" on **Sentosa** isn't such a bad idea if you have young children. On the downside, returning to your hotel for a short break from sightseeing downtown is a bit of a drag unless you catch a cab.

**Hotel Michael** ☎6577 8888, ⓦrwsentosa.com; see map p.107. The only hotel at *Resorts World* that's memorable, thanks to fittings and decor by the American architect and designer Michael Graves. Look out for packages that include Universal Studios, if you're so inclined. **$550**

**Mövenpick Sentosa** 23 Beach View, near Imbiah station ☎6818 3388, ⓦwww.moevenpick-hotels.com; see map p.107. Splendid new hotel, split into an elegant modern wing and a heritage wing housed in former British barracks dating from 1940. All rooms feature elegant contemporary fittings, but the most impressive are the pricey *onsen* suites with their own large outdoor Japanese hot tub. **$340**

**Rasa Sentosa Resort** Western end of Siloso Beach ☎6275 0100, ⓦwww.shangri-la.com; see map p.107. One of the best pre-casino-era hotels, in leafy grounds at the far end of Siloso Beach. Recently refurbished and family-friendly, it boasts a large freeform pool with water slides, a "kids' club" where staff take under-12s on activities such as treasure hunts and beach walks, plus a spa. **$400**

**Sentosa Resort and Spa** 2 Bukit Manis Rd ☎6275 0331, ⓦthesentosa.com; see map p.107. A swanky affair in secluded grounds above Tanjong Beach, with a spa featuring outdoor pools and imported mud from New Zealand that's said to be great for your skin. **$340**

**Siloso Beach Resort** 51 Imbiah Walk ☎6722 3333, ⓦsilosobeachresort.com; see map p.107. The central swimming pool is a stunner, its curvy fringes planted with lush vegetation and featuring a waterfall and slides; it far outshines the slightly dated rooms. Still, the resort is tranquil enough (the music from the nearby beach bars stops around 10pm) and rooms include breakfast. **$220**

**10**

# Eating

Along with shopping, eating ranks as the national pastime of Singaporeans, and a mind-boggling number of food outlets on just about every street cater to this obsession. One of the joys of the local eating scene is its distinctive and affordable street food, featuring Chinese and Indian dishes you won't find in China or India, served up in myriad hawker centres and food courts, as is great Malay and Indonesian food. Also worth discovering is Nonya cooking, a hybrid of Chinese and Malay cooking styles developed by the Peranakan community. Western food of all kinds is plentiful too, though it tends to be pricier than other cuisines from Asia, which are equally available. Quite a few of the more run-of-the-mill restaurants swing both ways by offering both Western and Asian dishes, and there's no shortage of upmarket places serving a fusion of the two.

## ESSENTIALS

**Alcohol** Hawker centres and *kopitiams* (see below) serve the most affordable alcohol, usually limited to bottled beer at $6–7 for 630 millilitres (1.1 Imperial pints or 1.4 US pints).

**Costs** Unlike many other things in Singapore, food is very good value if you eat at hawker centres, food courts or *kopitiams*; a meal of rice with toppings, or a serving of noodles, will cost $5–8 including a soft fizzy drink or juice. There are lots of affordable restaurants too, plus any number of swanky places charging as much as their counterparts in the West. One point to note is that if a stall's signboard or a restaurant menu lists more than one price next to a dish, it indicates that different portion sizes are available. Also note that restaurants may sell seafood by weight; make sure staff give you a clear idea of how those innocent-looking prices translate into platters of crab or prawn, as tourists have been known to get carried away when ordering and have then had to swallow a bill double what they expected to pay.

**Hawker centres and food courts** Elsewhere in Southeast Asia you can still see hawkers setting up simple pushcarts by the road to sell cooked food, with a few stools to sit at, but regulations long ago banished these from Singapore's streets and into purpose-built hawker centres, essentially indoor markets with alternating rows of tables and stalls. The oldest hawker centres often feature some of the best food, but their age also means they can be cramped and stuffy, and eating can be a hot and even smoky experience if the fumes from the stalls drift your way. Some more recent hawker centres are much more spacious affairs with air conditioning, and these are usually referred to as food courts; they're mostly found occupying one floor of a shopping mall. Some have become major franchises, notably the *Food Republic*, *Food Junction* and *Kopitiam* chains. Incidentally, don't assume that such places only serve local food – a minority of stalls offer other East Asian cuisines and some specialize in simple Western dishes, from steak to burgers with chips. As for ordering, there's no need to sit close to the stall you're want to buy from: find a free seat or table and tell the vendor roughly where you are (better still, quote the number on the table if there is one). At food courts you will probably be asked to pay when you order, though at hawker centres you tend to pay when the food reaches your table.

**Kopitiams** *Kopitiam* is a Hokkien Chinese term that literally means "coffee shop" – but don't go to one expecting it to serve croissants and cappuccinos. A *kopitiam* is like a mini version of a hawker centre, though of a much older provenance: it is the quintessential local diner, usually taking up the ground floor of a shophouse and containing perhaps a dozen tables with a four or five "stalls" serving a handful of standard dishes, though more elaborate places may have a range of *zichar* (see p.127) offerings from a kitchen at the back. Unfortunately *kopitiams* are increasingly vanishing from downtown, though they are worth seeking out wherever shophouses survive: on Chinatown side streets, in Little India, around Arab Street and off Beach Road.

**Opening hours** Only formal restaurants and Western-style cafés keep set hours, typically noon–2pm and 6–10.30pm in the case of restaurants. Because hawker centres and food courts are basically food markets, they seldom have precise opening times. As a rule food courts in shopping malls keep the same hours as the malls, while hawker centres are open from dawn until late at night, though individual stalls will open as they please, meaning that you may find fewer trading outside meal times or late in the evening. To the extent that *kopitiams* have formal opening times, they may likewise be prone to vary.

**Ordering** Chinese, Malay and, to a lesser extent, Indian restaurant meals tend to be shared affairs, where everyone tucks in to a common set of dishes with their own portion of rice as an accompaniment, so it's customary to order collectively in these situations. It's worth scanning the glossary on pp.134–135 to familiarize yourself with the most common dishes and terms. While English menus are always available at proper restaurants, note that many of the staff will be migrant workers and may not be able to understand anything but routine queries.

**Reservations** Only formal restaurants take bookings; hawker centres, food courts and *kopitiams* do not (and often do not have phone numbers, though we have given details where available). It is worth booking ahead for the more upmarket places, particularly for Friday or Saturday evening, or lunchtime on Sunday, when they are at their busiest.

**Special diets** Several Chinese and Indian restaurants and a few hawker stalls specialize in vegetarian food; the Chinese-run ones are often vegan, though they also tend to use mock meats made of gluten or soya that may be unappealing to some. If you're strict about your food being cooked separately from non-vegetarian items, you should stick to these outlets. Even if you're not so strict, when ordering elsewhere you may find that bits of meat or seafood will be added to food, and some dishes may be flavoured with meat stock, *hae ko* or *belachan*, the last two being pungent pastes made from shrimps; when ordering, make clear what you want to avoid. Halal food is predictably easy to find: most hawker centres have a row of stalls serving halal Indian or Malay food, there's a halal food-court chain (*Banquet*), and many international as well as local fast-food chains serve halal meat.

**Tipping** It is not customary to tip hawkers or when eating in food courts, *kopitiams* or cheap restaurants, and all upmarket and most mid-range restaurants add a ten percent service charge (in addition to the state's 7 percent GST) to your bill in any case. That leaves the lower end of mid-range as a grey area: here you may wish to offer a tip, though it's by no means expected.

11

## MARKETS AND SUPERMARKETS

Many hostels and guesthouses have cooking facilities, and if you want to take advantage of them, the most interesting places to buy produce and ingredients are **wet markets** – so called because the floors are perpetually damp, and sometimes actually quite wet, thanks to being hosed down from time to time. If you don't know a mango from a mangosteen, vendors are usually very helpful. Probably the most popular, well-stocked and atmospheric of downtown wet markets is the **Tekka Market** at the start of Serangoon Road, a worthwhile stopover on any trip to Little India (see p.50). In addition, Singapore has plenty of **supermarkets**, some of which are franchises of Western or Japanese chains; all stock imported beers and wines and have a deli counter. For more unusual imports, try Market Place (outlets include: Level B1, Tanglin Mall, 163 Tanglin Rd; Level B1, Paragon, 290 Orchard Rd, near Orchard MRT; both daily 9am–10pm), which is popular with expats for its specialist Western and Japanese food, including organic produce.

**11**

## RESTAURANTS, KOPITIAMS, HAWKER CENTRES AND FOOD COURTS

The reviews below cover all eating venues except Western-style cafés and specialist dessert places, for which see p.137. On the whole, proper restaurants are the places you go if you want a bit of comfort and the chance to savour more specialist local food or the best international cuisine. Note that for ordinary local food, restaurants aren't necessarily better than *kopitiams* or, indeed, food courts – they just charge quite a bit extra for posh surroundings and (often indifferent) service.

Given the cost of fine dining, consider taking advantage of the two- or three-course set lunches which are good value at many restaurants, and, for a blowout, look out for buffet and high-tea offers – for our picks, see box, p.132. All price indications in our reviews include any taxes and service charge that may apply.

### THE COLONIAL DISTRICT

Some of the genteel edifices of the Colonial District now house interesting restaurants, though on the whole the area is not the most exciting for food.

**Bobby's** #B1-03, CHIJMES, 30 Victoria St ☎6337 5477, ⓦbobbys.com.sg; see map p.34. With an atmospheric setting around the basement fountain courtyard, *Bobby's* specializes in barbecued beef rib and other meaty delights, including steaks and burgers, though veggie burgers, pizzas and pasta dishes are also available. Mains from $25. Sun–Thurs 3pm–1am, Fri & Sat 3pm–2am.

★ **Brussels Sprouts** #01-12 The Pier at Robertson Quay, 80 Mohamed Sultan Rd ☎6887 4344, ⓦbrussels sprouts.com.sg; see map p.34. This riverside restaurant specializes in – you guessed – mussels and clams (mains $47), available with a bewildering range of seasonings, from a strongly alcoholic white wine sauce to Thai tom yam, and accompanied by unlimited helpings of fries. Needless to say, you can also choose from a plethora of fruity Belgian beers, including Lindemans on draught. Mon–Thurs 5pm–midnight, Fri 5pm–1am, Sat noon–1am, Sun noon–midnight.

★ **Cedele** #03–28a Raffles City Shopping Centre ☎6337 8017, ⓦcedeledepot.com; see map p.34. Brilliant sandwiches plus light meals and cakes, at reasonable prices; see p.131 for more. Daily 11am–10.30pm.

**Coriander Leaf** Block A, Clarke Quay #02-03 ☎6732 3354, ⓦcorianderleaf.com; see map p.34. Pan-Asian and Mediterranean food in elegant upstairs premises,

encompassing everything from Lebanese meze to Vietnamese spring rolls. Main courses start at $30, or you can order a good-value sampler platter for $20. Mon–Fri noon–2pm & 6.30–10pm, Sat 6.30–10.30pm.

**Flutes at the Fort** 23b Coleman St ☎6338 8770, ⓦflutes.com.sg; see map p.34. If you think Singapore's colonial architecture is all about grand Palladian buildings, you'll be pleasantly put right at this restaurant, in a beautiful black-and-white wooden colonial house on the leafy slopes of Fort Canning Hill. You can sit indoors or out on the veranda to enjoy set lunches (two courses for around $40), or a full menu of modern European and fusion dishes. To get there, take the little path through the car park by the Freemasons' Hall. Mon–Fri noon–2pm & 6.30–10pm, Sat 11.30am– 2.30pm & 6.30–10pm, Sun 10am–5pm.

**Indochine** Asian Civilisations Museum, Empress Place ☎6339 1720 (café ☎6338 7596), ⓦindochine.com.sg; see map p.34. *Indochine* just about monopolizes the museum's river frontage with a restaurant, café and bar (see p.126). The restaurant has great views of Boat Quay and the Financial District, and both it and the *Siem Reap II* café have somewhat different menus from the original Club St premises, with the café's *pho bo* (beef noodle soup) particularly highly rated. Reckon on $20 per person for a one-dish meal plus a drink. Restaurant open for lunch Mon–Fri noon–3pm, dinner Mon–Fri & Sun 6.30– 11.30pm, Fri & Sat 6.30pm–12.30am; Siem Reap II café daily 11am–11pm.

★ **Shiraz** #01-06 Block A, Clarke Quay #01-06 ☎6334 2282, ⓦshirazfnb.com; see map p.34. The best Iranian restaurant in town, not that there's much competition, but the many Iranians among the clientele can't be misguided. The massive portions of tender kebabs and stews, all served with mounds of fluffy, aromatic saffron rice, aren't cheap – main courses from $30 – but the place is still better value than most of the competition in Clarke Quay. Belly-dancing some evenings, too, and they do serve alcohol. Mon 6.30–11pm, Tues–Thurs & Sun noon–3pm & 6.30–11pm, Fri & Sat noon–3pm & 6.30–12.30am.

**Tiffin Room** Raffles Hotel, 1 Beach Rd ☎6412 1190; see map p.34. High tea at this Anglo-Indian-themed restaurant is a splendid buffet of, oddly, dim sum plus servings of English scones, pastries, cakes and sandwiches – a real treat at $80. High tea daily 3.30–5.30pm.

**BRAS BASAH ROAD TO ROCHOR ROAD**

The area sandwiched between the Colonial District and Little India includes plenty of well-established restaurants, including a good cluster close to *Raffles Hotel*.

★ **Chao Shan Cuisine** 85 Beach Rd ☎6336 2390; see map pp.46–47. Formerly out in the suburbs, this Teochew restaurant retains a certain neighbourhood informality – witness the casually dressed proprietor wandering around chatting to customers. His wife takes orders for marvellous standards such as braised goose on a bed of beancurd, oyster omelette (in two styles, crispy or regular), fish maw soup (rather gelatinous) and cold crab. Around $30 a head, minus drinks. Daily 11.30am–2.30pm & 5.30–10.30pm.

**Fatty's Wing Seong** #01-31 Burlington Square, 175 Bencoolen St ☎6338 1087; see map pp.46–47. Run by an avuncular chubby cook in bygone decades, *Fatty's* was an institution on the now-vanished foodie paradise that was Albert St. Today this restaurant maintains the original's no-frills *zichar* approach, and also does classics such as chicken rice. Around $20 a head. Daily noon–2.30pm & 5.15–10.15pm.

★ **Haji Maimunah** 51 Bencoolen St ☎6338 5684, ⬚hjimaimunah.com; see map pp.46–47. Part of the

Bencoolen Mosque, this Malay diner serves great *nasi campur* plus a range of dishes to order; see p.125 for more. Daily 11am–9pm.

**Hock Lam Street Popular Beef Kway Teow** 38 Seah St ☎6339 9641; see map pp.46–47. Once a street stall, now a simple diner serving noodles with beef or beef dumplings, either stir-fried or in soup. Tues–Sat 10.30am–8pm.

**Kwan Im Vegetarian Restaurant** South East Asia Hotel, 190 Waterloo St ☎6338 2394; see map pp.46–47. More formal than the other Chinese veggie places clustered near the Kwan Im temple, this restaurant serves meatless versions of classic Chinese dishes (as opposed to street food). It's pricier too, though most dishes still cost under $10, and there's a good range of takeaway Chinese pastries. Daily 8.30am–8.30pm.

**Mr Bean's** 30 Selegie Rd ☎6333 3100; see map pp.46–47. Not to be confused with the *Mr Bean* chain of soya-milk outlets, this café-restaurant offers okay steaks and pizzas, plus good-value two-course lunches ($14) and dinners ($20) daily except Sun. Breakfasts also available for $10. Service may not be great but is still slicker than Mr Bean, whose visage is stuck over the *Mona Lisa* above the cake counter, would have managed. Daily 24hr.

**Yet Con Chicken Rice Restaurant** 25 Purvis St ☎6337 6819; see map pp.46–47. Cheap and cheerful old-time *kopitiam* known not just for chicken rice but also for its roast pork with pickled cabbage and radish. Around $15 for two people. Daily 11.30am–8.30pm.

**Yhingthai Palace** #01-04, 36 Purvis St ☎6337 1161; see map pp.46–47. A smartly turned-out Chinese-influenced Thai restaurant, where you can't go wrong with the deep-fried pomfret with mango sauce, Thai fishcakes or deboned chicken wings stuffed with asparagus and mushroom. Around $40 per head, excluding drinks. Daily 11.30am–2pm & 6–10pm.

**LITTLE INDIA TO LAVENDER STREET**

Little India is paradise if you're after maximum flavour for minimum outlay; the first part of Serangoon Rd and its side

**11**

---

**HAWKER AND KOPITIAM FOOD**

For taste and value, the inexpensive cooking served up by stalls in **hawker centres** and at the roadside diners called **kopitiams** simply can't be beaten. While not the healthiest food you could eat – much of it is fried, and cooks use salt and sugar liberally – it is likely to form an abiding and highly favourable impression of Singapore cuisine.

Perhaps the most basic meal is **mixed rice** (*nasi campur* in Malay), widely served up by Chinese, Malay and some Indian stalls; you'll instantly recognize it by the trays of stir-fries and stews behind the glass. Order simply by pointing at what you fancy, and expect plenty of entertaining culinary cross-fertilization – the Chinese stalls all serve curry, the Indian stalls have tofu, and so on. It's best had at mealtimes when the dishes will be freshly prepared, though food never really goes cold in Singapore's climate, so will be palatable at any time of day.

Otherwise, stalls offer literally dozens of classic one-plate rice and noodle dishes, plus other, more elaborate dishes.

streets, as well as Race Course Rd, are packed with inexpensive, excellent curry houses specializing in South Indian food, often dished out onto banana leaves and with plenty of vegetarian options; some places offer South Indian renditions of North Indian and Nepali dishes too. The only drawback to eating here is that there's not a lot that isn't Indian.

★ **Banana Leaf Apolo** 54 Race Course Rd ☎ 6293 8682; see map pp.46–47. Pioneering banana-leaf-type restaurant with a wide selection of Indian dishes, including fish-head curry ($22–30 depending on size) plus chicken, mutton and prawn curries ($12). The "South Indian vegetarian meal" is a steal, a huge thali of rice, poppadums, two main curries and several side ones, plus a dessert, for just $8. There's also a branch tucked away in the Little India Arcade (☎ 6297 1595). Daily 10.30am–10.30pm.

**Cocotte** Wanderlust Hotel, 2 Dickson Rd ☎ 6298 1188, ⓦ restaurantcocotte.com; see map pp.46–47. It's an obvious misfit in the area, but one that impresses with its eccentric decor and modern French cuisine using prime ingredients. The three-course executive lunch is best for value ($35), though it's a shame that its top main-course option, the superb duck leg confit, costs $11 extra. Mains from $40; reservations essential. Mon–Thurs noon–2.30pm & 6.30–10.30pm, Fri & Sat 6.30–11pm, Sun noon–3pm.

**Hillman** 135 Kitchener Rd ☎ 6221 5073; see map pp.46–47. For some reason this tiny old-fangled restaurant is popular with rowdy Japanese businessmen, though don't let that put you off. They come, as you should, for the tiptop *zichar* food. Particularly good are the claypot noodles and, if you're feeling adventurous, claypot sea cucumber – it's not a vegetable but a marine creature related to starfish and sea urchins. Slightly pricey for *zichar*, though, at $25 per head excluding drinks. Daily 11.30am–2.30pm & 5.30–10.30pm.

**Komala Villas** 76–78 Serangoon Rd ☎ 6293 6980; see map pp.46–47. A veteran, rather cramped vegetarian establishment with more than a dozen variations of dosai at just a few dollars each, plus fresh coconut to wash it down. They also do more substantial rice-based meals upstairs from 11am to 4pm. There's also a branch at 12–14 Buffalo Rd (☎ 6293 366; open from 8am). Daily 7am–10.30pm.

**Madras Woodlands Ganga** 22 Belilios Lane ☎ 6295 3750; see map pp.46–47. This simple vegetarian restaurant serves up great-value Indian buffets (Mon–Fri lunchtime $9, weekend lunchtimes and all eves $12), featuring several curries, rice, nan and a dessert, with the option of ordering a la carte as well. Daily 11.30am–2pm & 6.30–10pm.

**Saravana Bhavan** 84 Syed Alwi Rd ☎ 6297 7755, ⓦ saravanabhavan.com; see map pp.46–47. This South Indian vegetarian franchise, gone global out of Chennai, has a modern Singapore venue that offers all the staples, from *vada* (dhal-flour doughnuts) to dosai, plus their popular Indian take on Chinese food, typified by Gobi Manchurian (though not on the menu, it's usually available): stir-fried battered cauliflower with a spicy, tangy sauce. Also good for non-Tamil cuisine, such as *bisibelabeth*, a gooey rice, lentil and vegetable concoction from Karnataka. Daily 9am–midnight.

## INDIAN FOOD

As befits a country whose Indian community is largely Tamil, **Indian food** in Singapore tends to be synonymous with South Indian cooking, which is generally spicy, makes heavy use of coconut and tamarind and emphasizes starchy and vegetarian food. The classic southern Indian dish is the dosai or *thosai*, a thin rice-flour pancake. It's usually served accompanied by *sambar* a watery vegetable and dhal (lentil) curry; *rasam*, a spicy clear soup flavoured with tamarind; and perhaps a few small helpings of vegetable or dhal curries, plus coconut or mint chutney. Also very common are rotis – griddle breads – plus the more substantial *murtabak*, thicker than a roti and stuffed with egg, onion and minced meat. The latter is a particular specialty of Indian Muslim *kopitiams* and stalls, which form a sideshoot of the South Indian eating scene and tend to place much more emphasis on meat.

One endearing aspect of South Indian restaurants is that they often serve food on a banana-leaf "platter", the waiters dishing out replenishable heaps of various curries along with mounds of rice. In some restaurants you'll find more substantial dishes such as the popular fish-head curry (don't be put off by the idea – the "cheeks" between the mouth and gills are packed with tasty flesh).

South Indian restaurants tend to be very reasonably priced. North Indian food is usually pricier (though some cheap South Indian places will offer attempts at northern cooking) and tends to be richer, less fiery and more reliant on mutton and chicken. In Singapore, tandoori dishes – the *tandoor* being the clay oven in which the food is cooked – are the most common North Indian offerings, particularly tandoori chicken marinated in yoghurt and spices and then baked. Breads such as nan also tend to feature rather than rice, though just about every restaurant has a version of biriyani.

## MALAY AND INDONESIAN FOOD

Though Malays form the largest minority in Singapore, the **Malay eating scene** is a bit one-dimensional, mainly because the Malays themselves don't have a tradition of elaborate eating out. Every hawker centre has several Malay stalls, but these tend to serve fairly basic rice and noodle dishes. It's a shame, because Malay cuisine is a spicy and sophisticated affair with interesting connections to China in the use of noodles and soy sauce, but also to Thailand, with which it shares an affinity for such ingredients as lemon grass, the ginger-like galingale and fermented fish sauce (the Malay version, *budu*, is made from anchovies). Malay cooking also draws on Indian and Middle East cooking in the use of spices, and in dishes such as biriyani rice. The resulting cuisine is characterized by being both spicy and a little sweet. *Santan* (coconut milk) lends a sweet, creamy undertone to many stews and curries, while *belacan*, a pungent fermented prawn paste (something of an acquired taste), is found in chilli condiments and sauces. Unusual herbs, including curry and kaffir-lime leaves, also play a prominent role.

The most famous Malay dish is arguably satay (see p.135), though this can be hard to find outside the big cities; another classic, and this time ubiquitous, is *nasi lemak* (see p.134), standard breakfast fare. Also quintessentially Malay, rendang is a dryish curry made by slow-cooking meat (usually beef) in coconut milk flavoured with galingale and a variety of herbs and spices.

For many visitors, one of the most striking things about Malay food is the bewildering array of *kuih-muih* (or just *kuih*), or sweetmeats, on display at markets at street stalls. Often featuring coconut and sometimes *gula melaka* (palm-sugar molasses), *kuih* come in all shapes and sizes, and in as many colours (often artificial nowadays) as you find in a paints catalogue – rainbow-hued layer cakes of rice flour are about the most extreme example.

### INDONESIAN FOOD

Worth mentioning in the same breath as Malay food is **Indonesian cuisine** – the two can have much in common, given that native Malay speakers live in many parts of what is now Indonesia. One style of Indonesian cuisine is especially widespread in Singapore – *nasi padang*, associated with the city of Padang in Sumatra. Like mixed rice (see p.123), it's largely served up as curries and stir-fries in trays; point at what you want and servings will be dolloped on top of a generous portion of steamed rice.

**★ Tekka Food Centre** Start of Serangoon Rd; see map pp.46–47. Alongside Tekka market is one of the best old-school hawkers' centres on the island, generally steamy hot and busy. The Indian and Malay stalls are especially worthwhile, and look out for exceptional Indian *rojak* – assorted fritters with sweet dips. Daily 7am till late.

#### ARAB STREET AND AROUND

It seems logical that Arab St should boast several Middle Eastern and North African restaurants with meze to nibble at and *shishas* to puff on, but in fact these places have only been around for a few years; the mainstay of the area's dining has long been Malay and Indonesian food.

**★ Blu Jaz Café** 11 Bali Lane ☎ 6292 3800, ⒲ blujaz .net; see map pp.46–47. Chilled-out café-restaurant stretching between Bali and Haji lanes, and easily spotted with its gaudy decor. Reliable local and Western food – everything from chicken kebab to fish and chips – at affordable prices; a steak will set you back around \$23. Live jazz Wed, Fri & Sat evenings. Mon–Thurs noon–midnight, Fri noon–1am, Sat 4pm–1am.

**Bumbu** 44 Kandahar St ☎ 6392 8628, ⒲ bumbu.com .sg; see map pp.46–47. Boasting fine Peranakan artefacts

amassed by the owner, *Bumbu* is as much a social history document as a restaurant. Happily, the furnishings don't outshine the fine Thai cuisine, with a few Indonesian offerings too. Around \$25 per person. Tues–Sun 11am–3pm & 6–10pm.

**★ Café Le Caire** 33 & 39 Arab St ☎ 6292 0979, ⒲ cafelecaire.com; see map pp.46–47. This relaxed diner spearheaded the arrival of Arab cuisine in the area and is a good inexpensive bet for Lebanese and Egyptian kebabs, dips and wraps, plus Yemeni *harissa*, a spicy stew of minced lamb and cracked wheat. For those into hubble-bubbles, they do over a dozen tobaccos. Sun–Thurs 10am–3.30am, Fri & Sat 10am–5.30am.

**Haji Maimunah** 11 & 15 Jalan Pisang ⒲ hjmaimunah .com; see map pp.46–47. A cosy restaurant that's great for inexpensive Malay food, including good desserts and snacks; see p.123 for more. Mon–Sat 7am–8pm (closed during Ramadan).

**Islamic Restaurant** 745 North Bridge Rd ☎ 6298 7563; see map pp.46–47. The bland, modernized premises of today don't hint at this restaurant's impeccable pedigree, for which check out the photos of functions they catered for in the 1920s. Biriyanis are their trademark offering (\$7)

11

though they also do a huge range of North Indian chicken, mutton, prawn, squid and veg curries, with good-value set meals at around $8. Daily 10am–10pm; closed Fri 1–2pm.

★ **Kampong Glam Café** 17 Bussorah St; see map pp.46–47. Fantastic roadside *kopitiam* serving inexpensive rice and noodle dishes, cooked to order, plus curries. Come not just for the food but for a good chinwag with friends over *teh tarik* late into the evening. Daily 8am–1am.

**Piedra Negra** Corner of Haji Lane and Beach Rd 6291 1297; see map pp.46–47. The brashest restaurant in the area, the Mexican *Piedra Negra* is an offshoot of the *Blu Jaz Café* and sports similar gaudy walls. They do reasonably priced mains ($15–20) and snacks, including great guacamole, and plenty of margaritas. Gets packed out later in the evening; note that service can be a bit chaotic. Mon–Thurs noon–midnight, Fri noon–2am, Sat 5pm–2am.

★ **Rumah Makan Minang** 18a Kandahar St; see map pp.46–47. A street-corner place serving superb *nasi padang*, including the mildly spiced chicken *balado* and more unusual curries made with tempeh (fermented soybean cakes) or offal. For dessert there are freshly made sweet pancakes stuffed with peanuts and corn – much better than they sound. Just $8 per head for a good feed. Daily 8am–8pm.

**Zam Zam** 697/699 North Bridge Rd 6298 7011; see map pp.46–47. Staff at this venerable Indian Muslim *kopitiam* have the annoying habit of touting for custom – pointless, when the place draws crowds, especially on Fridays, with its *murtabak* and biriyani offerings (there's even a venison version of the latter). Avoid the house speciality drink, *air katira* – it's like one of Singapore's syrupy ice desserts, only melted. Daily 8.30am–10pm.

### CHINATOWN

Singapore's Chinatown is no Chinese ghetto, of course, and its places to eat are thus pretty diverse, though Chinese food retains a high profile in the heart of the area, on and around South Bridge Rd. A few touts on touristy Sago, Smith, Terengganu and Pagoda sts will try to lure you into the clutch of foreigner-friendly restaurants here, all decent enough though not the best in their class.

**Annalakshmi** #01-04 Central Square, 20 Havelock Rd 6339 9993, annalakshmi.com.sg; see map pp.60–61. Come here for excellent Indian vegetarian dishes served up by volunteers, with no prices specified; you pay what you feel the meal was worth. Profits go to Kala Mandhir, an association promoting South Indian culture. It's best to turn up for their superb buffets (at lunchtime plus dinner Fri–Sun), though note that they take a dim view of people helping themselves to more than they can finish. There's also a branch at 104 Amoy St ( 6223 0809)

which does buffets only (Mon–Sat 11am–3pm). Daily 11am–3pm & 6–9.30pm.

**Bee Heong Palace** 132–134 Telok Ayer St 6222 9074; see map pp.60–61. Less crowded than more famous rivals for Hokkien cuisine, this nondescript modern place nevertheless serves up creditable *hae cho*, minced pork and prawn fried up like little rissoles; plus *kong bak*, pork stewed in soy sauce and eaten stuffed into semicircular buns. Portions are quite large and prices reasonable – reckon on $20 per head, without alcohol. Mon & Wed 11.30am–3pm, Tues & Thurs–Sun 11.30am–3pm & 6–10.30pm.

**Hong Hock Eating House** South Bridge Rd opposite the Jamae Mosque; see map pp.60–61. Somewhere between a *kopitiam* and a small food court, this excellent place takes a multicultural approach: Chinese fare includes claypot curry fish and oyster omelette, while an Indian Muslim stall serves *nasi campur* and *tissue prata* – a sweet roti artfully folded up like a napkin. A good place to head after partying into the small hours. Daily 11.30am–7am.

**Indochine** Upstairs at 47 Club St 6323 7347, indochine.com.sg; see map pp.60–61. Classy Vietnamese, Lao and Cambodian cuisine in chic surroundings sums up this chain, and their Club St venue is no exception. The Vietnamese *chao tom* (minced prawn wrapped round sugar cane) and deep-fried Vietnamese spring rolls (in veggie and non-veggie versions) are mouthwatering starters, while the Lao *larb kai* (spicy chicken salad) is one of many excellent main courses. Mon–Fri noon–3pm & 6.30–11pm, Sat 6.30–11pm.

★ **Lee Tong Kee** 278 South Bridge Rd 6226 0417, ipohhorfun.com; see map pp.60–61. For years the speciality of this retro-styled restaurant, with old-fashioned fans and marble tables, has been *hor fun* (tagliatelle-type rice noodles) done in the style of Ipoh, a town in northern Malaysia, and supposedly smoother than regular noodles. Though you may have trouble discerning that difference, their many offerings are undeniably good whether served dryish or in soup (all around $6). Also available are assorted dumplings plus their signature lime juice, usually served with a pinch of salt. Get there early for lunch, when it gets packed out. Mon 10am–3.30pm, Wed–Sun 10am–8.30pm.

**Maxwell Food Centre** Corner of South Bridge Rd & Maxwell Rd; see map pp.60–61. One of Singapore's first hawker centres and home to a clutch of popular Chinese stalls, including Tian Tian for Hainanese chicken rice, plus others that are good for satay or *rojak*. Daily roughly 7am–midnight.

**Rongcheng** 271 New Bridge Rd 6536 4415; see map pp.60–61. One of several Sichuan hotpot places here, though not signed in English – look out for the Chinese name in black on a big red sign and for the cafeteria-style metal display of meats, seafood and vegetables. Hotpots

## CHINESE FOOD

The range of **Chinese cooking** available in Singapore represents a mouthwatering sweep through China's southeastern seaboard, reflecting the historical pattern of emigration from Fujian, Guangzhou and Hainan Island provinces. Frankly there aren't clear-cut differences between each province's style; it's more that each has its signature dishes (including some that were actually created by hawkers in Singapore and have subsequently become local standards). You'll also come across food from further afield in China, notably northern Beijing (or Peking) and western Sichuan cuisines. It's good to retain a sense of adventure when exploring menus: the Chinese eat all parts of an animal, from its lips to its entrails.

One popular feature of some Singapore Chinese *kopitiams* and restaurants is what's termed **zichar** – which basically means that their food has a home-cooked, less formal slant, with more flexibility to order dishes that don't correspond exactly to what's on the menu.

### CANTONESE

Cantonese food dominates in formal restaurants, reflecting that cuisine's pre-eminence in Chinese cooking. It's noted for its subtleties of flavour and memorable sauces, most famously sweet-and-sour. Fish and seafood weigh in heavily, either fried or steamed, and other specialities include pigeon, roast meats and frogs' legs. Dim sum is also a classic Cantonese meal: literally translated as "to touch the heart", it's a blanket term for an array of dumplings, cakes and tidbits steamed in bamboo baskets. Though you do occasionally see it on lunch menus, traditionally dim sum is eaten for breakfast, with one basket (of three or four pieces) costing as little as $3.

### HAINANESE

Hainanese cuisine in Singapore is synonymous with chicken rice, a simple but tasty platter featuring, predictably enough, slices of chicken laid on rice that has been cooked in chicken stock, with a chilli and ginger dip. Historically, though, the Hainanese were chefs to the British and kept their colonial employers happy with a range of fusion dishes such as pork chops, still found on menus.

### HOKKIEN

The Hokkien chef relies heavily upon sauces and broths to cook his meat and (primarily) seafood. Without doubt, the cuisine's most popular dish in Singapore is Hokkien *mee*, though confusingly it comes in two styles. The classic hawker version doesn't consist of just *mee* – yellow noodles – but also features white vermicelli, the combination fried with prawns and pork for flavour. In restaurants, however, Hokkien noodles are braised in a savoury brownish sauce.

### TEOCHEW

Chaozhou (Teochew in dialect) is a city in Fujian province where steaming is the most commonly used form of cooking, producing light but flavourful dishes such as fish steamed with sour plums. Other Teochew classics are braised goose, steamed crayfish and, at hawker stalls, *mee pok* – a spicy dish of flat noodles with round fishball dumplings.

### BEIJING

The sumptuous presentation of Beijing cuisine reflects that city's opulent past as the seat of emperors. Meat dominates, typically flavoured with garlic and spring onions, though the dish for which Beijing is most famous is roast duck, served in three courses: the skin is eaten in a pancake filled with spring onion and radish, and smeared with plum sauce.

### SICHUAN

Sichuan (or Szechuan) food is famously spicy and greasy, with chilli, pepper, garlic and ginger conspiring to piquant effect in classic dishes such as camphor-and-tea-smoked duck and chicken with dried chilli. One of the most common offerings in this vein in Singapore is the hotpot, akin to a fondue; you order raw ingredients, such as slices of meat and fish, and cook them at your table in a pot of boiling stock.

are akin to the steamboats you may encounter elsewhere in Singapore: help yourself to the raw ingredients, then cook them in your choice of stock, which will be boiling away on the stove at your table. You mix your own dips too, choosing from different chilli sauces, minced garlic and even tahini. Eat as much as you want for $20 per head. Things only really get going in the evening. Daily 11.30am until the small hours.

**Spizza** 29 Club St ☎ 6224 2525, ⓦ spizza.sg; see map pp.60–61. Modern, unpretentious pizzeria with a tempting A to Z of thin-crust offerings cooked in a traditional wood oven (from $20). They deliver all over the island, too (order on ☎ 6377 7773). Mon–Fri noon–3pm & 6–11pm, Sat & Sun noon–11pm.

**Tak Po** 42 Smith St ☎ 6225 0302; see map pp.60–61. Compact, competent and inexpensive Cantonese restaurant, refreshingly untouristy considering the location, with a/c inside and some tables out on the street. All the usual dim sum favourites, including *siu mai* dumplings, yam cake and excellent pork ribs with black beans, plus a wide range of *congees* (savoury rice porridges). For afters, try the baked egg tarts, which are spot on, the pastry not too flaky and the custard filling not oversweet. Reckon on $15 per person, without drinks. Daily 7am–10.30pm.

★ **Urban Bites** 123 Telok Ayer St ☎ 6327 9460, ⓦ urbanbites.com.sg; see map pp.60–61. It's nothing much to look at, but *Urban Bites* serves excellent Lebanese cuisine, from a tender *kafta khashkhash* (minced lamb kebab) to home-cooking favourites like *mujadara* (rice with lentils and fried onions). You can order meze-style or individual mains; reckon on $30 per head, minus drinks. Mon–Sat 9am–9.45pm.

**Yixin** 39 Temple St, no phone; see map pp.60–61. Workaday vegetarian *kopitiam* that turns out *zichar* dishes such as mock Peking duck ($8), plus rice and noodle standards like *lor mee* (noodles in a yummy, tangy, gloopy sauce). A picture menu makes ordering easy. Barely signed in English, but easy to spot by the Santa Grand Chinatown hotel. Daily 7.30am–9.30pm.

**Yum Cha** #02-01 20 Trengganu St (entry via Temple St) ☎ 6372 1717, ⓦ yumcha.com.sg; see map pp.60–61. Grand dim sum restaurant, with several dining rooms and a wide-ranging menu. They call their house speciality pomfret "tapino" – it's a fish hotpot for around $50. Mon–Fri 11am–11pm, Sat & Sun 9am–11pm.

## BOAT QUAY AND RIVERSIDE POINT

The south bank of the Singapore River is packed with busy restaurants and bars, at their most atmospheric in the restored shophouses of boisterous Boat Quay, though even the modern complexes can be a more enticing prospect than overpriced Clarke Quay on the north bank. All places reviewed here are in riverside buildings or no more than a couple of streets back from the river.

**Brewerkz** #01-05/06 Riverside Point, 30 Merchant Rd ☎ 6438 7438, ⓦ brewerkz.com; see map pp.60–61. This buzzing restaurant is popular for its highly rated beers, brewed on site, and American fare, including excellent

burgers and sandwiches, plus barbecued ribs, pizzas, nachos, grilled potato skins and the like. It's on the pricey side though, with burgers starting at $25. Busy at weekends. Sun–Thurs noon–midnight, Fri & Sat noon–1am.

★ **Café Iguana** #01-03 Riverside Point, 30 Merchant Rd ☎ 6236 1275, ⓦ cafeiguana.com; see map pp.60–61. This open-fronted restaurant features a huge mural of Frida Kahlo, plus assorted other Mexicana. Fajitas, tacos, burritos and all the other standards, with plenty for veggies; mains cost around $20. The avocado ice cream makes a tasty dessert. Great as a drinking venue too, and can get very crowded in the evenings. Mon–Thurs 4pm–1am, Fri 4pm–3am, Sat noon–3am, Sun noon–1am.

★ **Genesis** 1 Lorong Telok ☎ 6438 7118; see map pp.60–61. The most inconspicuous restaurant in the area, *Genesis* should have its name in lights for its brilliant take on vegan wholefood, with delicious *laksa*, dumplings and other Asian dishes, plus an excellent lasagne where the "cheese" is really a nut butter. The cooking is studiously low in fat and salt – a great way to detox after too many hawker meals. Mon–Thurs 8am–8pm, Fri & Sun 8am–3pm.

**Hock Lam Street Popular Beef Kway Teow** 6 North Canal Rd ☎ 6535 0084; see map pp.60–61. For decades this was a highly regarded stall on the now-vanished Hock Lam St, at the site of the present Funan DigitaLife Mall. The stall survives, albeit as a little shophouse restaurant, serving the same *kuay teow* noodles with beef slices or beefball dumplings, dry or with soup; servings cost around $6. Mon–Fri 11am–8pm, Sat & Sun 11am–4.30pm.

**Moomba** 52 Circular Rd ☎ 6438 0141, ⓦ themoomba .com; see map pp.60–61. With snazzy Aboriginal-influenced murals, this place has a great reputation for Australian fusion cuisine, including a dish or two of kangaroo and more conventional steaks. Most menu items have wine recommendations drawn from their on-site wine shop. A little pricey, with mains starting at $35, though there are also sandwiches and salads from their "tuck shop" section. Mon–Fri 11am–2.30pm & 6.30–10pm, Sat 6.30–10pm.

**Our Village** Entrance on fifth floor, 46 Boat Quay ☎ 6538 3092; see map pp.60–61. A hidden gem, with fine North Indian and Sri Lankan food, and peachy views of the river and Colonial District from its lamplit sixth-floor terrace. Mon–Fri noon–1.45pm & 6–11pm, Sat & Sun 6–11pm.

**Rendezvous** #02-72 The Central, 6 Eu Tong Sen St ☎ 6339 7508, ⓦ rendezvous-hlk.com.sg; see map pp.60–61. For decades *Rendezvous* has been serving up revered *nasi padang*, first as the Rendezvous *kopitiam* at the start of Bras Basah Rd, then in the hotel of that name that replaced it. Its new location in a mediocre mall doesn't suit at all, but thankfully the curries have stayed the course,

in particular the superb chicken korma, here a curried stew of just the right degree of richness, derived from coconut milk rather than cream or yoghurt. A couple of curries with rice and side dishes are unlikely to cost more than $25 a head. Daily 11am–9pm.

**Smiths** 50 Boat Quay ☎ 6536 7316; see map pp.60–61. British-style fish-and-chip shop that's excellent at what it does. Choose from cod or haddock or salmon fishcakes, or forgo the fish and have chicken or sausage (batter optional) with your chips. Mushy peas, curry sauce and chips butty (sic – basically a chips sandwich) available too. The lunch special is an excellent deal – $10 for fish and chips with a soft drink and side order. Daily 11.30am–11pm.

### TANJONG PAGAR AND THE FINANCIAL DISTRICT

You're unlikely to head to these areas bordering Chinatown for the food alone, but they do boast some excellent, if often pricey, independent restaurants.

**Blue Ginger** 97 Tanjong Pagar Rd ☎ 6222 3928, ⓦ theblueginger.com; see map pp.60–61. In a smartly renovated shophouse, this trendy Nonya restaurant has become a firm favourite thanks to such dishes as *ikan masal asam gulai* (mackerel in a tamarind and lemon-grass gravy), and that benchmark of Nonya cuisine, *ayam buah keluak* – chicken braised in soy sauce together with savoury black nuts. Daily noon–2.30pm & 6.30–10.30pm.

**BROTH** 21 Duxton Hill ☎ 6323 3353, ⓦ broth.com.sg; see map pp.60–61. The "Bar Restaurant On The Hill" serves beautifully presented Aussie-influenced fusion cuisine, including an exquisite spinach and portobello mushroom salad, and their trademark lamb loin in a "green coat" – a marinade of herbs, including mint. Not cheap though, with main courses at $35. Mon–Fri noon–2.30pm & 6.30–10.30pm, Sat 6.30–10.30pm.

**Cumi Bali** 66 Tanjong Pagar Rd ☎ 6220 6619, ⓦ cumibali.com; see map pp.60–61. Bamboo sieves and flutes line the walls at this tiny, inexpensive *nasi padang* joint. Both the beef *rendang* and satay Madura, marinated in sweet soy sauce, hit the spot, and they have generous $7 set lunches too. Mon–Sat 11.30am–2.30pm & 6–9.30pm.

★ **Lau Pa Sat** 18 Raffles Quay; see map pp.60–61. This historic market building is home to an excellent food court. Foods to try include Hokkien *mee* (stall #81) and satay – satay sellers set up just outside on Boon Tat St in the evenings. Pricier outlets offer cooked-to-order seafood such as chilli crab. Open 24hr.

★ **Sabio** 5 Duxton Hill ☎ 6223 4645 (no reservations), ⓦ sabio.sg; see map pp.60–61. Spanish-owned and -run, this elegant but tiny restaurant serves delicious tapas, including excellent pan-fried calamari, tender grilled lamb cutlets and aged ham from acorn-fed pigs, these last sold by weight (most tapas $10–15). Wash it down with sangria

or Estrella Damm beer from Barcelona. Often packed. Mon–Fri noon–late, Sat 6pm–late.

### MARINA BAY

**Paulaner Bräuhaus** #01-01 Millenia Walk, 9 Raffles Blvd ☎ 6883 2572, ⓦ paulaner.com.sg; see map p.74. The cavernous ceiling with a maypole sticking up into it is impressive, as is the menu of Bavarian delights such as the bitty spätzle pasta, but the best reason to come is the terrific Sunday brunch spread, including superb pork knuckle, sausages and salads, and desserts like strudel and cheesecake. It's good value at $55 with unlimited soft drinks, or $65 with unlimited beer from their microbrewery. Mon–Fri noon–2.30pm & 6.30–10.30pm, Sat 6.30–10.30pm, Sun 11.30am–2.30pm & 6.30–10.30pm.

**Pizzeria Mozza** #B01-42 Marina Bay Sands shopping mall, 1 Bayfront Ave ☎ 6688 8522, ⓦ pizzeriamozza .com/Singapore; see map p.74. An excellent range of reasonably priced thin-crust pizzas starting at $25, with plenty of salads, panini and soups, plus good desserts. Daily noon–11pm.

★ **Singapore Food Trail** Beneath the Singapore Flyer; see map p.74. Arguably more interesting than the Flyer itself, this retro-style food court evokes Singapore's street food scene of half a century ago, its stalls mocked up as pushcarts. The food can be retro too – for example satay *bee hoon*, rice vermicelli drenched in the peanut sauce normally eaten with satay, and popular in the 1970s – though it also features lots of evergreens, including oyster omelette and *popiah* (steamed spring rolls). Nothing costs more than $10. Mon–Thurs 10.30am–10.30pm, Fri–Sun 10.30am–11.30pm.

★ **Sky on 57** SkyPark at Marina Bay Sands ☎ 6688 8857; see map p.74. One of the best ways to circumvent that huge SkyPark admission charge is by eating at this fine restaurant featuring a harmonious marriage of Far Eastern and French cooking. Fiendishly expensive at dinner, when mains start at $50, but reasonable value at lunchtime when their superb king prawn *laksa* costs $30, or a three-course set menu is $60. Head up via tower 1 (the south tower). Daily 7.30–10am, noon–2.30pm, 6–10.30pm.

### ORCHARD ROAD AND AROUND

Eating in the heart of Singapore's shopping nexus – Orchard Rd, Tanglin Rd and Scotts Rd – is almost completely about restaurants in malls and hotels, though a few venues are housed in two rows of refurbished shophouses on Emerald Hill Rd and at Cuppage Terrace next to the Centrepoint mall; both are near Somerset MRT.

**Bistro Du Vin** #02-12 Shaw Centre, 1 Scotts Rd ☎ 6733 7763; see map pp.80–81. Reasonably priced, informal French restaurant that does an exceptional duck leg confit and even a tender suckling pig confit, plus standards such as escargot and French onion soup. The lunch deals are great value at $36 for three courses; mains ordered a la carte cost just about as much. Daily noon–2.30pm & 7–10pm.

★ **Cedele** #B1-37, Ngee Ann City, 391 Orchard Rd ☎6235 2380, ⓦcedeledepot.com; see map pp.80–81. A café/bakery combo, *Cedele* serves up some of the very best sandwiches in Singapore ($6–8) – think, say, honey dijon chicken on rosemary focaccia – and sells a vast variety of specialist breads and rich cakes. Some branches, like this one, also have a restaurant with soups, pies and inventive light meals such as the beetroot burger, which even non-veggies love. Daily 10am–10pm.

★ **Crystal Jade La Mian Xiao Long Bao** #04-27, Ngee Ann City ☎6238 1661, ⓦcrystaljade.com; see map pp.80–81. *Crystal Jade* is an umbrella for several linked Chinese restaurant chains, each with a different emphasis. Their mid-priced La Mian Xiao Long Bao outlets focus on Shanghai and northern Chinese cuisine, as exemplified by *xiao long bao*, succulent Shanghai pork dumplings, and the northwestern speciality *la mian*, literally "pulled noodles", the strands of dough being stretched and worked by hand. Not fantastic for veggies though. Daily 11am–10pm.

★ **Delicious** #B1-16 Scotts Square, Scotts Rd ☎6636 0913, ⓦthedeliciousgroup.com.sg; see map pp.80–81. How a Malaysian clothing store specializing in gear for larger ladies spawned a restaurant chain serving healthy fusion food is a little mysterious, but no matter: the food is its own recommendation. Trusty favourites include their tender masala lambshank with pilau rice, salad and poppadums, and their unusual take on beef *rendang*. Mains start at around $20 and portions are always generous. Daily 11am–9pm.

★ **Food Republic** Level 5, 313@Somerset mall, above Somerset MRT; see map pp.80–81. One of the nicest examples of this all-conquering food court chain, spacious, comfortable and with a wealth of excellent stalls, including one that does great *nasi padang* – it's hard to go wrong, whichever stall you choose. Daily 8am–10pm.

**Kiseki** #08-01 Orchard Central mall, 181 Orchard Rd ☎6736 1216, ⓦkisekirestaurant.com.sg; see map pp.80–81. If you come here often enough you might end up as rotund as the sumo wrestler statue at the entrance. This "mega Japanese buffet" has everything from sushi to Japanese curry pizza, via tempura, yakitori and (at dinner) steak and chicken teriyaki. Prices range from $24 Mon–Fri lunchtime to nearly double that Fri–Sun eves. Daily 11.30am–3pm & 6–10.30pm.

★ **Lao Beijing** #03-01 Plaza Singapura, 68 Orchard Rd ☎6738 7207, ⓦlaobeijing.com.sg; see map pp.80–81. Styled like a classy, old-fangled Chinese teahouse, this restaurant specializes in northern Chinese fare, including Peking duck and "Chairman Mao's Favourite Braised Pork" – suitably red in colour – plus dishes from elsewhere in China. There's also a high-tea buffet featuring not scones and cream but plenty more Chinese specialities (3–5pm;

$15 weekdays, $20 weekends). Daily 11.30am–5pm & 6–10pm.

★ **Marché** Ground floor and basement, 313@Somerset, 313 Orchard Rd ☎6834 4041; see map pp.80–81. Never mind that Mövenpick's *Marché* restaurants are formulaic: what a formula, when you can have rösti, sausages or crêpes cooked to order in front of you, or help yourself to the superb salad bar. Daily lunch specials offer a meal and drink for $10, while the bakery counter does takeaway sandwiches (from $5), bread sticks and Berliners, doughnuts with a range of fillings. Daily 11am–11pm; bakery from 7.30am.

**Maharajah** 39 Cuppage Terrace ☎6732 6331, ⓦmaharajah.com.sg; see map pp.80–81. This splendid North Indian restaurant has a large terrace and a tempting menu that includes several tandoori options plus the sublime fish *mumtaz* – fillet of fish stuffed with minced mutton, almonds, eggs, cashews and raisins. Around $35 per person without alcohol. Daily 11am–11pm.

**Min Jiang** Goodwood Park Hotel, 22 Scotts Rd ☎6730 1704; see map pp.80–81. This stylish affair serves some Cantonese food and lunchtime dim sum, though their spicy Sichuan specialities are the most interesting. Good choices include the prawn fried with dried chillies, Sichuan smoked duck and long beans fried with minced pork. Reasonably priced for a top hotel. Daily 11am–2.30pm & 6–10.30pm, plus dim sum buffet Sat & Sun 3–5.30pm.

**Newton Circus Hawker Centre** Corner of Clemenceau Ave North and Bukit Timah Rd, near Newton MRT; see map pp.80–81. A venerable open-air place with a wide range of cooking. It's noted for its seafood, for which you can end up paying through the nose; prices are on the high side for stalls anyway, as the place is very much on the tourist trail. Mostly gets going in the late afternoon and stays open till the small hours.

★ **PS Café** Level 2, Palais Renaissance, 390 Orchard Rd ☎9834 8232, ⓦpscafe.sg; see map pp.80–81. Marvellous if pricey restaurant set in something resembling a glasshouse and offering an inventive, constantly revised menu of fusion fare and great desserts; mains from $30. There's also a branch – actually the original *PS Café* – in the Project Shop home-furnishings store (Level 3, The Paragon, 290 Orchard Rd ☎9297 7008), that serves lighter meals (daily 9.30am–10.30pm, with breakfast served until 11.30am). Mon–Fri 11.30am–midnight, Sat & Sun 9.30am–midnight.

**Sakae Teppenyaki** #B2-52 Plaza Singapura, 68 Orchard Rd ☎6337 5676, ⓦsakaeteppenyaki.com; see map pp.80–81. One of many mini-restaurants squeezed into the shopping mall's basement food court, with tables set around hot stoves all geared up to prepare *teppenyaki*, Japanese fry-ups of meat or seafood. Choose from various set combinations of ingredients and a chef will cook them with aplomb, and more than a dash of seasoning, in front of

**11**

## TOP 5 BLOWOUT JOINTS

The best way to stuff yourself silly in Singapore is to take advantage of **buffet** spreads. Several restaurants offer these, though sometimes only for Sunday brunch or for **high tea** – a colonial tradition now elastically recast to cover just about any cuisine that seems to work as part of a mid-afternoon banquet. These are some of the best.

**Café l'Espresso** see p.137
**Kiseki** see p.131
**Paulaner Bräuhaus** see p.130
**Straits Kitchen** see below
**Tiffin Room** see p.123

**11**

you. About $20 per head at lunchtime (more at dinnertime), excluding drinks. Daily 11.30am–9.30pm.

★ **Straits Kitchen** Grand Hyatt Hotel 10 Scotts Rd ☎ 6738 1234; see map pp.80–81. If you never had the guts to try anything more adventurous than fried noodles when you were at a food court, this place will disabuse you of your misgiving. *Straits Kitchen* is a tour de force of Singapore food, covering hawker favourites like satay, *murtabak*, savoury carrot cake and prawn *mee*, all expertly prepared. There's a vast range of desserts too, including Nonya classics like *kueh lapis*, an eggy layer cake. Lunch $52, dinner $64. Daily noon–2.30pm & 6.30–10.30pm.

**Swensen's** #03-23 Plaza Singapura, 68 Orchard Rd ☎ 6733 6461, ⓦ swensens.com.sg; see map pp.80–81. Wins no prizes for trendiness, but for what is essentially a chain of ice-cream parlours, the food menu is extensive – salads, pasta dishes, jumbo-sausage subs, etc. Prices are reasonable, with soups and many of the huge range of ice-cream concoctions weighing in at around $8. Breakfasts served at weekends. Mon–Fri 10.30am–10.30pm, Sat & Sun 8am–10.30pm.

**Thai Express** #03-24 Plaza Singapura, 68 Orchard Rd ☎ 6339 5442, ⓦ thaiexpress.com.sg; see map pp.80–81. A modern chain with plenty of wood and chrome fittings and where everything is chop-chop. The menu is packed with Thai rice and noodle dishes (from $12) plus lots of desserts. Daily 11.30am–10.30pm.

**Warung M Nasir** 69 Killiney Rd ☎ 6734 6228; see map pp.80–81. Tiny but well-established Indonesian *nasi padang* joint, with standards such as fried chicken *balado*, beef and chicken *rendang* and tofu or beans fried with *sambal*, plus one or two sticky dessert options. Daily 10am–10pm.

### THE BOTANIC GARDENS AND DEMPSEY (TANGLIN) VILLAGE

The so-called Dempsey Village, off Holland Rd and a couple of kilometres west of the start of Orchard Rd, is a sprawling collection of lawns and fields dotted with bungalows. If it feels like something out of rural England, that's because it was originally a British military camp; later it housed Singapore's Ministry of Defence, and nowadays it's home to a jumble of posh restaurants and bars, plus health spas, antique shops and so forth. The venues reviewed here are not too far from the main road, and can be reached on foot. Opposite the village, the Botanic Gardens is itself home to a few worthwhile restaurants. Buses #7, #77 and #174 head along this stretch of Holland Rd from Orchard Blvd.

**Halia** Botanic Gardens, near the ginger garden and Burkill gate on Tyersall Ave ☎ 6476 6711, ⓦ halia.com.sg; see map p.100. A sophisticated menu of modern fusion cooking, some dishes seasoned with – surprise – ginger. Lunch specials are sensibly priced at around $35 for two courses; otherwise expect to pay upwards of $40 for mains. Arriving by taxi, ask the driver to drop you on Tyersall Ave rather than at Tanglin gate. Daily noon–4pm & 6.30–10.30pm, Sat & Sun 10am–5pm (brunch until 4pm, high tea 3–5pm) & 6.30–10pm.

**Long Beach Seafood** Block 25, Dempsey Rd ☎ 6323 2222, ⓦ longbeachseafood.com.sg; see map p.100. Once you had to trek to the beaches to find Singapore's finest Chinese-style seafood, but no longer, now that this beachside stalwart has set up here. The best dishes really are magic, including treacly crisp baby squid, chunky Alaska crab in a white pepper sauce, steamed *soon hock* (goby) and, of course, chilli crab. Worthwhile but pricey – depending on the degree to which you let seafood dominate the meal, you can pay anything from a few tens of dollars per head to a hundred or more. Dempsey Rd is a 10min walk west of the Botanic Gardens' Tanglin gate. Daily 11am–3pm & 5.30pm–1.30am.

★ **Samy's** Block 25, Dempsey Rd ☎ 6472 2080, ⓦ samyscurry.com; see map p.100. Housed in a colonial-era hall with ceiling fans whirring overhead, *Samy's* is an institution that's been serving superb banana-leaf meals for decades. Choose from curries of jumbo prawn, fish-head, crab or mutton, and either plain rice or the delicate, fluffy biriyani. There's excellent freshly squeezed lemonade or *teh tarik* – made the old-fashioned way with much ostentatious pouring of fluid – to wash it all down. You'll eat well for $20 a head excluding drinks. Daily except Tues 11am–3pm & 6–10pm.

### GEYLANG AND KATONG

**328 Katong Laksa** 51 East Coast Rd, at the corner of Ceylon Rd; see map p.94. Run by a brother-and-sister team, this *kopitiam* is famed for its classic *laksa*, featuring noodles cut into short strands so you can slurp them with a spoon, and prepared only in classic style with just prawns and seafood, no meat as used by more modern variants. Daily 8am–10pm.

## PERANAKAN FOOD

**Peranakan cuisine**, also called Nonya/Nyonya food (Nonya being the term for a Peranakan woman), is the product of the melding of Chinese and Malay (and also Indonesian) cuisines. It can seem more Malay than Chinese thanks to its use of spices – except that pork is widely used.

*Nonya popiah* (spring rolls) is a standard dish: rather than being fried, the rolls are assembled by coating a steamed wrap with a sweet sauce made of palm sugar, then stuffed mainly with stir-fried *bangkwang*, a crunchy turnip-like vegetable. Another classic is *laksa*, noodles in a spicy soup flavoured in part by *daun kesom* – a herb with a distinctive taste and fittingly referred to in English as the laksa leaf. Other well-known Nonya dishes include *asam* fish, a spicy, tangy fish stew featuring tamarind (the *asam* of the name); *otak-otak*, fish mashed with coconut milk and chilli paste, then put in a narrow banana-leaf envelope and steamed or barbecued; and *ayam buah keluak*, chicken cooked with "black nuts" which are actually the large, creamy seeds of a local plant.

**Betel Box Living Bistro** 200 Joo Chiat Rd ⊙6440 5440, ⊛betelbox.com/bistro; see map p.94. Run by the socially committed hostel upstairs, this restaurant and community space serves up a mixture of Peranakan food (including *roti babi*) and colonial-era favourites like mulligatawny soup. Western fry-up breakfasts available too. Most mains are around $10. Daily 8am–10pm (Tues 8am–noon).

★ **Everything With Fries** 458 Joo Chiat Rd ⊙6345 5034, ⊛everythingwithfries.com; see map p.94. Main courses built around their French fries with a range of seasonings, plus suitably sickly desserts; see p.136 for more. Daily noon–10pm (Fri & Sat until 10.30pm).

**Glory** 139 East Coast Rd ⊙6344 1749; see map p.94. This cafeteria-style place doesn't look like much, but it's run by the main manufacturer of Peranakan goodies sold in supermarkets across Singapore. They offer the standard Nonya dishes, as well as an amazing range of sweetmeats and desserts, and you can eat reasonably well for around $15 per person. Tues–Fri 8.30am–8.30pm, Sat & Sun 8.30am–7.30pm.

★ **Guan Hoe Soon** 38/40 Joo Chiat Place ⊙6344 2761, ⊛guanhoesoon.com; see map p.94. Open in one form or another for more than half a century, this restaurant turns out fine Nonya cuisine in home-cooked style, including *ngoh hiang*, a yummy sausage-like item in which minced prawn is rolled up in a wrapper made from bean curd, and *satay babi* – not as in Malay satay, but a sweetish pork curry. They also do a mean, crisp *sio bak* (roast pork; not on the menu). Around $25 per head, excluding drinks. Daily 11am–3pm & 6–9.30pm.

★ **Haji Maimunah** 20 Joo Chiat Rd #01-02 ⊛www .hjmaimunah.com; see map p.94. Inexpensive Malay diner serving good breakfasts (*nasi lemak*, *lontong* etc) and a fine *nasi campur* spread, featuring the likes of *ayam bakar sunda* (Sundanese-style barbecued chicken), with cooked-to-order choices such as *siput lemak sedut* (snails with coconut milk) and assorted *kuih* for afters. Daily except Mon 8am–9pm (buffet in Ramadan noon–10pm).

**Mr Teh Tarik** Ground floor, Tristar Complex, 970 Geylang Rd; see map p.94. This neighbourhood hawker centre is a cut above the average. Besides the usual rice and noodle offerings, look out for the fritter stall at the front selling everything from sardine puffs to sweet potato in batter, and the incredibly popular *putu piring* stall, where you can line up to pay $2 for five little spongy rice-flour puddings, flavoured with palm sugar and individually steamed in metal cups. Daily 24hr.

**Peranakan Inn** 210 East Coast Rd ⊙6440 6195; see map p.94. As much effort goes into the food as went into the renovation of this immaculate, bright green shophouse restaurant, which offers a great range of authentic Nonya favourites such as a delectable *bakwan kepiting*, a pork meatball soup. Reckon on $30 for two, without alcohol. Daily 11am–3pm & 6–9.30pm.

### NORTHERN SINGAPORE

**Adam Road Hawker Centre** Corner of Adam and Dunearn rds, near Botanic Gardens MRT; see map p.85. This old-school, 1970s hawker centre is well worth a visit if you're at the northern end of the Botanic Gardens or at Bukit Brown. The Chinese food is indifferent, but the Malay and Indian stalls are great – look out for the *Selera Rasa nasi lemak* stall (closed Fri), which is so renowned that when the sultan of neighbouring Johor in Malaysia is in town, he sends his chauffeur to buy supplies. Daily 7am till late.

**Al-Ameen Eating House** 4 Cheong Chin Nam Rd, opposite ⊙6464 8052; see map p.85. Conveniently close to the Bukit Timah Nature Reserve, this popular Malay/ Indian Muslim *kopitiam* offers a vast range of Thai and quasi-north Indian curries. Daily 24hr.

### HOLLAND VILLAGE

The well-established expat stronghold of Holland Village is well worth a visit for its plethora of Western restaurants and shops. Get here on bus #7 from the Botanic Gardens, Orchard Blvd and the Colonial District, or ride the Circle

**11**

**11**

## A MENU READER

### NOODLES (MEE) AND NOODLE DISHES

| | |
|---|---|
| *Bee hoon/mee fun* | Thin rice noodles, like vermicelli. |
| *Hokkien fried mee* | Yellow and white noodles fried with pieces of pork, prawn and vegetables. |
| *(Char) kuey teow* | *Kuey teow* (*hor fun* in Cantonese) are flat rice noodles, like tagliatelle. *Char* indicates the noodles are stir-fried, usually with prawns, Chinese sausage, egg and greens. |
| *La mian* | "Pulled noodles", made by spinning dough skipping-rope-style in the air. |
| *Laksa* | Noodles, beansprouts, fishcakes and prawns in a spicy coconut soup. |
| *Mee* | Yellow wheat noodles |
| *Mee goreng* | Spicy Indian/Malay fried noodles. |
| *Mee rebus* | Classic Malay dish of boiled *mee*, the Singaporean version being served in a sweet sauce based on yellow-bean paste, garnished with tofu, boiled egg and bean sprouts. |
| *Sar hor fun* | Flat rice noodles served in a chicken stock soup, to which, prawns fried shallots and bean sprouts are added. |
| *Wonton mee* | Roast pork, noodles and vegetables in a light soup. |

### RICE (NASI) DISHES

| | |
|---|---|
| *Biriyani* | Saffron-flavoured rice served with curries or fried chicken. |
| *Claypot rice* | Rice topped with meat (as diverse as chicken and turtle), cooked in an earthenware pot over a fire to create a smoky taste. |
| *Hainanese chicken rice* | Steamed or boiled chicken slices on rice cooked in chicken stock, served with chicken broth and chilli and ginger sauce. |
| *Mixed rice* | The simplest and most popular choice at food courts, this is a spread of meat, fish and vegetable dishes which you point at to order; a large portion of plain rice comes as standard. |
| *Nasi goreng* | Malay- or Indian-style fried rice with diced meat and vegetables. |
| *Nasi kunyit* | Yellow rice, cooked with turmeric; a side dish. |
| *Nasi lemak* | A classic Malay breakfast: fried anchovies, cucumber, peanuts and fried or hard-boiled egg slices served on rice cooked in coconut milk. |
| *Nasi padang* | Mixed rice featuring dishes cooked in the style of Padang, the town in Sumatra, Indonesia. |
| *Nasi puteh* | Plain cooked rice. |

### OTHER SPECIALITIES

| | |
|---|---|
| *Ayam goreng* | Malay-style fried chicken. |
| *Bak kut teh* | Literally "pork bone tea", a Chinese broth of pork ribs in soy sauce, herbs and spices. |
| *Chye tow kueh* | Also known as "carrot cake", this is a delicious sort of scramble made with white radish, flour and egg; it's available plain ("white") or "dark", the latter cooked with sweet soy sauce. |
| *Congee* | Watery rice gruel, either unsalted and eaten with slices of egg and salt fish, or else boiled up with chicken, fish or pork. |
| *Dosai/thosai* | South Indian pancake, made from ground rice and sometimes other ingredients, and stuffed with dhal or other fillings. |
| *Fishballs/fishcake* | Fish-flavoured dumplings, round or in slivers (the "cake" version), used to add substance to noodle dishes and stews. |
| *Fish-head curry* | Another Singapore classic, the head of a red snapper (usually), cooked in a spicy curry sauce with tomatoes and okra. |

Line's Holland Village MRT, which is only a few stops from HarbourFront.

**Café 211** #04-01 Holland Road Shopping Centre ☎ 6462 6194, ⊛ www.cafe211.com.sg; see map p.102. The "hidden gem" cliché does apply to this rooftop café-restaurant, serving decent pizza and pasta dishes, snacks and cakes. In the cool of evening you can sit out in their terrace garden area for surreal views of residential tower blocks all around. Cooked breakfasts are available too. Cheaper than similar places downtown, with mains

| | |
|---|---|
| *Gado gado* | Malay/Indonesian salad of lightly cooked vegetables, boiled egg, sticky-rice cubes and a crunchy peanut sauce. |
| *Ikan bilis* | Anchovies, usually deep-fried. |
| *Kai pow* | Similar to *char siew pow* (see below), but contains chicken and boiled egg. |
| *Kaya* | A coconut and egg curd "jam", great with toast. |
| *Keropok* | Originally a kind of fish or prawn dumpling, but used in Singapore to mean crackers made of the dumpling mixture, sliced thinly and fried. |
| *Murtabak* | A much more substantial take on *roti prata*, stuffed with onion, egg and chicken or mutton. |
| *Otak-otak* | Fish mashed with coconut milk and chilli paste and steamed in a banana leaf; a Nonya dish. |
| *Popiah* | Spring rolls, steamed rather than fried, and filled with egg, vegetables and a sweet sauce; sometimes known as *lumpia*. |
| *Pow* | Cantonese steamed bun; the most popular variety is *char siew pow*, filled with sweet roast pork. |
| *Rendang* | Dry, slow-cooked curry of beef, chicken or mutton. |
| *Rojak* | A salad of greens, beansprouts, pineapple and cucumber in a peanut-and-prawn paste sauce, similar to *gado gado*. There's also a totally different Indian version, comprising a selection of fritters (as ever, order by pointing) served with sweet spicy dips. |
| *Roti john* | French bread spread with egg, chopped onion and spicy chilli sauce (sometimes meat too), then shallow-fried. |
| *Roti prata* | Indian griddle bread served with a thin meat or fish curry sauce or dhal – a standard breakfast or snack. |
| *Satay* | Marinated pieces of meat, skewered on small sticks and cooked over charcoal; served with peanut sauce. |
| *Sop kambing* | Spicy Malay/Indian mutton soup. |
| *Steamboat* | Chinese fondue: raw vegetables, meat or fish dunked into a steaming broth until cooked. |

**11**

### DESSERTS

| | |
|---|---|
| *Bubor cha cha* | Sweetened coconut milk with pieces of sweet potato, yam and tapioca balls. |
| *Cheng tng* | Surprisingly refreshing Chinese sweet stew of unusual dried fruits and fungi, served hot or iced. |
| *Cendol* | Coconut milk, palm sugar syrup and pea-flour noodles poured over shaved ice. |
| *Ice kachang* | Slushy ice with beans, cubes of jelly, sweet corn, rose syrup and evaporated milk. |
| *Pisang goreng* | Fried banana fritters. |

### DRINKS

| | |
|---|---|
| *Bandung* | Pink drink made with rose-flavoured syrup and a little milk. |
| *Chinchow* | Looks like cola gone flat but is actually a sweet drink made from a kind of seaweed, with bits of agar jelly floating around inside. |
| *Kopi* | Coffee, normally served with sweetened condensed milk. |
| *-o* | Suffix meaning "black" – so say *kopi-o* for black coffee. |
| *Lassi* | Sweet or sour Indian yoghurt drink. |
| *Tarik* | Meaning "pulled" (*tarik*), it refers to pouring tea or coffee between two cups to produce a frothy drink. |
| *Teh* | Tea, usually with condensed milk. |

from $15. Daily 9am–10.45pm.

**Cha Cha Cha** 32 Lorong Mambong, Holland Village ☎6462 1650; see map p.102. Classic Mexican dishes, including enchiladas and chimichangas, in this vibrantly coloured restaurant. Book ahead for the few open-air patio tables outside, ideal for posing with a bottle of Dos Equis beer. Mains from $15. Sun–Thurs 11am–11pm, Fri & Sat 11am–midnight.

★ **Crystal Jade La Mian Xiao Long Bao** 241 Holland Ave ☎6463 0968, ⓦ crystaljade.com; see map p.102.

This chain is best known for its Shanghai and northern Chinese dumplings and noodles, though in the evenings they also do a Sichuan-style hotpot, where you cook raw ingredients in boiling stock at the table (around $30). Daily 11.30am–3pm & 6.30–11pm.

★ **Everything With Fries** 40 Lorong Mambong ☎6463 3741, ⓦeverythingwithfries.com; see map p.102. As the name suggests, all mains come with shoestring or straight-cut fries, featuring such seasonings as garlic and herbs. Have, say, a burger or grilled pork chop, then mess up your blood-sugar level with a sickly cupcake or their flan that uses a well-known chocolate spread to good advantage. Small wonder it's popular with 20-somethings when mains are reasonably priced at $10–15; takeaway fries $5. Sun–Thurs noon–11pm, Fri & Sat noon–1am.

**Indochine Café Siem Reap** 44 Lorong Mambong ☎6468 5798, ⓦindochine.com.sg; see map p.102. Swanky representative of the Indochine empire, with a slightly different menu from its other venues. The rice vermicelli with beef and the *Lao laksa* are among dishes that hit the spot, for at least $20 per head. Daily noon–2.30pm & 6–11.30pm.

**Original Sin** #01-62 Block 43, Jalan Merah Saga ☎6475 5605, ⓦoriginalsin.com.sg; see map p.102. The only upmarket Western vegetarian restaurant focuses on Mediterranean cooking, though rather unadventurously – much of the menu is taken up by pizza and pasta dishes, with only the odd fusion item thrown in. Pricey for what it is, too, with mains from $25, yet the place is often full. Daily 11.30–2.30pm & 6–10.30pm.

**Pho Hoa** 18 Lorong Mambong ☎6467 3622; see map p.102. This international Vietnamese chain offers a zillion variations on beef noodle soup at around $12 a bowl. The menu is divided into "beginner's" (lean cuts), "regular" (more fatty meat) and "adventurous" sections (with tripe), and you can opt for vermicelli instead of the standard coarse rice noodle. Naturally, Vietnamese drip coffee is available too. Daily 11am–10pm.

**Swensen's** 251/253 Holland Ave ☎6467 1825, ⓦswensens.com.sg; see map p.102. Ice-cream desserts plus sandwiches, soups and other light Western meals, round the clock; a main course and drink will cost $15–20 per person. Daily 24hr.

### SENTOSA AND VIVOCITY

★ **Food Republic** Level 3 Vivocity, above HarbourFront MRT; see map p.107. Perhaps the best example of this upmarket food court, the stalls styled to resemble something out of prewar Chinatown. The cuisine, from hand-picked stallholders, is top-notch too. Try the scissors-cut curry rice – basically mixed rice (see p.134) but with the hawker slicing up the rice serving with scissors and heaping curry gravy onto it, on request. Avoid the place at peak times, though, as it will be rammed. Daily 8am–10pm (Fri–Sun until 11pm).

**Koufu** Palawan Beach; see map p.107. The cheapest place to eat on the island, this food court offers standard such as chicken rice and other rice and noodle dishes, notably *bak chor mee* – a Teochew dish of thin yellow noodles and minced pork, flavoured with vinegar. There's also a good range of juices and desserts. Daily 9am–9pm.

★ **Soup** #02-141 Vivocity, above HarbourFront MRT ☎6376 9969; see map p.107. So-called *samsui* women once sailed from China's Guangdong province in droves, incredibly, to work on Singapore building sites. This fine little restaurant celebrates the cuisine of these redoubtable women, most famously their ginger chicken; similar to the steamed chicken in chicken rice, it comes with a gingery dip and iceberg-lettuce leaves to roll it up in. Reckon on $20 per head, excluding drinks. Mon–Fri 11.30am–2.30pm & 5.30–10pm, Sat & Sun 11.30am–10pm.

**Trapizza** Siloso Beach ☎6376 2662; see map p.107. Of the eating places on Siloso Beach, *Trapizza* stands out for its excellent pizzas and pasta dishes starting at $20, with drinks served after the kitchen closes for the evening. Daily noon–9pm.

---

## TABLE MANNERS

Local dishes are generally eaten with **fork and spoon** – never a knife as the food is usually sliced up enough that one is unnecessary – and it's the spoon you eat off, with the fork playing the supporting role of helping to pick up and move morsels of food, plus rice, onto the spoon. Of course you have the option of using **chopsticks** with Chinese food, but don't make the mistake of trying to consume rice off a plate with them, as that's where the spoon comes into play. Chopsticks go together with a rice bowl, which you hold right to your mouth so you can snaffle the rice using the chopsticks as a shovel. More familiarly, they also serve as tongs: one chopstick is laid between thumb and forefinger, and supported by your fourth and little fingers, while the second chopstick is held between thumb, forefinger and second finger, and manipulated to form a pincer. Indian and Malay food is traditionally eaten using the **right hand** as a scoop and the right thumb to flick food into your mouth, and there are always sinks near the tables for washing before and after the meal.

## STREET ICE CREAM

A couple of generations ago, **ice cream** in Singapore often meant stuff sold by hawkers from pushcarts, in exotic flavours like sweetcorn, red (aduki) bean and yam. This was so-called **potong** ("cut" in Malay) ice cream because it came in bricks and the seller would use a cleaver to slice it into slabs, to be served either between wafers or, oddly, rolled up in white bread.

The general elimination of street stalls put paid to that trade in Singapore, but in recent years the ice-cream vendors have made a comeback. They're often to be seen at Cavenagh Bridge, on Orchard Road near Somerset MRT and outside Bugis MRT. The bread option complements the ice cream surprisingly well, serving as a sort of neutral sponge cake.

## CAFÉS AND DESSERT VENUES

**2am Dessert Bar** 21a Lorong Liput, Holland Village ☎6291 9727, ⊕2amdessertbar.com; see map p.102. Hidden down a side street, this slick upstairs venue features a slew of sinful puddings (from $18), plus simpler delights such as Spanish churros dunked in hot chocolate, though portion sizes can be disappointingly small for the price. There's a full range of wines and cocktails, too. Daily except Sun 6pm–2am.

★ **Ah Chew Desserts** #01-11, 1 Liang Seah St ☎6339 8198; see map pp.46–47. Taking up two restored shophouses, *Ah Chew* confronts you with nothing but strange local sweets containing beans or other unexpected ingredients. The cashew-nut paste is not bad if you like the sound of a broth made of nut butter; also available are the likes of *pulot hitam*, made with black sticky rice and better warm than with the optional ice cream. Cautiously sample a few items by ordering the small servings; most bowls cost $4 or so. Mon–Thurs 12.30–11.30pm, Fri 12.30pm–12.30am, Sat 1.30pm–12.30am, Sun 1.30–11.30pm.

★ **Brunetti** #01-35 Tanglin Mall, 163 Tanglin Rd ☎6733 9088; see map pp.80–81. This incredible Australian café boasts cabinet after cabinet stuffed with exquisite macaroons, cakes and ice creams that together come in almost as many colours as you find in a paint catalogue. Not too pricey – cheesecake costs $8, a macaroon $2 – though the light meals and savoury snacks aren't such good value. Daily 8am–9pm.

**Dôme** Singapore Art Museum, Bras Basah Rd; see map pp.46–47. Slick Australian café with an impressive list of coffees and teas. There's also a branch at #01-02 UOB Plaza 1, 80 Raffles Place (by Boat Quay, see map pp.60–61) with river views. Daily 8.30am–10.30pm (Raffles Place Mon–Fri 8am–8pm, Sat 8am–3pm).

**Café l'Espresso** Goodwood Park Hotel, 22 Scotts Rd ☎6730 1743; see map pp.80–81. A legendary array of English cakes, scones and speciality coffees, not to mention chocolate fondue, for high tea – so successful they've extended it to lunchtimes at weekends. $53. Daily 10am–midnight; high tea Mon–Thurs 2–5.30pm, Fri–Sun noon–2.30pm & 3–5.30pm.

**Island Creamery** Ground floor, Holland Village Shopping Mall, 3 Lorong Liput; see map p.102. This tiny takeaway place is one of the new breed of upmarket

ice-cream parlours, exploiting traditional flavours never previously seen in frozen desserts – like *teh tarik*, the frothy tea so beloved of Singaporeans, and *pulut hitam*, the sticky rice dessert. More conventional flavours available too, including a rich black forest, and prices start at around $3 – about a third less than at Häagen-Dazs. Daily 11am–10pm.

**Novus Café** National Museum, 93 Stamford Rd ☎6337 1397, ⊕novus.sg; see map p.34. A refined, cosy café, slightly pricier than elsewhere but perfect for an intimate tête-à-tête or a catch-up with old friends. Besides coffees, muffins and so forth, the menu includes light bites such as *croque monsieur* or risotto. Daily 10am–6pm.

**The Pigeonhole** 52 Duxton Rd ☎6226 2880, ⊕thepigeonhole.com.sg; see map pp.60–61. So unlike its upmarket Tanjong Pagar neighbours, this unpretentious café-bar is, to quote the management, "like visiting a cool Singaporean friend's home" – the place is filled with preloved furniture and totally chilled out. They do good coffee, sweet treats like bread-and-butter pudding and some light meals, but even more appealing is the rolling programme of art exhibits, acoustic nights and socially aware talks – their website has details. Tues–Thurs 10am–11pm, Fri 10am–1am, Sat 11.30am–1am, Sun 11.30am–8pm.

**Soho Coffee** Loke Yew St, off Hill St ☎6634 7977; see map p.34. Indie coffee outlets are a rarity in corporate-dominated Singapore. Here's a proud exception to that rule, a tiny, friendly venue offering most things you'd get in Starbucks, but using blends of beans that they select and roast themselves. Daily 9am–8pm.

**Spinelli's** Ground floor, Peninsula Excelsior Hotel, 3 Coleman St; see map p.34. Part of a chain that's generally a safe bet for a good coffee, with croissants, muffins, and a few sandwiches available too. Daily at least 9am–8pm.

**Ya Kun Kaya Toast** #01-31 The Central, 6 Eu Tong Sen St ☎6534 7332; see map pp.60–61. Now a ubiquitous chain, *Ya Kun* started out in the prewar years as a Chinatown stall offering classic *kopitiam* breakfast fare – *kaya* toast plus optional soft-boiled eggs eaten with white pepper and soy sauce. Of course there's strong local coffee too, normally drunk with condensed or evaporated milk. Daily 7am–10pm.

**11**

RAFFLES BAR

# Drinking and nightlife

With its affluence and large expat community, Singapore supports a huge range of drinking holes, from elegant colonial chambers through hip rooftop venues with skyline views to slightly tacky joints featuring karaoke or middling covers bands. There's also a bunch of glitzy and vibrant clubs where people let their hair down to cutting-edge sounds minus – this being Singapore – any assistance from illicit substances. Some venues regularly manage to lure the world's leading DJs to play, too.

## ESSENTIALS

**Cover charges** Most clubs have a cover charge, if not all week then at least on Friday and Saturday. The charge almost always includes your first drink or two, and varies between $15 and $30 (weekends are pricier, and men pay slightly more than women). Some clubs advertise weekly "ladies' nights" when women can get in free or enjoy discounted drinks, perhaps paying for the first drink and then getting free refills of the house cocktail at certain times.

**Drink costs** A pint of Tiger beer served in a bar or club will generally cost at least $12 – double what you would pay at a hawker centre – and prices can be much higher in fancier venues or for imported brews. A glass of house wine usually costs much the same as a beer, spirits and cocktails

a few dollars more. At least during happy hour, which can last the whole first half of the evening, you'll either get a considerable discount off drinks or a "one-for-one" deal (meaning two drinks for the price of one). Many bars and clubs also have a "house pour" – basically a discounted cocktail on offer all night.

**Opening hours** Bars tend to open in the late afternoon, closing around midnight or later (certainly an hour or two later on Friday, Saturday and the day before a state holiday), and may close on Sunday, depending on the district; a few places are also open at lunchtime. Nightclub hours are predictable – many throw their doors open no earlier than 9pm, and will keep going until the wee hours, even dawn in a few cases.

## BARS AND PUBS

Singapore's best **bars** cluster mainly in Orchard Rd and along the Singapore River, though anywhere where expats like to hang out is bound to have a cluster of watering holes, such as at Holland Village and on Ann Siang Hill off South Bridge Rd in Chinatown.

### THE COLONIAL DISTRICT

**Bar Opiume** Asian Civilisations Museum, 1 Empress Place ☎ 6339 2876; see map p.34. Cool-as-ice venue, graced by chandeliers, modish leather furniture and lordly Buddha statues, with a vast range of cocktails and plenty of Indochinese snacks, courtesy of its sibling restaurant and café next door. The views across to Boat Quay are splendid at night. Mon–Thurs 5pm–2am, Fri & Sat 5pm–3am, Sun 5pm–1am.

**The Long Bar** *Raffles Hotel*, 1 Beach Rd ☎ 6412 1816; see map p.34. It's still just about mandatory to have a Singapore Sling amid the old-fashioned elegance of the bar where Ngiam Tong Boon invented it in 1915. No happy hour, and only the standard beers on draught. Daily 11am–12.30am; Fri & Sat until 1.30am.

### BRAS BASAH, LITTLE INDIA AND ARAB STREET

**Bar Stories** Level 2, 55/57a Haji Lane ☎ 6298 0838; see map pp.46–47. This tiny venue, secreted away on the top floor of a couple of shophouses, majors on custom-made cocktails created to suit your tastebuds by a young and enthusiastic team of mixologists. It's a strange combination of somewhat pricey – concoctions cost around $25 – and yet quite domestic, with home-style low couches and armchairs to relax in. Daily 3pm–1am, Fri & Sat until 2am.

⭐ **The Countryside Café** 71 Dunlop St ☎ 6292 0071; see map pp.46–47. A delightfully plain, low-key, convivial establishment, with something of the feel of a middle-class Singapore household of yesteryear, at least in its middle-of-the-road music – complemented by posters of Kenny Rogers and Johnny Cash on the wall. Run by a

friendly Indian woman, it offers an incredible list of bottled beers – five dozen, at reasonable prices – and the menu of bar snacks and food, partly Indian, partly Western, is nearly as impressive. Monday 6pm–2am, Tues–Thurs & Sun 10am–2am, Fri & Sat 10am–3am.

⭐ **Loof** Top of the Odeon Towers Extension, 391 North Bridge Rd #03-07 ☎ 6338 8035, ⦾ loof.com.sg. A rooftop chill-out joint with views into the back of the *Raffles* hotel opposite, lots of low sofas to lounge in, Asahi beer on draught, a good range of cocktails, and delicious snacks such as spicy chicken wings and minced prawns on toast. DJs spin varied sounds at weekends, too. Happy hour Mon–Fri until 8pm. Daily 5pm–1am; Fri & Sat until 3am.

**Lot, Stock and Barrel Pub** 30 Seah St ☎ 6338 5540; see map pp.46–47. Cheerful, unpretentious venue frequented by a post-work crowd in the early evening, with some backpackers making their presence felt later on, drawn partly by a jukebox featuring everyone from Sinatra to Beyoncé. Happy hour until 8pm. Daily 4pm–3am.

**Night and Day** 139a/c Selegie Rd ☎ 6884 5523; see map pp.46–47. Funky cartoons on the walls hint that this is not just a bar but also a gallery space, though it's also down to earth with nothing self-important about it. It's tucked away upstairs in a restored 1950s building, but not hard to spot as there's a touch of Art Deco about the facade. Happy hour until 9pm. Daily 6pm until late.

**Prince of Wales** 101 Dunlop St ☎ 6299 0130; see map pp.46–47. The ground floor of this hostel is taken up by a buzzing travellers' bar with live acoustic music or bands most nights, plus Australian Pilsner-style microbrewery beer and pale ale on tap at keen prices. Sun–Thurs 9am–1am, Fri & Sat 9am–2am.

**12**

## CHINATOWN, BOAT QUAY AND THE FINANCIAL DISTRICT

★ **1-Altitude Gallery and Bar** Levels 61-63, One Raffles Place ☎6336 9366, ⓦ1-altitude.com; see map pp.60–61. Even if this isn't "the world's highest alfresco bar", as it styles itself, but merely one of the loftiest, the views of the Colonial District, Marina Bay and Chinatown from the roof of the One Raffles Place tower are simply stunning. It's best to drop by towards the end of your stay, when you can make sense of the cityscape and ponder the myriad changes that half a century of rapid growth has wrought upon this island. En route you'll have to ascend through a sports bar with virtual reality golf and a modern European restaurant, all part of the same establishment, but they pale in comparison. Cover charge $25 (Fri & Sat $30 after 9pm) including house pour; smart casual dress only, and no men under 25 or women under 21 after 10pm. Daily 6pm–2am; Fri & Sat until 4am, Sun until 1am.

**BQ Bar** 39 Boat Quay ☎6536 9722, ⓦbqbar.com; see map pp.60–61. One of Boat Quay's cooler venues, thanks to the friendly staff, memorable views of the river from upstairs and diverse sounds, anything from dance to rock. Kebabs available too from a nearby outlet run by the same management. Kirin beer on draft; happy hour until 8pm. Mon & Tues 11am–1am, Wed–Fri 11am–3am, Sat 5pm–4am.

★ **Brewerkz/Café Iguana** #01-03/05/06 Riverside Point, 30 Merchant Rd ☎6438 7438, ⓦbrewerkz.com; see map pp.60–61. Owned by the same company, *Brewerkz* serves up a range of highly rated beers from its own microbrewery, including some interesting seasonal faves that use local ingredients such as Thai honey. *Café Iguana*, meanwhile, offers a huge selection of tequilas and margaritas, plus the same beers. Happy hour until 8pm and, at *Cafe Iguana*, also after 11pm. Daily noon–midnight; Fri & Sat until 1am.

**Harry's** 28 Boat Quay ☎6538 3029; see map pp.60–61. One of the best located of this well-established, ubiquitous chain of bars, with a good range of draught beers, plus light meals and snacks; happy hour is until 8pm. Daily 11.30am–1am; Fri & Sat until 2am.

**Helipad** #05-22 The Central, 6 Eu Tong Sen St ☎6327 8118, ⓦhelipad.com.sg; see map pp.60–61. It's not encouraging that the entrance is via the fifth-floor car park, but the reward is a relaxing rooftop bar, an actual helipad where you can sit out on the "H" symbol and enjoy marvellous views over the river. There's also a less interesting dance club below. Ladies' night is Wed. Mon–Sat 6pm–2am (club Wed, Fri & Sat 10pm–3am).

**The Penny Black** 26 & 27 Boat Quay ☎6538 2300, ⓦpennyblack.com.sg; see map pp.60–61. Not a convincing evocation of a "Victorian London pub" as their sign states, but pleasant enough, with one table built around a red pillar box to evoke the UK. There's Strongbow cider and Old Speckled Hen on draught, plenty of pub grub – cottage pie, ploughman's lunches and the like – and live British football on TV. Happy hour until 8pm. Mon–Thurs 11.30am–1am, Fri & Sat 11.30am–2am, Sun 11.30am–midnight.

**Screening Room** 12 Ann Siang Hill ☎6221 1694; see map pp.60–61. The unpretentious rooftop bar here (officially *La Terraza*, though few people know it as that) is a convivial spot for an evening drink, with the bonus of views of Chinatown's shophouses and modern towers, plus plenty of tapas-style snacks and burgers. Daily 6pm–1am; Fri & Sat until 3am.

★ **Speakeasy** 50 Tanjong Pagar Rd ☎6224 4171; see map pp.60–61. Not the first bar to be themed around 1920s Prohibition America, and the old wooden furniture here doesn't quite make the connection stick. Rather more effective are the cocktails, based on spirits such as rye whiskey; some are served using teapots or teacups as speakeasies once did, and actually contain tea as one of the ingredients. On a quite unrelated note, they also have the Swiss Calvinus Blanche wheat beer on draught, and a great range of bottled beers at reasonable prices. Happy hour until 8.30pm. Mon–Sat 11.30am till late.

## MARINA BAY

**Ku Dé Ta SkyBar** North tower, SkyPark at Marina Bay Sands, 1 Bayfront Ave ☎6688 7688, ⓦkudeta.com.sg; see map p.74. The bar at the SkyPark's fanciest venue is one of the best ways to bypass the 57th-floor admission fee and enjoy fabulous views over downtown Singapore. Stella and Hoegaarden on draft; no happy hour, though, and you'll need to dress fairly smartly in the evening (no shorts). Daily noon–1am; Fri & Sat until 2am.

★ **Orgo** Roof terrace, Esplanade – Theatres On The Bay ☎6438 0410, ⓦwww.orgo.sg; see map p.74. They make a big thing of their huge range of cocktails, which emphasize fresh fruit and herbs, but the views of the spires of the Financial District sell themselves. Happy hour 5–8pm. Daily 5pm–2am.

## ORCHARD ROAD AND TANGLIN VILLAGE (DEMPSEY)

★ **The Dubliner** 165 Penang Rd ☎6735 2220, ⓦdublinersingapore.com; see map pp.80–81. Set up in a colonial-era mansion, this isn't the predictable ersatz Irish pub but simply a homely, congenial place to enjoy good company. The grub – fish and chips, Irish stew and burgers – is a cut above as well, you can enjoy Old Speckled Hen on draught, and there's a band every Fri. Happy hour until 9pm. Daily 11.30am–1am; Fri & Sat until 2am.

**Ice Cold Beer** 9 Emerald Hill Rd ☎6735 9929; see pp.80–81. Noisy, happening place where the beers are kept in ice tanks under the glass-topped bar. Shares a

**12**

kitchen and a menu with *No. 5 Emerald Hill*. Happy hour until 9pm. Daily 5pm–2am; Fri & Sat until 3am.

**KPO** 1 Killiney Rd ☎ 6733 3648; see map pp.80–81. You'd never have guessed that *KPO*, with its big black sofas and slick roof terrace, was once part of the now much-reduced post office next door. It's convivial and relaxed in the afternoon, but can get raucously noisy after dark, with DJ sets some evenings. Happy hour until 8pm. Mon–Thurs 3pm–1am, Fri & Sat 3pm–2am.

★ **No. 5 Emerald Hill** 5 Emerald Hill Rd ☎ 6732 0818; see map pp.80–81. Set in one of Emerald Hill Rd's restored houses, *No. 5* is not only a feast for the eyes but also offers speciality cocktails plus great chicken wings and thin-crust pizzas. Tetley's and Kronenbourg on tap, there's some outdoor seating and a pool table upstairs. Happy hour until 9pm. Mon–Thurs noon–2am, Fri & Sat noon–3am, Sun 5pm–2am.

**Outdoors Café & Bar** Peranakan Place, corner of Orchard Rd and Emerald Hill Rd ☎ 6732 6966; map pp.80–81. Pleasant alfresco place with a canopy for shade, a great spot to watch the hordes on Orchard Rd. There's Erdinger on draught, plus other beers and a range of cocktails, and an extensive menu of Western and Asian mains and light meals. Happy hour until 7pm. Daily 11am–2am; Fri & Sat until 3am.

**Que Pasa** 7 Emerald Hill ☎ 6235 6626; see map pp.80–81. A tapas-themed bar with a creaky wooden staircase and scattered with wine bottles. No happy hour. Mon–Thurs 1.30pm–2am, Fri & Sat 1.30pm–3am, Sun 5.30pm–2am.

**White Rabbit** 39C Harding Rd, Tanglin Village ☎ 6473 9965; see map p.100. This restaurant, housed in a restored old church, just happens to have a marvellous open-air bar at the back that buzzes after 10pm at weekends. A great spot for a drink away from the bustle of downtown. Tues–Thurs & Sun 6.30pm–midnight, Fri & Sat 6.30pm–1.30am.

## HOLLAND VILLAGE

**Harry's** 27 Lorong Mambong ☎ 6467 4222; see map p.102. Nothing special to look at, but popular as a place to unwind after a meal elsewhere in the area. Strongbow cider plus various beers on draught. Happy hour until daily until 9pm. Mon–Thurs 3pm–1am, Fri 3pm–2am, Sat noon–2am, Sun noon–1am.

**Wala Wala Café Bar** 31 Lorong Mambong, Holland Village ☎ 6462 4288; see map p.102. This rocking joint has Tetley's, Kronenbourg and other beers on draught, and acoustic and electric acts nightly upstairs from 10pm. Happy hour until 9pm. Mon–Thurs 4pm–1am, Fri 4pm–2am, Sat 3pm–3am, Sun 3pm–1am.

## SENTOSA

**Bora-Bora Beach Bar** Palawan Beach ☎ 6278 0838; see map p.107. The quietest and simplest of Sentosa's handful of beach bars, and all the better for it. A good place for a chinwag as you imbibe one of their speciality mojitos or margaritas. Mon–Thurs 11am–8pm, Fri–Sun 10am–9pm.

## DISCOS AND NIGHTCLUBS

European and American dance music dominates in the best **Western-style clubs**, though some venues feature **bands** playing covers of current hits and pop classics (for venues that focus on live music, see Chapter 13). There are also more **Asian-oriented places**, with signage in Chinese and English. Even if you enjoy the Chinese pop or karaoke they specialize in, they can be worth avoiding as some are slightly seedy, with hostesses trying to hassle you into buying them a drink.

★ **Avalon** South Crystal Pavilion, *Marina Bay Sands* ☎ 6597 8333; see map p.74. A Far Eastern outpost of the Hollywood original, *Avalon* is entombed within a squat glass islet, reached by a walkway out over the water. The music extends from trance through house to general electronica, and the see-through architecture ensures all-round views of the Financial District and Singapore Flyer. Cover charge $25–35. Thurs–Sun 10pm–late.

★ **Butter Factory** Level 2, One Fullerton, 1 Fullerton Rd ⓦ thebutterfactory.com; see map p.60. This fun, glossy venue has two spaces: *Bump*, where it's all hip-hop and R&B, and the trance-dominated *Fash*. Men pay around $28 for *Bump*, slightly less for *Fash*; women pay slightly less than men; and anyone who gets into *Bump* can also access *Fash*, but the converse doesn't hold true. More straightforwardly, Wednesday is ladies' night, when women get in free. Wed, Fri & Sat 10pm–4am.

**Home Club** #B01-06 The Riverwalk, 20 Upper Circular Rd ☎ 6538 2928, ⓦ homeclub.com.sg; see map pp.60–61. This cosy venue makes the best of its riverside location with a chilled-out patio area outside; inside DJs spin cutting-edge sounds, from trance to grime and dubstep. Friday nights see a bit of a switch to indie and metal, however, as local bands play original material that wouldn't sound out of place on US college radio (9–11pm). Cover charge $12–15. Tues–Thurs 6pm–3am, Sat until 4am.

**Powerhouse** St James Power Station, next to VivoCity and HarbourFront MRT ☎ 6270 7676, ⓦ stjames powerstation.com; see map p.107. Arguably the best of the venues at this renovated power station, the cavernous *Powerhouse* spins R&B on Wed & Sat and house on Fri. Only men pay the $20 cover charge. Happy hour until 10pm. Wed, Fri & Sat 9pm–4am.

**Tanjong Beach Club** Tanjong Beach ☎ 6270 1355, ⓦ tanjongbeachclub.com; see map p.107. If you needed

**12**

like a luxury beach bungalow, it boasts an incongruous infinity pool, a pricey restaurant and a bar, with monthly beach parties (usually Sun) featuring guest DJs. Daily 11am–11pm.

**Zouk/Phuture/Velvet Underground** 17 Jiak Kim St ☏ 6738 2988, ⓦ zoukclub.com; see map pp.60–61. Launched in the 1990s, *Zouk* is one of Singapore's most successful clubs and still the best for many, though for others it's getting a little mainstream. House remains the mainstay, with guest sets from world-renowned DJs from time to time. *Zouk* also houses two smaller clubs, *Phuture*, majoring in hip-hop and R&B, and *Velvet Underground*, with a more relaxed mix of everything from Afrobeat to jazz. The cover charge depends on the venue and the night, but typically starts at $25. Bus #16 from Somerset/Orchard MRT; ask to be let off close to the *Grand Copthorne Waterfront* hotel, next door. Zouk Wed 11pm till late, Fri & Sat midnight till late; Phuture Wed, Fri & Sat 9pm till late; Velvet Underground Wed–Sat 10pm till late.

## GAY AND LESBIAN VENUES

Singapore's **gay scene**, though modest, is one of the liveliest in Southeast Asia, and in recent years the country has seen the annual Pink Dot rally (a gay pride event by another name; June; ⓦ pinkdot.sg) grow into one of the most well-attended mass meetings on the island. That said, attitudes toward homosexuality remain a bit schizophrenic. Colonial-era legislation banning sex between men remains on the statute book following a failed attempt in 2007 to get parliament to repeal it, though the government has said it will not enforce the law. Despite the generally tolerant atmosphere, it makes sense to be discreet: gay issues are seldom discussed in public, and open displays of affection, whether gay or straight, aren't really the done thing in Singapore. Gay venues themselves keep a low profile, functioning largely unhindered but scarcely using the word "gay" in promotional material, for example.

The scene centres on Chinatown and Tanjong Pagar, where there are some half a dozen bars and clubs; note that they only really get busy at weekends, and even then only after 10pm. In addition, a few mainstream clubs have gay nights – notably, at the time of writing, *Avalon* (see p.141) on Sundays – and ladies' nights promotions may be popular with lesbians. The gay personals website ⓦ fridae.asia lists new venues, though it doesn't always drop places that have shut; lesbians can try ⓦ twoqueens.me for personal ads and details of events. Another source of information is a small gay library project, the Pelangi Pride Centre, in Geylang (ⓦ pelangipridecentre.org).

**Backstage** 13A Trengganu St ☏ 6227 1712, ⓦ www .backstagebar.moonfruit.com; see map pp.60–61. Entered through a side door in Temple St (look for the discreetly placed rainbow flag on the floor above), this tiny bar offers a view over the souvenir stalls of Trengganu St. Daily 6pm–2am (Fri & Sat until 3am).

**DYMK** 41 Neil Rd ⓦ dymk.sg; see map pp.60–61. Probably the friendliest gay bar in town, with music that's slightly quieter than elsewhere, making it a good place for a relaxed chat. Most of the crowd are Chinese 20- and 30-somethings. Mon–Thurs & Sun 7pm–midnight, Fri 7pm–1am, Sat 8pm–2am.

**Play** 21 Tanjong Pagar Rd ☏ 6227 7400; see map pp.60–61. Low-key club spinning house, with a well-attended lesbian night on Thursdays. Thurs & Fri 9pm–3am, Sat 9pm–4am.

**Taboo** 65 & 67 Neil Rd ☏ 6225 6256, ⓦ taboo97.com; see map pp.60–61. Small mixed club spinning the usual mix of house, trance and other pulsating sounds. Wed & Thurs 10pm–2am, Fri 10pm–3am, Sat 10pm–4am.

**Tantric** 78 Neil Rd ☏ 6423 9232; see map pp.60–61. Pleasant enough shophouse bar with a clientele that's slightly more reflective of Singapore's multi-ethnic make-up than the largely Chinese crowd you find elsewhere. Daily 8pm–3am; Sat until 4am.

**12**

CHINESE OPERA

# Entertainment and the arts

Singapore offers an excellent range of cultural events in all genres, drawing on both Asian and Western traditions, and even on a brief visit it's hard not to notice how much money has been invested in the arts. Prime downtown property has been turned over to arts organizations in areas like Waterloo Street and Little India, and prestige venues like Theatres on the Bay bring in world-class performers – at top-dollar prices. This isn't to say that all is hunky-dory: questions remain over whether creativity is truly valued when censorship lingers, if not as overtly as in the 1970s and 1980s, then in terms of there being well-established red lines concerning party politics, ethnicity and religion which no one dare cross. More cynically, some say that support for the arts is a way to keep Singapore attractive to expats and its own sometimes restive middle class.

**13**

## ESSENTIALS

**Festivals** There are two major international arts festivals annually: the Singapore Arts Festival (four weeks in May & June; ⓦ singaporeartsfest.com), running the gamut from theatre through dance and film to concerts; and the Singapore Fringe Festival (Feb; ⓦ singaporefringe.com), which concentrates on theatre, dance and the visual arts. There's also the annual Singapore Writers' Festival (ⓦ singaporewritersfestival.com), featuring international as well as local writers working in all four of the country's official languages.

**Information** Events are widely advertised in the press and in listings magazines such as the weekly *I-S* (free in print, and at ⓦ is-magazine.com).

**Tickets** You can buy tickets directly from venues or through agencies such as SISTIC (the largest, with outlets in many downtown malls; ☎ 6348 5555, ⓦ sistic.com.sg) and Gatecrash (☎ 6100 2005, ⓦ gatecrash.com.sg). Alternatively, head to TicketCube, which brings together the main ticketing agencies under one roof; it's on Orchard Rd between the Ngee Ann City and Wisma Atria malls (daily 10.30am–9pm).

## THEATRE

Singapore's arts scene is probably at its best when it comes to **drama**: a surprising number of small theatre companies have sprung up over the years, performing works by local playwrights which dare to include a certain amount of social commentary. Foreign theatre companies tour regularly too, and lavish Western musicals are staged from time to time.

### COMPANIES

**Action Theatre** 42 Waterloo St ☎ 6837 0842, ⓦ action.org.sg. Stages work by Singaporean playwrights as well as the standard repertoire, with its own 100-seater venue on site.

**The Necessary Stage** Marine Parade Community Building, 278 Marine Parade Rd ☎ 6338 0611, ⓦ necessary.org. Pioneering socially conscious theatre group. Their premises are out near Katong though some of their productions are staged downtown.

**Singapore Repertory Theatre** DBS Arts Centre (see p.146), ⓦ srt.com.sg. English-language theatre, performing more than just the most obvious British and American plays.

**Theatreworks** #72-13 Mohamed Sultan Rd ☎ 6737 7213, ⓦ theatreworks.com.sg. Another of the early pioneers of the Singapore stage.

## CLASSICAL AND TRADITIONAL MUSIC AND DANCE

At the heart of Singapore's healthy Western classical music scene is the **Singapore Symphony Orchestra**, whose concerts often feature stellar guest soloists, conductors and choirs from around the world. Dance is an another thriving art, with several active local troupes and regular visits by international companies.

### COMPANIES AND ORCHESTRAS

**Chinese Opera Teahouse** 5 Smith St ☎ 6323 4862, ⓦ ctcopera.com.sg/teahouse.html. For an interesting culinary and musical experience, come here for the *Sights and Sounds of Chinese Opera* (Fri & Sat 7pm), a set dinner followed by performances of excerpts from Chinese operas. The package costs $35, though you can watch the opera selections alone for $20 (includes tea and snacks; admission at 7.50pm).

**Nanyang Academy of Fine Arts City Chinese**

**Orchestra** ☎ 6742 9359, ⓦ cityco.com.sg. Chinese classical and folk music recitals.

**Singapore Chinese Orchestra** Singapore Conference Hall, 7 Shenton Way (Financial District) ☎ 6440 3839, ⓦ sco.com.sg. Performances of traditional Chinese music through the year, plus occasional free concerts.

**Singapore Dance Theatre** ☎ 6338 0611, ⓦ singaporedancetheatre.com. Contemporary and classical works, sometimes in the open air at Fort Canning Hill.

---

## STREET THEATRE

Walk around Singapore long enough and you're likely to stumble upon some sort of streetside cultural event, most usually a **wayang** – a Malay word used in Singapore to denote Chinese opera. Played out on outdoor stages next to temples and markets, or in open spaces in the new towns, wayangs are highly dramatic and stylized affairs, in which garishly made-up characters enact popular Chinese legends to the accompaniment of the crashes of cymbals and gongs. They're staged throughout the year, but the best time to catch one is during the Festival of the Hungry Ghosts, when they are held to entertain passing spooks. Another fascinating traditional performance, **lion-dancing**, takes to the streets during Chinese New Year, and **puppet theatres** may appear around then, too. Chinatown and the Bugis/Waterloo Street area are places where you might stumble upon performances.

**Singapore Lyric Opera** ⓦsingaporeopera.com.sg. Western opera and operetta.

**Singapore Symphony Orchestra** ⓦsso.org.sg. Performances throughout the year at Esplanade – Theatres on the Bay and other venues; occasional free concerts at the Botanic Gardens too.

**Siong Leng Musical Association** 4B Bukit Pasoh Rd ☎6222 4221, ⓦsiongleng-nanyin.blogspot.co.uk. A unique body dedicated to preserving what they call *nanyin*

(literally "southern sound") – distinctive music and opera from southeast China, sung in dialect. Occasional demonstrations take place at their Chinatown headquarters, with full-scale shows several times a year, notably some free opera stagings against the exceptional temple backdrop of Thian Hock Keng.

**Temple of Fine Arts** ☎6535 0509, ⓦtempleoffinearts .org. This Indian cultural organization puts on occasional shows of classical music and dance.

## FILM

Postwar Singapore was the nexus of the Malay-language movie industry (as recounted at the National Museum's film gallery; see p.43), with some films in Chinese also shot here. That flowering lasted all of twenty years until, following independence, Malay film-making drifted off to Kuala Lumpur while in Singapore censorship grew more problematic as tastes were, in any case, gravitating away from locally made films towards slicker efforts from the West and Hong Kong. It wasn't until the 1990s that local film-making saw a renaissance, and today a thriving independent scene releases full-length features, shorts and documentaries.

The best time to appreciate locally made movies is at the **Singapore International Film Festival** (ⓦsiff.sg; usually in Sept). If you intend to be in Singapore for a while, you might want to join the Singapore Film Society (ⓦsfs.org.sg), which puts on its own monthly screenings of films (members-only) and mounts occasional film festivals (with discounts for members). Otherwise, Singapore's cinemas offer up all the latest blockbusters from Hollywood, Bollywood and Hong Kong, with English subtitles as appropriate. Turn up early or book in advance to secure tickets (at around $10) if the film is newly released – and take a sweater, as the air-conditioning units are perpetually on full blast. Be prepared, also, for chatter, as Singaporeans often talk incessantly at the cinema.

### MULTIPLEX CHAINS

**Cathay Cinemas** include: Cathay Cineplex, 2 Handy Rd (near Dhoby Ghaut MRT); Cineleisure Orchard, 8 Grange Rd (near Somerset MRT) ⓦcathay.com.sg. The Art Deco Cathay Cineplex is a city landmark and includes a gallery of memorabilia from Cathay's own involvement in local film-making in the mid-twentieth century (see p.79).

**Golden Village Cinemas** include: Level 7, Plaza Singapura, 68 Orchard Rd; Levels 2 & 3, VivoCity, HarbourFront; #03/04-01 Marina Leisureplex, near the Mandarin Oriental hotel, Marina Centre; ⓦgv.com.sg.

**Shaw Cinemas** include: Lido 8 Cineplex, levels 5 & 6, Shaw House, 350 Orchard Rd (IMAX-equipped); Bugis Cineplex, Bugis Junction, 200 Victoria St; ⓦshaw.sg.

**WE** Downtown at #03-51 Suntec City Mall, 3 Temasek Blvd, Marina Centre ☎6836 9074, ⓦwecinemas.com.sg.

### INDEPENDENT CINEMAS

**Alliance Française** 1 Sarkies Rd (10min walk from Newton MRT) ⓦalliancefrancaise.org.sg/cineclub .html. Weekly French-language films with English subtitles; tickets through SISTIC.

**National Museum Cinematheque** National Museum, 93 Stamford Rd ⓦnationalmuseum.sg. The museum mounts its own laudable programme of films from around the world. Tickets from the museum itself or SISTIC.

**Omni-Theatre** See p.100. One of Singapore's two IMAX cinemas.

**The Picturehouse** Cathay Building, 2 Handy Rd ☎6337 8181, ⓦwww.thepicturehouse.com.sg; see map p.104. Though part of the Cathay empire and not strictly indie, unlike its multiplexes, it's devoted to art-house films.

**Rex** 2 Mackenzie Rd ☎6337 0025. On the edge of Little India, this is one of the oldest cinemas in town, now the place to come for the latest Tamil and Bollywood movies, plus the occasional Malay flick.

**The Screening Room** 12 Ann Siang Hill ☎6221 1694, ⓦscreeningroom.com.sg. "Where food meets film" is the motto of this complex, incorporating a basement lounge, restaurant, gallery space and a cinema screening the relatively intellectual end of Hollywood's output plus the odd Asian flick.

## LIVE MUSIC

Singapore is an established part of the East Asian circuit for **Western stadium-rock outfits** as well as indie bands, though gigs can be marred by a rather staid atmosphere as locals are often still uncomfortable about letting their hair down. **Local bands** do exist and some aren't at all bad, but these are more likely to perform in community centres, rather than decent venues. Rivalling Western music in terms of popularity in Singapore is **Canto-pop**, a bland hybrid of Cantonese lyrics and Western disco beats whose origins lie in the soundtracks of 1950s Cantonese movie musicals; Hong

**13**

Kong Canto-pop superstars visit periodically, and the rapturous welcome they receive make their shows quite an experience. No matter who else is in town, you can always catch a set of cover versions at one of Singapore's bars and clubs; the main venues are picked out below. Jazz and blues ensembles are also popular.

The most exhaustive lists of what's on are to be found in the weekly magazine *8 Days* and the fortnightly *I-S*, though the "Life!" section of the *Straits Times* is also worth a scan. The best music festival is **Mosaic** (March; ⓦ mosaicmusicfestival. com), showcasing an excellent range of jazz and rock acts at Theatres on the Bay.

**Bar Opiume** Asian Civilisations Museum, 1 Empress Place ☎ 6339 2876; see map p.34. This sleek bar features a couple of live bands most nights, with perhaps a jazz or lounge act at 9pm, then a more upbeat R&B/pop band after 11pm. Mon–Thurs 5pm–2am, Fri & Sat 5pm–3am, Sun 5pm–1am.

**Blu Jaz Café** 11 Bali Lane ☎ 6292 3800, ⓦ www .blujaz.net; see map pp.46–47. Live jazz music Fri & Sat 9.30pm–midnight, plus a mixture of other musical styles, even a smattering of comedy, some other nights.

**Crazy Elephant** 3e River Valley Rd, #01-03 Block E Clarke Quay ☎ 6337 7859, ⓦ www.crazyelephant.com; see map, p.34. Of the hotchpotch of brash venues along Clarke Quay, this bar has more street cred than most, with live music – blues and rock – practically every night and an open-mike jam session on Sun. Some tables are by the water's edge. Daily 5pm–2am; Fri & Sat until 3am.

**Home Club** #B01-06 The Riverwalk, 20 Upper Circular Rd, near Boat Quay ☎ 6538 2928, ⓦ www.homeclub .com.sg; see map, pp.60–61. Local indie bands play original material here on Fridays (9–11pm). Tues–Thurs 6pm–3am, Sat until 4am.

**Singapore Indoor Stadium** Stadium Rd (Stadium MRT) ☎ 6348 5555. The usual venue for big-name bands in town; tickets are available through SISTIC.

**TAB** #02-29 *Orchard Hotel*, 442 Orchard Rd ☎, ⓦ tabclub.com.sg; see map, pp.80–81. This compact venue tends to feature slightly poppy shows by local and East Asian acts, though it sees a stream of up-and-coming Western bands stopping by as well. Daily 7pm till late.

**Timbre** Substation, 45 Armenian St ☎ 6338 8030, ⓦ timbre.com.sg; see map, p.34. Open-air venue by the car park at the back of Substation, with local bands and singer-songwriters serving up their own material, though it can be a little derivative. Daily 6pm–1am; Fri & Sat until 2am.

**Timbre** The Arts House, 1 Old Parliament Lane ☎ 6336 3386, ⓦ timbre.com.sg; see map, p.34. More sets by local musicians, though with a slightly slicker feel than at the Substation in view of the high-visibility riverside location. Mon–Sat 6pm–1am; Fri & Sat until 2am.

## ARTS CENTRES AND GENERAL-PURPOSE VENUES

In addition to the venues listed here, the two casino-resorts of *Marina Bay Sands* (see p.75) and *Resorts World* (see p.106) also play host to some concerts and musical extravaganzas.

**The Arts House** 1 Old Parliament Lane, near Empress Place ☎ 6332 6919, ⓦ theartshouse.com.sg. Plays, concerts, films and art exhibitions.

**DBS Arts Centre** 20 Merbau Rd, Robertson Quay ☎ 6733 8166. Plays and concerts.

**Drama Centre** Level 3, National Library, 100 Victoria St ☎ 6837 8400. Mainly plays by local companies.

**Esplanade – Theatres on the Bay** 1 Esplanade Drive ☎ 6828 8222, ⓦ esplanade.com.sg. Sucks up most of the high-profile events.

**MAX Pavilion** Singapore Expo, 1 Expo Drive ⓦ singaporeexpo.com.sg. Big-name concerts at this huge hall, inconveniently located out by Changi Airport.

**NAFA Lee Foundation Theatre** Campus 3, Nanyang Academy of Fine Arts, 151 Bencoolen St ☎ 6513 4000. Plays and other performances.

**Singapore Indoor Stadium** 2 Stadium Walk, Kallang ⓦ sportshub.com.sg. The usual venue for big-selling bands in town.

**Substation** 45 Armenian St ☎ 6337 7535, ⓦ substation.org. Self-styled "home for the arts" with a theatre as well as a gallery hosting art, sculpture and photography exhibitions.

**Victoria Concert Hall and Theatre** 11 Empress Place ⓦ vch.org.sg. Concerts and plays, due to reopen perhaps in 2013 after a major refurbishment.

MOON CAKES

# Festivals

With so many ethnic groups and religions present in Singapore, it would be unusual if your trip didn't coincide with some sort of traditional festival, ranging from exuberant, family-oriented pageants to blood-curdlingly gory displays of devotion. Below is a chronological round-up of Singapore's major festivals (excluding commercial events themed around shopping or the arts, for example, which are covered in the relevant chapters), with suggestions of where best to enjoy them. The dates of many of these change annually according to the lunar calendar; we've listed rough timings, but for specific dates it's a good idea to check with the Singapore Tourism Board (ⓦyoursingapore.com). Some festivals are also public holidays, when many shops and restaurants may close. For a full list of public holidays, see p.30.

**14**

## JANUARY–MARCH

### PONGGAL (OR PONGAL)

**Mid-Jan** A Tamil thanksgiving festival marking the end of the rainy season and the onset of spring. In Hindu homes, rice is cooked in a new pot and allowed to boil over, to symbolize prosperity. At the Sri Srinivasa Perumal Temple on Serangoon Rd, food is prepared against a cacophony of drums, bells, conch shells and chanting, offered up to the gods, and then eaten by devotees as a symbol of cleansing.

### CHINESE NEW YEAR

**Jan–Feb** Singapore's Chinese community springs spectacularly to life to welcome in the new lunar year. The festival's origins lie in a Chinese legend telling of a horned monster that was awoken by the onset of spring, terrorizing nearby villagers until they discovered it could be held at bay by noise, light and the colour red. Essentially, Chinese New Year is a family affair – old debts are settled, friends and relatives visited, mandarin oranges exchanged, red envelopes (*hong bao*) containing money given to children, and red scrolls and papers bearing the character *fu* pasted to front doors as a sign of good fortune. Even so, there's still plenty to see in Chinatown, whose streets are ablaze with lanterns and fairy lights. Two major celebrations take place at Marina Centre – the traditional Chingay procession, a carnival like display with dragon and lion dancers that has now grown into a major ticketed event that includes some international performers, and River Hongbao, with displays of lanterns and yet more performances of music and dance.

### THAIPUSAM

**Jan/Feb** Not for the faint-hearted, this Hindu festival sees entranced penitents walking the 3km from Little India's Sri Perumal Srinivasa Temple to the Chettiar Temple on Tank Road, carrying *kavadis* – elaborate steel arches decorated with peacock feathers and attached to their skin by hooks and prongs – and with skewers spiked through their cheeks and tongues – to honour the Lord Murugan. Some join the procession to pray for assistance, others to give thanks for heavenly aid already granted. Coconuts are smashed at the feet of the penitents for good luck as they set off, and friends and relatives jig around them en route, singing and chanting to spur them on.

## APRIL–AUGUST

### QING MING (OR CHING MING)

**April** At the beginning of the third lunar month, the Chinese remember their ancestors by cleaning and restoring their graves and making offerings of joss sticks, incense papers and food.

### VESAK DAY

**May** Saffron-robed monks chant sacred scriptures at packed Buddhist temples, and devotees release caged birds to commemorate the Buddha's birth (May), enlightenment and the attainment of Nirvana; in the evening, candlelit processions are held at temples. The Buddha Tooth Relic Temple in Chinatown (see p.62) is a good place to experience this festival.

### DUMPLING FESTIVAL

**June** Pyramid-shaped sticky-rice dumplings, wrapped up in leaves and steamed, are often sold at stalls all over Singapore, but are especially common in the run-up to the Dumpling Festival, celebrated on the fifth day of the fifth lunar month. The festival commemorates Qu Yuan, a Chinese scholar who drowned himself in protest against political corruption. Local people, it is said, tried to save him from sea creatures by beating drums, disturbing the waters with their oars, and throwing in rice dumplings to feed them, but to no avail.

### DRAGON BOAT FESTIVAL

**June/July** Rowing boats, bearing a dragon's head and tail, their crews spurred on by the pounding of a great drum in the prow, race across Bedok Reservoir in the east of the island to commemorate Qu Yuan.

### RAMADAN

**July/Aug** Muslims spend the ninth month of the Islamic calendar fasting from dawn to dusk in order to intensify awareness of the plight of the poor and to identify with the hungry. The fast (which includes abstaining from drinking even water, smoking and sex by day) is broken nightly with delicious Malay sweetmeats served at stalls outside mosques. The biggest collection of stalls sets up along Bussorah and Kandahar streets, outside the Sultan Mosque. Muslims mark Hari Raya Puasa (Eid-al-Fitr), the end of Ramadan, by feasting, donning their best traditional clothes and visiting family and friends.

### NATIONAL DAY

**Aug 9** Singapore's gaining of independence in 1965 is celebrated with a national holiday and a huge show at Marina Bay, featuring military parades and fireworks.

### FESTIVAL OF THE HUNGRY GHOSTS

**Aug/Sept** Sometimes called Yue Lan, this festival is held to appease the souls of the dead released from Purgatory during the thirty days of the seventh lunar month, and thereby forestall unlucky events. Chinese street operas and concerts are held for the entertainment of the "wandering spirits", and joss sticks – some the size of a man – red candles and paper money are burnt outside Chinese homes. Paper effigies of worldly goods such as houses, cars and servants are sometimes burnt, too. Elsewhere, marquees are set up in the street to hold festive banquets, followed by auctions of pieces of charcoal, cake and flowers – all thought to be auspicious.

## SEPTEMBER–DECEMBER

### BIRTHDAY OF THE MONKEY GOD

**Sept** To celebrate the birthday of one of the most popular deities in the Chinese pantheon, mediums possessed by the Monkey God's spirit pierce themselves with skewers at the Qi Tian Temple at 44 Eng Hoon St (⊛ qitiangong.com; Outram Park MRT, then a 10min walk), while a sedan chair said to be possessed by the god himself is carried by worshippers. In the evening the temple hosts performances of street opera.

### MOON CAKE FESTIVAL

**Sept** Also known as the Mid-Autumn Festival (held on the fifteenth day of the eighth lunar month), this is when Chinese people eat moon cakes – generally made from aduki-bean paste and sometimes stuffed with salted egg yolk for good measure, though in Singapore durian-flavoured versions and other weird tropical variants are available. One story is that the cakes commemorate the fall of the Mongol Empire, plotted, so legend has it, by means of messages secreted in cakes. Others say the cakes represent the full moon, which is said to be at its brightest at this time of year. Besides seeing the cakes on sale all over the island, you may come across children walking around with multicoloured candlelit lanterns by night in the open areas around high-rise estates.

### NAVARATHIRI

**Sept/Oct** Hindu temples such as the Chettiar Temple on Tank Road, and Chinatown's Sri Mariamman Temple, devote nine nights to classical dance and music in honour of Durga, Lakshmi and Saraswathi, the consorts of the Hindu gods Shiva, Vishnu and Brahma. Visitors are welcome at the nightly performances that take place at temples across the island. On the tenth night, a silver horse is carried at the head of a procession that begins at the Tank Road temple.

### FESTIVAL OF THE NINE EMPEROR GODS

**Oct** The nine-day sojourn on earth of the Nine Emperor Gods, thought to cure ailments and bring good health and longevity, is celebrated at a few temples, notably the Hougang Tou Mu temple (779a Upper Serangoon Rd; Serangoon MRT then continue north on bus #101 or #107 for a couple of stops). Besides Chinese opera and mediums conducting their trade in the streets, there's a procession during which effigies of the nine gods are carried in sedan chairs.

### HARI RAYA HAJI

**Oct** An auspicious day for Singapore's Muslims, who gather at mosques to honour those who have completed the annual Hajj pilgrimage to Mecca, the birthplace of the prophet Muhammad. Goats are sacrificed and their meat is given to the needy.

### DEEPAVALI (DIWALI)

**Oct/Nov** Serangoon Road is festooned with colourful lights during this, the most auspicious of Hindu festivals, celebrating the victory of the Lord Krishna over Narakasura, and thus of light over dark. Oil lamps are lit outside homes to attract Lakshmi, the goddess of prosperity, and prayers are offered at all temples.

### THIMITHI

**Oct/Nov** Another dramatic Hindu ceremony, this one sees devotees proving the strength of their faith by running across a four-metre-long pit of hot coals at the Sri Mariamman Temple in Chinatown. Outside the temple, devotees in their hundreds line up awaiting their turn, and building up their courage by dancing, shouting and singing.

### PILGRIMAGE TO KUSU ISLAND

**Oct/Nov** Locals visit Kusu island in their thousands to pray for good luck and fertility at the island's temple and Muslim shrines; for more, see p.111.

### CHRISTMAS

**Dec 25** December in Singapore is generally very wet, and somehow the weather lends something appropriate to Christmas in the tropics. It's a particularly colourful and atmospheric time for shopping, as shopping centres vie for the best decorations in town.

14

ORCHARD ROAD

# Shopping

Choice and convenience make the Singapore shopping experience a rewarding one, but the island's affluence and strong currency mean most things are priced at Western levels. Perhaps the best time to bargain-hunt is during the Great Singapore Sale (from late May to late July; ⓦgreatsingapore sale.com.sg), when prices are marked down across the island. Unsurprisingly, Orchard Road boasts the biggest cluster of malls, bulging with designer names. Malls elsewhere tend to be more informal; the most interesting ones in Chinatown are like multistorey markets, home to a few traditional outlets stocking Chinese foodstuffs, medicines, instruments and porcelain. Singapore's remaining shophouses are worthy of attention too, as many are still home to independent stores selling books, jewellery, souvenirs and so on.

## ESSENTIALS

**Bargaining** Haggling is not as widespread as you might assume – it's expected in smaller family-owned or independent shops, but nowhere else.

**Complaints** In the unlikely event that you encounter a problem with a retailer that you cannot resolve mutually, you may be able to recover your money by initiating proceedings at Singapore's Small Claims Tribunal. It only costs $10 to have your case heard, though you will need to attend in person; see ⓦsmallclaims.gov.sg for more information.

**Opening hours** Department stores and other big retailers are typically open daily from 10am to 9pm (perhaps 10pm in the biggest malls), while hours vary for smaller shops. In the reviews that follow, times are not given for shopping malls as the buildings themselves are accessible from the early morning until late at night, but their tenants keep hours as they please.

**Tax refunds** On leaving the country, tourists can claim a refund of Singapore's goods and services tax (GST; 7.7 percent at the time of writing) on purchases over a certain amount (at least $100, though some retailers require a larger outlay), provided the shop in question is participating in the tax refund scheme. You will either have to complete a form which must be signed by the retailer, and then present the goods, forms and receipts to the customs authorities when you leave, or else ask the shop to link your purchases to one of your debit or credit cards, in which case you claim the tax back by, for example, scanning a barcode at a booth at the airport. For detailed information on the intricacies of all of this, have a look at the "GST for consumers" section of ⓦiras.gov.sg, or pick up the appropriate leaflet from a tourist office.

**15**

## SHOPPING MALLS

### ORCHARD ROAD AND AROUND

**313@Somerset** 313 Somerset Rd (above Somerset MRT) ⓦ313somerset.com.sg; see map pp.80–81. Uniqlo is the star name at this new mall.

**Centrepoint** 176 Orchard Rd ⓦfrascentrepoint malls.com; see map pp.80–81. This all-round complex has for many years housed Robinsons, Singapore's oldest department store. It's likely to be shut for much of 2013 for a major refit, however, during which time you will find Robinsons at The Heeren, just slightly further west on Orchard Rd opposite the Mandarin Gallery.

**Forum the Shopping Mall** 583 Orchard Rd (near the Orchard Parade hotel) ⓦforumtheshoppingmall.com; see map pp.80–81. Plenty of items for pampered brats – upmarket kids' clothes, toys and so forth.

**ION Orchard** 2 Orchard Turn (above Orchard MRT); see map pp.80–81. Despite the impressive hyper-modern facade and a sprinkling of designer names, Armani included, by far the most popular section of this cavernous mall is the *Food Opera* food court on basement 4.

**Ngee Ann City** 391a Orchard Rd ⓦngeeanncity.com.sg; see map pp.80–81. A brooding twin-towered complex, home to the Japanese Takashimaya department store and the excellent Kinokuniya bookshop, plus several jewellers.

**Palais Renaissance** 390 Orchard Rd; see map pp.80–81. Prada, DKNY and yet more top brands.

**Paragon** Opposite Ngee Ann City ⓦparagon.sg; see map pp.80–81. This swanky mall is holding its own despite upstart competition. Come here for Calvin Klein, Gucci, Versace and many more big names.

★ **Plaza Singapura** 68 Orchard Rd ⓦplazasingapura.com.sg; see map pp.80–81. Veteran mall with a bit of everything: Marks & Spencer, the Singapore department store John Little, sportswear and sports equipment, musical instruments, audio, video and general electrical equipment. Always rammed.

**Tanglin Shopping Centre** 19 Tanglin Rd (next to the Orchard Parade hotel) ⓦtanglinsc.com; see map pp.80–81. Good for art, antiques and curios.

**Tangs** Junction of Orchard and Scotts Rd ⓦtangs.com; see map pp.80–81. Tangs is a department store dating back to the 1950s, and the only one to have its own building on Orchard Rd, topped by a pagoda-style construction occupied by the *Marriott* hotel. The store sells a wide range of reasonably priced clothes and accessories.

**Wisma Atria** 435 Orchard Rd (opposite Tangs) ⓦwismaonline.com; see map pp.80–81. Hosts a good range of middle-market local and international fashion shops, plus the Japanese department store Isetan.

### THE COLONIAL DISTRICT

**Funan DigitaLife Mall** 109 North Bridge Rd ⓦfunan.com.sg; see map p.34. A variety of stores here sell computer and electronics equipment.

**Raffles City** 252 North Bridge Rd (above City Hall MRT) ⓦrafflescity.com; see map p.34. Home to a branch of Robinsons department store with a Marks & Spencer within it, plus numerous fashion chains.

### MARINA BAY

**Marina Square** 6 Raffles Blvd ⓦmarinasquare.com.sg; see map p.74. Nowhere near as large as its sprawling neighbour, Suntec City, but better laid out and with a very diverse range of outlets.

**The Shoppes at Marina Bay Sands** 10 Bayfront Ave; see map p.74. A hotchpotch of swish designer outlets and some quite humdrum stores.

### BRAS BASAH ROAD TO ROCHOR ROAD

**Bugis Junction** Junction Victoria St and Rochor Rd

(above Bugis MRT) ⓦ bugisjunction-mall.com.sg; see map pp.46–47. Mall encasing several streets of restored shophouses, and featuring the Japanese/Chinese department store BHG.

**Sim Lim Square** 1 Rochor Canal Rd ⓦ simlimsquare .com.sg; see map pp.46–47. Electronics, computers and cameras – with some bargaining, it can be better value than the slicker Funan DigitaLife Mall.

### LITTLE INDIA

★ **Mustafa** Syed Alwi Rd ⓦ mustafa.com.sg; see map pp.46–47. Totally different in feel to the malls of Orchard Rd, Mustafa is a phenomenon, selling electronics, fresh food, luggage, you name it – and it never closes. Daily 24hr.

### 15 CHINATOWN

**Hong Lim Complex** 531–531a Upper Cross St; see map pp.60–61. One of several Chinatown shopping centres where ordinary people buy ordinary things – dried mushrooms, cuttlefish and crackers from provisions shops, for example.

**Pearl's Centre** 100 Eu Tong Sen St; see map pp.60–61.

Home to some Chinese medicine clinics and a few shops selling Buddhist paraphernalia.

**People's Park Centre** 101 Upper Cross St; see map pp.60–61. Stall-like shop units selling Chinese handicrafts, CDs, electronics, silk, jade and gold.

★ **People's Park Complex** 1 Park Rd; see map pp.60–61. A venerable shopping centre that, like the Hong Lim Complex and adjacent People's Park Centre, is among the most entertaining places to browse in Chinatown because it's so workaday. Also here is the Overseas Emporium on level 4, selling Chinese musical instruments, calligraphy pens, lacquerwork and jade.

### ELSEWHERE IN SINGAPORE

**Holland Road Shopping Centre** 211 Holland Ave, Holland Village; see map p.102. The shops above the supermarket are good places to browse for curios.

★ **VivoCity** Next to HarbourFront Centre and above HarbourFront MRT ⓦ vivocity.com.sg; see map p.107. A humdinger of a mall, containing a branch of Tangs department store, a cinema, three food courts and several restaurants.

## ANTIQUES, CRAFTS, CURIOS AND SOUVENIRS

Singapore bulges with stores selling Asian antiques and crafts, ranging from Chinese snuff bottles to Malaysian pewter. If it's antiques you're specifically after, try trawling through Tanglin Shopping Centre at the western end of Orchard Road, or Holland Road Shopping Centre.

**Antiques of the Orient** #02-40 Tanglin Shopping Centre ☎ 6734 9351; see map pp.80–81. Antiquarian books and maps, engravings and old photos. Mon–Sat 10am–6pm, Sun 11am–4pm.

**Artrium** MICA Building, 140 Hill St ⓦ www .artriumatmica.com; see map p.34. The glass-ceilinged atrium here – artfully named the ARTrium – is home to half a dozen galleries selling work from around Southeast Asia. Typically daily 11am–7pm.

**Dulu-Dulu** 11 Jalan Pinang ☎ 6341 7743; see map pp.46–47. Ancient typewriters, brass spittoons and beaded necklaces are among the items jostling for space at this friendly Indian Muslim-run junk shop. Daily 10.30am–7pm.

**Elliott's Antiques** #02-13 Raffles Hotel Arcade ☎ 6337 1008; see map p.34. Chinese antique furniture and art. Daily 11am–7pm.

**Eng Tiang Huat** 284 River Valley Rd ☎ 6734 3738; see map p.34. Oriental musical instruments, wayang costumes and props. Mon–Sat 11am–6pm.

**Far East Inspirations** 33 Pagoda St ☎ 6224 2993; see map pp.60–61. The classiest of several antique shops here, offering Asian furniture, porcelain-based lamps and vases. Daily 10.30am–6.30pm.

**The Heritage Shop** 93 Jalan Sultan; see map pp.46–47. An incredible range of bric-a-brac, from antique radios to beautiful enamelware tiffin carriers – little pots for

cooked food, stacked and held together within a metal frame for easy carrying. Daily 1.30–8pm.

**Jasmine Fine Arts** #03-01 Mandarin Gallery (in front of the Mandarin Orchard hotel) ☎ 6734 5688; see map pp.80–81. Appealing artwork from all over the world. Daily 11am–8pm.

★ **Katong Antiques House** 208 East Coast Rd, Katong ☎ 6345 8544; see map p.94. Peranakan artefacts and Chinese porcelain (see p.65.) Tues–Sun 11am–5pm.

**Kwok Gallery** #03-01 Far East Shopping Centre, 545 Orchard Rd ☎ 6235 2516; see map pp.80–81. A broad, impressive inventory of traditional Chinese pottery, jade and sculpture. Mon–Sat 11am–6pm.

★ **Lim's Arts & Living** #02-01 Holland Rd Shopping Centre ☎ 6732 6486; see map p.102; #02-154 VivoCity ☎ 6376 9468; see map p.107. A sort of Asian Conran Shop, packed with bamboo pipes, dainty teapots, cherrywood furniture and lamps crafted from old tea jars. Daily: Holland Rd 10am–8.30pm, Vivocity 10.30am–10pm.

**Little Shophouse** 43 Bussorah St, near Sultan Mosque ☎ 6295 2328; see map pp.46–47. Well named, this tiny outlet boasts some beautiful examples of Peranakan beaded slippers (from $300), plus replica Peranakan crockery. Daily 10am–6pm.

**Lopburi** #01-04 Tanglin Place, 91 Tanglin Rd ☎ 6738 3834; see map pp.80–81. Seriously fine – and seriously

**15**

expensive – antique Buddhas and Khmer sculptures, as well as some old silk textiles. Mon–Sat noon–7pm, Sun noon–4pm.

**Malay Art Gallery** 31 Bussorah St ☎ 6294 8051; see map pp.46–47. Stocks *kerises* (traditional daggers) from Malaysia and Indonesia. Mon–Sat 8.30am–5.30pm, sometimes also Sun 9am–4.30pm.

**Maya Gallery** 666 North Bridge Rd ☎ 6291 1760, ⓦ mayagallery.com.sg; see map 46–47. Represents a number of top Singapore artists working in a variety of media, including master potter Iskandar Jalil, and also has several Indonesian artists on its books. Daily noon–6pm.

**Rishi Handicrafts** 5 Baghdad St, close to Arab St ☎ 6298 2408; see map pp.46–47. Specializes in a range of baskets made from rattan, bamboo and other materials, with some knick-knacks, too. Daily 10am–5.30pm (Sun from 11am).

**Rumah Bebe** 113 East Coast Rd ☎ 6247 8781, ⓦ rumahbebe.com; see map p.94. Peranakan products, including beaded shoes and handbags, costume jewellery and the traditional *kebaya* garb of Nonyas. They also offer

courses in beading and Nonya cookery. Tues–Sun 9.30am–6.30pm.

**Singapore Tyler Print Institute** 41 Robertson Quay ☎ 6336 3663, ⓦ stpi.com.sg; see map p.34. In a nineteenth-century godown, the STPI is a state-of-the-art print- and paper-making workshop and art gallery. Tues–Sat 10am–6pm.

**TeaJoy** #01-05 North Bridge Centre, 420 North Bridge Rd ☎ 6339 3739; see map pp.46–47. Close to the National Library, this sells Chinese tea sets with special attention paid to oolong accoutrements. Daily noon–8pm.

**Tong Mern Sern** 51 Craig Rd, Tanjong Pagar ☎ 6223 1037, ⓦ tmsantiques.com; see map pp.60–61. "We buy junk and sell antiques", proclaims the banner outside this great little establishment. The owner is quite a character and will gladly tell you all about the collection of crockery, old furniture and other bric-a-brac he has amassed. Mon–Sat 9am–6pm, Sun 1–6pm.

**Zhen Lacquer Gallery** 1 Trengganu St, Chinatown ☎ 6222 2718; see map pp.60–61. Specializes in lacquerware boxes and bowls. Daily 10.30am–9pm.

## BOOKS

Singapore's bookshops are as well stocked as many in the West; all the larger outlets carry a good selection of Western and local fiction, plus books on Southeast Asia and a range of magazines.

★ **Kinokuniya** Level 3, Ngee Ann City ☎ 6737 5021; branch at Level 3, Bugis Junction ☎ 6339 1790, ⓦ kinokuniya.com.sg; see map pp.80–81. The main outlet is one of Singapore's largest and best bookshops, with titles on every conceivable subject and some foreign-language literature too. Daily 10.30am–9.30pm.

**Littered With Books** 20 Duxton Rd ☎ 6220 6824; see map pp.60–61. Despite its name, this indie outlet has a neatly laid out, though somewhat random, collection of literary fiction, thrillers and travel writing. Daily at least noon–8pm, slightly longer hours Fri–Sun.

**MPH** #B1-21 Raffles City ☎ 6336 4232, ⓦ mph.com.sg;

see map p.34. Veteran of the local book trade, though not as comprehensive these days as it should be. Daily 10am–10pm.

★ **Select Books** 51 Armenian St ☎ 6337 9313, ⓦ selectbooks.com.sg; see map p.34. A great range of books on Singapore, Malaysia and the rest of Southeast Asia, with a mail-order service, too. Mon–Sat 9.30am–6.30pm, Sun 10am–4pm.

**Times Bookstores** Level 4, Centrepoint; Level 4, Plaza Singapura; ⓦ timesbookstores.com.sg; see map pp.80–81. A reasonably stocked local chain. Daily 10.30am–9.30pm.

## CDS AND DVDS

Plenty of Western CDs and DVDs are available in Singapore. If you want to buy Asian material, you'll find Chinese music and DVDs widely available; for Indian releases, there are several outlets in Little India, and for Malay music, head to the Joo Chiat Complex, Geylang (see p.92).

**Earshot Café** Arts House, 1 Old Parliament Lane ☎ 6337 1086; see map p.34. Stocks some CDs and DVDs by Singaporean musicians and film-makers. Mon–Fri 11.30am–7pm.

**Gramophone** Cathay Building, 2 Handy Rd (where Orchard Rd becomes Bras Basah Rd) ☎ 6235 4105; see map pp.80–81. Largely mainstream CD releases. Daily noon–10pm.

**HMV** Level 4, 313@Somerset ☎ 6733 1822; see map pp.80–81. Best bet for mainstream releases with dedicated jazz and classical music sections. Daily 10am–10pm.

**Roxy Records** #02-15 Excelsior Shopping Centre (at the Hill St end of the Peninsula Excelsior Hotel) ☎ 6337 7783; see map p.34. A range of imported indie and other hard-to-find releases – even secondhand vinyl. Mon–Sat noon–9.30pm.

**Straits Records** 24 Bali Lane ☎9681 6341; see map pp.46–47. Stocking CDs and vinyl by obscure US metal/ thrash bands and better-known 1970s punk and reggae acts, plus a little Malay music, this minuscule shop epitomizes the strange mix of sensibilities at play in and around Arab St. Daily 3–10pm.

## JEWELLERY

Singapore isn't a bad place to buy jewellery, particularly if you share the Chinese affection for jade or the local fondness for high-purity gold (22 or 24 carat).

**CT Hoo** #01-22 Tanglin Shopping Centre ☎6737 5447; see map pp.80–81. Specializing in pearls. Mon–Sat 9.30am–6.30pm.

**Flower Diamond** #03-02 Ngee Ann City ☎6734 1221; see map pp.80–81. Contemporary designs as well as more traditionally styled bling, at sensible prices. Daily 10am–9pm.

**Poh Heng** #01-17, People's Park Complex ☎6535 0960; see map pp.60–61. Old-fangled Chinese jewellers dating back to 1948, though now housed in modern premises. Daily 11am–9pm.

**Risis** National Orchid Garden, Botanic Gardens ☎6475 5104; see map p.100. Singaporeans tend to regard gold-plated orchids – available as brooches, pendants, earrings, even on tie clips – as clichéd, but tourists snap them up here as well as at a few malls and at Changi Airport. Daily 8.45am–6.30pm.

**Wong's Jewellery** 62 Temple St ☎6323 0236; see map pp.60–61. Chinese-style outlet, good for jade, gold and pearls. Daily 10am–7.30pm.

## FABRICS AND FASHION

Arab Street and Geylang Serai are among the main areas for old-fashioned fabric stores packed with bolts of cloth. Some of these stock Malaysian and Indonesian **batik**, produced by applying hot wax to a piece of cloth with either a pen or metal stamp; patterns appear when dye is applied as it cannot penetrate the waxed areas. Also available is the exquisite style of brocade known as **songket**, made by handweaving gold and silver thread into plain cloth. Not cheap, it's traditionally worn as a *sampin*, a sarong-like garment. Chinese, Japanese and Thai silks are all available, too, and there are multi-hued silk **saris** on sale in Little India. It might seem odd to shop for high **fashion** items in Singapore as big-name designer goods are no cheaper than elsewhere; the trick is to look out for the best of the local designers, who offer quality clothes and shoes at decent prices.

**Boutique by Ashley Isham** #01-27 Orchard Central, 181 Orchard Rd ☎6509 5408; see map pp.80–81. Elegant dresses by the London-based Singapore designer. Daily 11am–9pm.

**Charles & Keith** Several outlets, including #B3-58 ION Orchard ☎6238 1840; see map pp.80–81. Singapore's answer to Malaysia's Jimmy Choo, the brothers Charles and Keith Wong design stylish, surprisingly affordable women's shoes and handbags too. Daily 10.30am–10pm.

**Dakshaini Silks** 65 Serangoon Rd ☎6291 9969; see map pp.46–47. Premier Indian embroidered silks. Mon–Sat 10am–9pm, Sun 10am–8pm.

**Jim Thompson** Level 1, Raffles Hotel Arcade, 328 North Bridge Rd ☎6336 5322; see map p.34. Though businessman Jim Thompson disappeared under mysterious circumstances in Malaysia's Cameron Highlands in 1967, his name is still a byword for quality silk. Daily 10.30am–7.30pm.

**M)phosis** Several outlets, including #01-24 Plaza Singapura ☎6334 1736; see map pp.80–81.

Eveningwear and shoes styled for 20-somethings and at prices they can afford, by the Singaporean designer, Colin Koh. Daily 10.30am–9.30pm.

**Malay Art Gallery** 31 Bussorah St ☎6294 8051; see map pp.46–47. *Songket* cloth, suitable for wearing or framing. Mon–Sat 8.30am–5.30pm, sometimes also Sun 9am–4.30pm.

**Raoul** Several outlets, including #02-49 Paragon ☎6737 0682, ⚲raoul.com; see map pp.80–81. Sensibly priced designer clothes for men and women by a Singaporean/Lebanese husband-and-wife team. Daily 10am–9pm.

**Rossi Apparel** Level 1, Millenia Walk, Marina Centre ☎6336 2818; see map p.74. For the male executive who just has to have bespoke shirts, starting at $130 apiece in high-quality cotton. Mon–Sat 11.30am-7.30pm, Sun 12.30–6.30pm.

**Toko Aljunied** 91 Arab St ☎6294 6897; see map pp.46–47. Batik cloth and *kebaya* – the blouse/sarong combinations traditionally worn by Nonyas. Mon–Sat 10.30am–7pm, Sun 11am–5pm.

**15**

MARINA BAY SANDS SAMPAN RIDES

# Kids' Singapore

Slick yet suitably exotic, Singapore can feel like a gigantic theme park to children, and just wandering Little India or even Orchard Road should unearth plenty to interest them. Reactions to the Hindu and Buddhist temples covered throughout this book will vary: some children are utterly fascinated by them, while for others the colourful statuary and religious ceremonies just sail over their heads. Traditional festivals are generally entertaining too, but Thaipusam (see p.148) is one event which might freak some kids out. Otherwise, there are several theme parks around Singapore, and of course Sentosa is one giant theme park (see Chapter 9 for more). Upmarket shops geared to kids cluster within the Forum mall on Orchard Road (see p.151). For childcare products, try Mothercare, with various outlets in the city centre (⊚ mothercare.com.sg).

## ATTRACTIONS FOR KIDS

Prices for children's tickets, where available, are given throughout this book after the adult prices, and generally weigh in at a third less.

**Bukit Timah Nature Reserve;** see p.84. Come for the rainforest trails and macaques – kids are fascinated by the latter, though note the critters hiss and bare their teeth if you get very close. The trails are probably a bit too strenuous for under-6s.

**Cable cars to Sentosa** See p.101. Not only is this the way to arrive in style at Sentosa, but the vertiginous views always go down well.

**DuckTours and river cruises** See p.25. Children love the amphibious Ducktour; the Singapore River cruise is fun but unlikely to make quite such an impression.

**E2Max** Level 9, Cathay Cineleisure, 8 Grange Rd (off Orchard Rd; Somerset MRT) ☎6235 9249, ✆e2max .com.sg. Computer gaming might save the day if there's a tropical downpour that just won't blow over. PC games cost $2–3.50/hr to play while Playstation, Xbox and other consoles cost $8/hr, with a small additional fee to rent the controller. Mon–Thurs & Sun noon–midnight, Fri & Sat noon–3am.

**Forest Adventure** Bedok Reservoir Rd ☎8100 7420, ✆forestadventure.com.sg. There's a treetop obstacle course at Sentosa, but this one out in the eastern suburbs just might appeal if you are tackling, say, Changi on the same day. The park includes a children's course featuring the usual assortment of elevated bridges and ending with a zip line. Bedok MRT, then bus #67 to the eastern end of Bedok Reservoir Park, opposite the Clearwater apartments. $30 (the adult course is $42). Sat & Sun 10am–6pm.

**Go-Go Bambini** Block 8, Dempsey Rd ☎6474 4176, ✆gogobambini.com. Part of the Dempsey Village complex near the Botanic Garden, this indoor playground features lots of bouncy playpens, climbing walls etc. Best reached by taxi. Children pay $25 for unlimited play ($12 for kids under 24 months) while accompanying adults get in free. Mon–Thurs 9.30am–6pm, Fri–Sun 9.30am–8pm.

**Haw Par Villa** See p.99. No rides at this Buddhist theme park, where lurid statues, murals and dioramas dramatize Chinese myths. The occasional shock-horror touch tends to amuse rather than scare.

**Jacob Ballas Garden** Northern edge of the Botanic Garden ☎6465 0196. Under-12s will appreciate splashing about in and around the fountains of the water-play area (bring swimming gear), and there's a treehouse and maze to explore, too. Botanic Garden MRT or head up Bukit Timah Rd on bus #171 from Orchard Rd or bus #170 from Little India, getting off just after Evans Rd, when you see the National University of Singapore running track. Tues–Sun 8am–7pm; free.

**Jurong Bird Park** See p.103. Penguins and flamingos are among the obvious highlights, but do catch at least one bird show – the ones featuring birds of prey are especially good.

**Marina Bay Sands Sampan Rides** 10 Bayfront Ave. The idea of navigating the hotel's internal "canal" system in little wooden boats sounds preposterous, but it actually goes down really well with children. All rides $10, regardless of age. Daily 11.30am–8pm.

**Marina Bay Sands Skating Rink** 10 Bayfront Ave. The casino resort's own skating rink, using synthetic ice, is well run and reasonably priced: $7/$6 for 1hr, plus $3 for skate rental. Daily 11.30am–5pm & 6–8.30pm.

**Port of Lost Wonder** Palawan Beach, Sentosa ✆polw .com.sg. A playground centred on a pirate ship, with a picnic area and a garden where kids can familiarize themselves with plants and animals. There's a daily programme of guided activities featuring storytelling, dance and water fights (have swimwear ready). Children Mon–Fri $8, Sat & Sun $15; no charge for accompanying adults. Daily 10am–6.30pm (last admission 4.30pm).

**Singapore Flyer** See p.73. This can be a space-age experience for kids, even though they're merely being raised aloft in a glass-and-metal cage. The views are incidental.

**Singapore Science Centre** See p.103. Uncover your children's latent scientific bent by setting them loose amid zillions of interactive displays.

**Singapore Zoo and Night Safari** See p.88. Animal exhibits aside, the zoo also has a Rainforest Kidzworld section featuring pony rides and a water-play area, but it's the night safari that some young 'uns find magical.

**Snow City** 21 Jurong Town Hall Rd, close to the Omni-Theatre and Science Centre ☎6560 1297, ✆snowcity .com.sg. Hi-tech machines let it snow year-round in this corner of equatorial Singapore, though the slope at this indoor centre is just 60m long and less than three storeys high, leaving scope only for tobogganing on rubber rings. $15/hr including use of their jackets and boots, though glove rental costs extra. Daily 10am–6pm.

**Superbowl** #03-200 Marina Square mall, Marina Centre. Yet another option in wet weather – ten-pin bowling, costing $4.20 ($3.20 for kids) per game on weekdays during, a tad more during the evening and at weekends.

**Universal Studios** See p.106. Bear in mind that many rides have age or height restrictions and so aren't suitable for young children.

**16**

RAFFLES PLACE STATUE

# Contexts

# History

Not much is known of Singapore's pre-colonial history. Third-century Chinese sailors could have been referring to Singapore in their account of a place called Pu-Luo-Chung, a corruption of the Malay for "island at the end of a peninsula". In the late thirteenth century, Marco Polo reported seeing a place called Chiamassie, which could also have been Singapore. By then the island was known locally as Temasek and was a minor trading outpost of the Sumatran Srivijaya Empire. According to the Sejarah Melayu (or Malay Annals, a historical document commissioned by the Malay sultans in the seventeenth century), by the late fourteenth century the island was called Singapura, meaning "Lion City" in Sanskrit, though the origins of the name are mysterious. The annals mention a Sumatran noble who saw what he took to be a lion while sheltering on the island from a storm, but this must be regarded as legend.

Around 1390, a Sumatran prince called **Paramesvara** broke with the Majapahit Empire of Java and escaped to what is now Singapore. There he ruled until a Javanese offensive forced him to flee up the Malay Peninsula, where he and his son, **Iskandar Shah**, founded the **Malacca sultanate**. With the rise of Malacca, Singapore declined into a low-key fishing settlement and remained so after the Portuguese and then the Dutch took Malacca in 1511 and 1641 respectively.

## The founding of Singapore

In the late eighteenth century the **British East India Company** embarked on a drive to establish ports along the strategic Straits of Malacca. Penang was secured in 1786 and Malacca taken in 1795 at the request of the Dutch Republic (whose government was in exile in London after being brought down by French-backed revolutionaries), but a port was needed further south to counter the Dutch presence in what is now Indonesia. Enter the visionary **Thomas Stamford Raffles** (see p.42), the British lieutenant-governor of Bencoolen in Sumatra. In 1818 he was tasked with setting up a colony at the southern tip of the Malay Peninsula, and the following year he stepped ashore on the northern bank of the Singapore River, accompanied by Colonel William Farquhar, a former senior British official in Malacca who was fluent in Malay.

Swampland and tiger-infested jungle covered Singapore, and its population was probably no more than a thousand, but Raffles recognized that the area at the southern tip of the island could make a superb deep-water harbour. With a view to setting up a trading station, he quickly struck a treaty with Abdul Rahman, *temenggong* (chieftain) of Singapore and a subordinate of the sultan of Johor, the region occupying the

| 7th c. | c.14th c. | c.1390 |
|---|---|---|
| The Sumatran Srivijayan Empire, encompassing the Malay Peninsula, rises to prominence | Srivijaya is challenged by the Majapahit Empire of Java and declines | Prince Paramesvara, fleeing Majapahit, takes control of Singapore – then Temasek – which prospers for a few years |

southern part of the Malay Peninsula. Raffles also exploited a succession dispute in the ruling house of Johor, bypassing the man who had until then been ruling as sultan, and who was sympathetic to the Dutch. Instead Raffles recognized his half-brother as sultan and signed a second treaty with both him and the *temenggong*. This riled the Dutch, for whom Singapore was part of their domain, but Farquhar managed to divert a contingent of British troops to Singapore and an immediate confrontation was averted. The matter was settled by the **Anglo-Dutch treaty** of 1824, a classic colonial carve-up in which the Dutch let the British keep Malacca and Singapore in exchange for Bencoolen and British recognition of the Riau Archipelago, the islands just south of Singapore, as being part of the Dutch sphere of influence.

## The early boom years

With its duty-free stance and ideal position at the gateway to the South China Sea, Singapore experienced a meteoric expansion. The population had reached ten thousand by the time of the first census in 1824, with Malays, Chinese, Indians and Europeans arriving in search of work and commercial opportunities.

Two years earlier, Raffles had begun dividing up what is now downtown Singapore, earmarking the area south of the Singapore River for the Chinese, while Muslims were settled around the sultan's palace near today's Arab Street. Sultan Hussein and the *temenggong* were bought out in 1824, and Singapore ceded outright to the British. Three years later, the fledgling colony united with Penang and Malacca to form the **Straits Settlements**, which became a British crown colony in 1867. Singapore's laissez-faire economy boomed throughout this time, though life was chaotic and disease was rife. By 1860 the population had reached eighty thousand; Arabs, Indians, Javanese and Bugis (from Sulawesi) all came, but most populous of all were the Chinese from the southeastern provinces of China.

The advent of steamships and the Suez Canal made Singapore a major staging post on the Europe–East Asia route at the close of the nineteenth century. Singapore had also become a world centre for rubber exports thanks to **Henry Ridley**, who led a one-man crusade to introduce the rubber plant to Southeast Asia. As all of the Malay Peninsula gradually fell into British clutches, the island benefited further from its hinterland's tin- and rubber-based economy.

## The Japanese occupation

Singapore's Asian communities began to find their political voice in the 1920s, but pro-independence activity had not gone far when the spectre of war reared its head. Within the space of a few hours in December 1941, Japan had bombed Pearl Harbor and landed on the Malay Peninsula, whose raw materials were vital for the Japanese war effort. By the end of January 1942 they were at Johor Bahru, facing Singapore across the Straits of Johor. But the guns of "Fortress Singapore" pointed south from what is now Sentosa island; received wisdom had it that a Japanese attack would come from the sea. The view of one British intelligence officer that "the Japanese are very small and short-sighted and thus totally unsuited physically to tropical warfare" embodied the complacency of the Allied command under Lieutenant-General Arthur Percival.

| 1511 | 1641 | 1795 | 28 Jan 1819 |
| --- | --- | --- | --- |
| The Portuguese capture Malacca, creating the first European outpost in the Malay Peninsula | The Dutch East India Company seizes Malacca | The British East India Company captures Dutch possessions in Southeast Asia, including Malacca | Stamford Raffles sets foot on Singapore for the first time |

After a week's bombing, on February 7 the Japanese General Tomoyuki Yamashita launched his invasion of Singapore with an attack on Pulau Ubin, northeast of the main island. More landings from the north followed, and between February 11 and 14 the Japanese won decisive victories at Bukit Timah and Pasir Panjang, the site of today's museums at the former Ford car factory (see p.84), and Bukit Chandu (see p.99). On February 15, Percival went to Yamashita's new base at the Ford factory and surrendered. Winston Churchill called it "the largest capitulation in British history"; later, it transpired that the Japanese forces had been outnumbered and their supply lines hopelessly stretched prior to the surrender. Three and a half years of brutal Japanese rule ensued, during which Singapore was renamed Syonan, or "Light of the South", and Europeans were either herded into Changi Prison or sent to work on Thailand's infamous "Death Railway". Less well known is the vicious **Operation Sook Ching**, mounted by the military police force, or **Kempeitai**, during which upwards of 25,000 ethnic Chinese men were executed at Singapore's beaches as enemies of the Japanese.

## Postwar transformation

Even though the island was back in British hands following the end of World War II in 1945, the aura of colonial supremacy had gone and Singaporeans were demanding a say in the island's administration. The subsequent quarter-century would be a time of enormous political upheaval in Singapore, whose resolution laid the foundations for the regimented and wealthy city-state of today.

Though Britain was beginning to divest itself of its colonial possessions, it was unsure what to do with Singapore. One "obvious" option, for Singapore and the Malay Peninsula to become a new state together, was fraught with difficulty: Singapore had so many Chinese that its inclusion would have led to the politically awkward result of Malays being in a minority in the new state. So it was that when the Straits Settlements were dissolved in 1946, Malacca and Penang joined the newly formed **Malayan Union** together with the rest of the Peninsula, while Singapore became a crown colony in its own right. However, even the Singapore-less union was opposed by Malay nationalists, who did not want the Chinese and Indian communities to be afforded citizenship under the terms of the union, arguing that the Malays should retain special privileges. The British caved in and reinvented the union in 1948 as the **Federation of Malaya**, with rights for the Chinese and Indians to be decided later. Now it was leftists that were disgruntled, and that same year a communist insurgency was launched in Malaya by largely Chinese guerrillas, who had gained experience of jungle warfare in resisting the Japanese. This created another area of potential friction between the two territories: Malayan Chinese politicians tended to be conservative and looked askance at Singapore, where many Chinese were developing leftist sympathies.

In April 1955, Singapore held elections for the newly created legislative assembly, 25 of whose 32 members were directly elected. The **Labour Front** emerged as the biggest party and its leader, **David Marshall**, an idealistic, British-trained lawyer of Iraqi Jewish stock, became the island's first chief minister. The elections were also notable for the emergence of the brand-new **People's Action Party (PAP)**, which came third. Led by another British-qualified lawyer, the shrewd, calculating **Lee Kuan Yew**, a Peranakan, the party had at its core several more graduates of British universities who were generally of

| **1824** | **1845** |
|---|---|
| The Anglo-Dutch treaty is signed, under which the British dominate the Malay Peninsula while the Dutch focus on what would become Indonesia; the same year, the Malay rulers cede Singapore to the East India Company under the Crawfurd treaty | *The Straits Times*, Singapore's oldest surviving newspaper, begins publication |

the centre left. Lee's key insight was that to take power, the party had to reach out beyond the English-speaking elite. He steered the PAP into absorbing new members further to the left, chiefly trade unionists as well as Chinese activists who were unhappy over the lack of support for Chinese-language education.

Just before the elections, the PAP's left wing had been involved in mass action by ten thousand Chinese high-school students demanding recognition for their union. The following month the bus workers' union, led by two PAP activists, was embroiled in a strike that descended into violence, with a number of deaths. Marshall made concessions to restore order while attacking the PAP for fomenting disorder, but just a year later, he resigned over differences on defence after talks with the British on further constitutional reform. He was replaced by his deputy, **Lim Yew Hock**, who confronted the unions and the students and, in 1957, arrested several PAP left-wingers. Ironically, this aided his political rivals by strengthening the hand of the moderates in the PAP.

## Marriage with Malaysia, and divorce

Malaya achieved independence in 1957, and two years later Singapore achieved full self-government, with the PAP winning 43 of the 51 seats in the newly enlarged, totally elected legislative assembly. Lee became Singapore's first prime minister and quickly looked for a merger with Malaya, with a high degree of autonomy for the island. The talk was of Singapore playing New York to Kuala Lumpur's Washington DC, and it made sense: Singapore was Malaya's financial hub and main port, as well as a centre for publishing and the arts. For its part, Malaya, still recovering from the communist insurgency, feared that PAP leftists could yet turn Singapore into an extremist hotbed and so wanted the island under its wing, though with its Chinese element diluted by having Sarawak and British North Borneo (now Sabah) join as well. That was duly achieved in September 1963 with the proclamation of a new country, the **Federation of Malaysia**. Soon afterwards Singapore went to the polls, with the PAP again winning despite a major challenge from ex-PAP left-wingers.

Singapore's presence within Malaysia, was, however, an uneasy one, with the PAP challenging the mainstream Malaysian parties over their ethnically based politics. Racial incidents in Singapore developed into full-scale riots, with several deaths. Within two years Singapore was given its marching orders from the Federation, in the face of outrage in Kuala Lumpur at the PAP's attempts to break into Peninsular politics in 1964.

## The new nation takes shape

On August 9, 1965, hours after announcing that Singapore would be going it alone as an **independent state**, a tearful Lee Kuan Yew appeared on local TV and called the event "a moment of anguish". With no natural resources, the tiny island seemed destined to fade into obscurity. Against all the odds, the PAP's vision transformed Singapore into an Asian economic heavyweight, but this also meant the government orchestrating seemingly every aspect of life on the island as it saw fit, brooking little opposition.

While the port and shipyards were thriving, the first task was for Singapore to diversify economically and lessen its dependence on Malaysia. For all its leftist credentials, the PAP went all-out to seek **foreign investment**, and new industries sprang up in Jurong and other areas. The government also clamped down on union militancy,

| **1858** | **Feb 1915** | **15 Feb 1942** |
|---|---|---|
| The British East India Company closes, its possessions transferred to direct British government control | Indian troops stationed in Singapore mutiny for more than a week, killing tens of British soldiers and civilians | The British surrender to the Japanese at the Ford factory near Bukit Timah |

a process that had begun in 1961 when it formed the National Trades Union Congress to replace a leftist union grouping; now the unions were told to swallow a **no-strike philosophy** in return for government intervention in resolving industrial disputes fairly.

Soon after the split with Malaysia, Singapore set up military **conscription**, modelled in part on the Israeli system (and, indeed, with Israeli help), but the stakes were raised after the surprise announcement, in 1968, that the British were to close all their military bases east of Suez. Singapore was still a major British outpost, an arrangement which boosted both the island's security and the local economy. While the vacuum left by the British was cushioned by new industries and American investment, conscription has remained a fundamental element of Singapore life ever since, with a sizeable chunk of the budget spent on defence.

There was also the pressing matter of the country's high birth rate and lack of decent housing. In 1966 the Land Acquisition Act was passed, enabling the government to buy land compulsorily for minimal compensation. This allowed the building of **new towns** all over the island, where people from kampongs (villages) or the slums of Chinatown could be resettled in affordable apartments within uniform concrete towers. However, ethnic quotas in each town, meant to prevent ghettoes forming, had the effect of breaking communities apart and of making one area much like another demographically – with electoral implications.

## The 1970s and 1980s

Over the next two decades, the PAP consolidated its grip on Singapore as its project for the nation continued to roll. The economy largely enjoyed healthy growth, and by 1980 Singapore was practically an industrialized country. The opposition was moribund: between 1968 and 1980, the PAP held every seat in parliamentary elections, and when the opposition Workers' Party unexpectedly won a by-election in 1981, the new MP, **J.B. Jeyaretnam**, found himself charged with several offences and chased through the Singaporean courts for the next decade. The government was also not averse to using the colonial-era **Internal Security Act**, which allows detention without trial, and used it to keep the leftist Chia Thye Poh either in jail or under some form of detention for more than two decades for allegedly advocating violence.

Having transformed the trade unions, the government now turned its attention to the **press**, which they felt should articulate the policies of the party that the electorate had voted for rather than offering an independent perspective. Press reform culminated in the early 1980s with a wholesale restructuring of the industry: two established Chinese newspapers were closed and two new ones created out of their ashes, while papers in all languages were brought under the umbrella of a new company whose chairman, **S.R. Nathan**, was once a civil servant involved in security and intelligence matters.

Another significant development of the time was in **education**. Back in the 1950s, the PAP had appeased Chinese-speaking voters by permitting the launch of a Chinese-language university, Nantah, but thirty years on the public had largely decided that English offered better prospects, and Chinese-language institutions were in decline. In 1980 the government absorbed Nantah into the new National University of Singapore, which used English, and a few years later the remaining state schools that taught mainly in Chinese were switched to English. Though most Singapore students still

| Sept 1945 | Aug 1957 | 1959 |
| --- | --- | --- |
| The Japanese occupation ends with the surrender at City Hall by the Padang | The Federation of Malaya – the Malay Peninsula, minus Singapore – gains independence from the British | Singapore attains full self-government under Lee Kuan Yew while remaining a British colony |

learn Chinese, Malay or Tamil as a subsidiary language, it is English that now reigns supreme – with all the potential implications that has for the island's identity, cultures and values.

Cementing the PAP's grip on power was a major change to the electoral system, the introduction in the late 1980s of "group representation constituencies" or **GRCs**. These were essentially winner-takes-all super-constituencies where only one party wins all seats in area by gaining the largest share of the combined vote. The system was brought in apparently to make parliament more diverse (candidates for a GRC must form an ethnically balanced slate), though considering how hard it was for the opposition to win any single seats, let alone a cluster, the change had the effect of raising the barrier faced by anyone wishing to challenge the PAP.

## New leaders

As the 1990s began, Singapore was an obvious economic miracle, yet it was also bland and rigid, a consumerist showcase where the historic Chinatown had been partly demolished and the remnants sanitized, and where patronizing state campaigns exhorted citizens to, among other things, be nice to each other and not spit in the street. So when Lee Kuan Yew stepped down in 1990 in favour of his deputy, **Goh Chok Tong**, Singaporeans hoped for a degree of loosening up. Goh promised to lead in a more consultative way, and there were some liberalizing changes: films began to be rated so that they could be viewed intact instead of being cut to shreds in order to be family-friendly, and the arts scene began to take off, though there were still written and unwritten rules curbing freedom of expression. However, the government has kept a lid on the press, and on the surface little has changed since Lee's eldest son, **Lee Hsien Loong**, took over as prime minister in 2004, though he comes across as much more managerial than his sometimes ruthless father.

## Prospects

In many respects, Singapore today feels more at ease with itself and is a great deal more culturally rich than a generation ago. And yet there are clouds on the horizon. The wisdom of the island's reliance on **financial services** was questioned when Singapore suffered a sharp recession in the wake of the global banking crisis of 2008. In this light, government approval for two **integrated resorts** – as the casinos at Sentosa and Marina Bay are euphemistically termed – was not only controversial with the public but was viewed by some as a sign that the country lacked new economic avenues. Other observers single out the country's record on **human rights** and press freedom, but international scrutiny is limited to rare episodes such as in 1994 when the American teenager Michael Fay, then at school in Singapore, was flogged for minor crimes. In general, however, Western countries prefer to view Singapore as a wealthy trading partner and a useful little ally in the so-called war on terror.

### Stresses and strains

More significant is the growing level of internal disquiet, something that more perceptive visitors often pick up on. They observe that Singaporeans, despite apparently

| Sept 1963 | 9 Aug 1965 | May/June 1987 |
| --- | --- | --- |
| Singapore plus Sarawak and Sabah in Borneo join Malaya to form a new federation, Malaysia | After protracted bickering with Malaysian political parties over economic and social policies, Singapore is forced to leave the Federation and goes it alone as an independent country | The government cracks down on an alleged Marxist conspiracy, imprisoning lawyers and Catholic activists |

rolling in wealth, are sometimes far less sanguine about their prospects and the system that envelops their lives than is obvious from the state-run media.

Ordinary people have, for example, questioned the government's much-vaunted water-management schemes in the wake of flash **floods** in no less significant a location than Orchard Road. There have also been howls of dismay over repeated breakdowns on the MRT system, which had run flawlessly until recent years. More tellingly, there was an outcry over losses suffered by **Temasek Holdings**, the state-owned company that helps manage Singapore's huge foreign reserves. Following losses when the company grabbed stakes in two foreign banks, it was announced in 2009 that the company's head, Ho Ching – who also happens to be the prime minister's wife – was to step down, though in the event she clung on to her job.

Perhaps the most significant area of discontent concerns **immigration**. On occasion, this can turn into public expressions of xenophobia, though not out of racism, as many new arrivals hail from China and India as Singapore's own citizens once did. Rather, people see the increasing pace of inward migration as taking jobs from them at all levels and making even state housing unaffordable, even as luxury apartments shoot up downtown to tempt super-rich foreigners. If only the island had a **minimum wage** policy, people argue, Singaporeans would be tempted to do more basic jobs and fewer migrants would be needed – not realizing that the cheap food and transport they take for granted are partly the result of migrant labour. Ordinary people also complain that high inflation and healthcare costs squeeze the lower and middle classes, and statistics bear out that Singapore has a more unequal distribution of wealth than, for example, Australia or the UK, neither of which is a beacon in this regard.

All this adds up to a gradual attrition of the unwritten pact under which Singaporeans have, for decades, voted in an authoritarian government in exchange for supposedly foolproof management of the country. Even so, when the island went to the polls in May 2011, it was a shock that the opposition managed to win 6 out of the 87 parliamentary seats, including its first ever GRC, with the foreign minister among government casualties. This was a minor political earthquake, and in the aftermath, Lee Kuan Yew gave up his "minister mentor" post – a role created to give him continuing influence despite no longer being prime minister.

Singapore approaches its sixth decade of independence as a nation of wealth tempered by internal restrictions and contradictions. The government rules paternalistically, yet complains that citizens do not show more initiative; capitalism appears to have triumphed over the welfare state, yet the state owns eighty percent of the land and state-dominated institutions play a crucial role in shipping, property, banking and other key sectors of the economy. It remains to be seen if places like Singapore and China truly present some kind of "**neo-Confucian**" alternative to liberal Western democracy, or if Singapore, always a hybrid of East and West, might one day soon embark on a more tolerant and pluralistic path.

| **May 1989** | **May 2011** | **Nov 2012** |
| --- | --- | --- |
| After 23 years of imprisonment without trial, former left-wing opposition MP Chia Thye Poh is released to a kind of internal exile on Sentosa | Singapore's opposition enjoys its best electoral showing since independence | More than 100 migrant bus drivers from China launch an unofficial strike – Singapore's first strike in more than two decades |

# Religion

Singaporeans enjoy freedom of worship, and the island's multicultural nature is reflected in its wide range of creeds. More than half of the population are adherents of Buddhism, with elements of Taoism and Confucianism. Malays, who make up around fifteen percent of the population, are predominantly Muslim, while the nation's Indians are either Hindu, Muslim or Sikh. In addition, one in ten Singaporeans are Christian, and there is a tiny Jewish community worshipping at two synagogues. This section gives an outline of traditional Chinese beliefs, plus Islam and Hinduism, and their places of worship.

## Chinese beliefs

The majority of Singaporean Chinese describe themselves as **Buddhist, Taoist** or **Confucianist**; in practice, they are often a mixture of all three. These different strands of Chinese religion ostensibly lean in different directions, but the combination amounts to a system of belief that is first and foremost pragmatic. The Chinese use religion to ease their passage through life, whether in the spheres of work or family, while temples double as social centres, where people meet and exchange views.

### Buddhism

Buddhism states that the suffering of the world can only be achieved by attaining a state of personal enlightenment, or Nirvana, through meditation. The founder of Buddhism, **Siddhartha Gautama**, was born a prince in Lumbini in present-day Nepal, around 500 BC. Shielded from knowledge of suffering and death for the first decades of his life, he later renounced his pampered existence and spent years meditating before finding enlightenment under a bodhi tree. At this point he became the Buddha or "Awakened One". In Singapore and elsewhere in Southeast Asia he is sometimes called Sakyamuni, or "Holy Man of the Sakya tribe".

In his first sermon, Buddha taught the four noble truths: that suffering exists; that its source should be recognized; that one should strive for a cessation of suffering; and that this can be achieved by following the **Eightfold Path** – practising right views, intentions, speech, action, livelihood, effort, mindfulness and concentration. The religion is split into two schools: **Hinayana** (or Theravada) Buddhism, which focuses on people attaining enlightenment for themselves, and **Mahayana** Buddhism – more common in Singapore – which teaches that one who has become a Bodhisattva, that is, attained enlightenment, should then help others do the same.

### Taoism

Unity with nature is the chief tenet of Taoism (also spelt Daoism), a philosophical movement dating from the sixth century BC, and propounded by the Chinese scholar **Lao Tze** or Laozi. Taoism advocates that people follow a central *Tao* or "way", and cultivate an understanding of the nature of things. This search for truth has often expressed itself in Taoism by way of superstition on the part of its devotees, who engage in fortune-telling and the like. The Taoist gods are mainly legendary figures – warriors, statesmen, scholars – with specific powers that can generally be determined by their form; others represent incarnations of the forces of nature.

## Confucianism

Confucianism began as a philosophy based on piety, loyalty, humanitarianism and familial devotion. In the 2500 years since **Kongzi** or **Confucius**, its founder, died, it has transmuted into a set of principles that permeate every aspect of Chinese life. A blueprint for social and moral harmony, the Confucian ideology stresses one's obligation to family, community and the state, hinging on the individual's need to recognize his or her position in the social hierarchy and act accordingly – son must obey father, student must obey teacher, subject must obey ruler.

## Chinese temples

The rules of **geomancy**, or **feng shui** (wind and water), are rigorously applied to the construction of **Chinese temples** to ensure they are free from malign influences. Visitors wishing to cross the threshold of a temple have to step over a low barrier intended to trip up evil spirits, and walk through doors painted with fearsome door gods; fronting the doors are two stone lions, providing yet another defence. Larger temples typically consist of a front entrance hall opening on to a walled-in courtyard, beyond which is the hall of worship, where joss sticks are burned below images of the deities.

Temples are usually constructed around a framework of huge, lacquered timber beams, adorned with intricately carved warriors, animals and flowers. More figures are moulded onto outer walls, which are dotted with octagonal, hexagonal or round windows. Elsewhere in the grounds, you'll see sizeable ovens stuffed constantly with slowly burning fake money, prayer books and other offerings. Pagodas – tall, thin towers thought to keep out evil spirits – are common too.

The most important and striking element of a Chinese temple is its roof. They are grand, multi-tiered affairs, with low, overhanging eaves, the ridges alive with auspicious creatures such as dragons and phoenixes and, less often, with miniature scenes from traditional Chinese life and legend. One particular feature of Singapore temple roofs is the use of **jiannian**, a southern Chinese art form in which pottery fragments in multicoloured pastel hues are used to create ornamentations such as finials. Temples are open from early morning to early evening and devotees go in when they like, to make offerings or to pray; there are no set prayer times. They also play an important part in Chinese community life, and some hold occasional musical and theatrical performances.

# Islam

**Islam** ("submission to God") was founded in Mecca in what is now Saudi Arabia by Muhammad (570–632 AD), the last in a long line of prophets that included Abraham, Moses and Jesus. Muhammad transmitted Allah's final and perfected revelation to mankind through the writings of the divinely revealed "recitation", the **Koran**. The official beginning of Islam is dated as 622 AD, when Muhammad and his followers, exiled from Mecca, made the **hijra**, or migration, north to Yathrib, later known as Medina. The *hijra* marks the start of the Islamic calendar.

The first firm foothold made by Islam in Southeast Asia was the conversion of the court of Melaka, in modern-day Malaysia, in the early fifteenth century. One after another, the powerful Malay court rulers of the region took to Islam, adopting the title sultan. Today, almost all of Singapore's Malays are Muslims, as well as a proportion of its Indian population. Islam as practised here may be devout but is not overt, largely because of the secularizing influence of the state, which has banned headscarves from government-run schools.

All the central tenets of Islam are embodied in the Koran, with the most important known as the **Five Pillars of Islam**. The first pillar is *shahada* – the confession of faith, "There is no god but God, and Muhammad is his messenger." The *shahada* is recited at the *salat*, the second pillar, which enjoins the faithful to make five daily prayers facing in the direction of Mecca. The other three tenets are: giving alms (*zakat*); fasting during the ninth month of the Muslim lunar calendar, **Ramadan**; and making the great annual pilgrimage (**hajj**) to Mecca at least once in a devotee's lifetime.

## Mosques

While only a small proportion attend the mosque every day, all Muslims converge on their nearest **mosque** on Friday for the weekly congregational prayer at midday. Once there, the men wash their hands, feet and faces three times in the outer chambers, before entering the prayer hall to recite sections of the Koran. Standard fixtures in the prayer hall are the *minbar* (pulpit), from where the imam preaches, and women cannot enter the main prayer hall during prayers and must congregate in a chamber to the side of the hall. Visitors are welcome outside the set prayer times, provided that their shoulders and legs are covered.

# Hinduism

**Hinduism** reached the Malay Peninsula and Singapore long before Islam, brought by Indian traders more than a thousand years ago. Its base of support grew in the nineteenth century, when large numbers of indentured workers and convicts arrived from the subcontinent to labour on rubber estates and in construction.

Hinduism had no founder, but grew slowly over thousands of years. Its central tenet is the belief that life is a series of rebirths and reincarnations (*samsara*) that eventually leads to spiritual release (*moksha*). An individual's progress is determined by his or her *karma*, very much a law of cause and effect, in which negative decisions and actions slow up the process of upward reincarnation and positive ones accelerate it.

A whole variety of deities are worshipped, which on the surface makes Hinduism appear complex, but even with a loose understanding of the **Vedas**, the religion's holy books, the characters and roles of the main gods quickly become apparent. The deities you'll come across most often are the three manifestations of the faith's Supreme Divine Being: **Brahma the Creator**, **Vishnu the Preserver** and **Shiva the Destroyer**. Other enduring favourites among Hindus include: elephant-headed Ganesh, the son of Shiva, who is evoked before every undertaking except funerals; Vishnu's consort, the comely Lakshmi, worshipped as goddess of prosperity and wealth; and Saraswati, wife to Brahma, and seen as a goddess of purification, fertility and learning.

## Hindu temples

Step over the threshold of a Hindu temple and you enter a veritable Disneyland of colourful gods and fanciful creatures. In Singapore, the style is typically **Dravidian** (South Indian), as befits the largely Tamil population, with a soaring *gopuram*, or entrance tower, teeming with sculptures, and a central courtyard leading to an inner sanctum (off-limits to tourists) dedicated to the presiding deity.

# Books

Singapore's bookshops stock imported titles and the output of the island's thriving English-language publishing industry, covering everything from political biographies to encyclopedic tomes on design, though fiction tends to have a low profile. Of the bookshops listed on p.154, the best for more specialist titles is Select Books, which offers a mail-order service. In the reviews below, books marked ★ are particularly recommended while o/p signifies out of print. Note that authors with Chinese names usually have their surname appearing first, as is the Chinese custom; Malay and Indian names are alphabetized according to the given name which appears first, the second name being the father's name.

## TRAVEL WRITING AND MEMOIR

**Charles Allen** *Tales from the South China Seas*. Recollections of the last generation of British colonists in which predictable Raj attitudes prevail, though some of the drama of everyday lives, often in inhospitable conditions, is evinced with considerable pathos.

**Hidayah Amin** *Gedung Kuning: Memories of a Malay Childhood*. A simple, heartfelt account of life in the little yellow mansion on Kandahar Street (see p.76), taking in Muslim festivals, family weddings, neighbourhood characters and stories handed down over the generations, culminating with the author's family being pitiably turfed out in 1999 when the state took over the property.

**Isabella Bird** *The Golden Chersonese*. The intrepid author's adventures in the Malay states in the 1870s ranged from strolls through Singapore's streets to elephant-back rides and encounters with alligators. Periodically reissued, it's also available from various websites as a free download.

**Russell Braddon** *The Naked Island*. Braddon's disturbing and moving first-hand account of the POW camps of Malaya, Singapore and Thailand displays courage in the face of appalling conditions and treatment.

**Eric Lomax** *The Railway Man*. An artless, redemptive and moving story of capture during the fall of Singapore, torture by the Japanese and reconciliation with the author's tormentor after fifty years.

★ **Lucy Lum** *The Thorn of Lion City*. You might think a memoir of a wartime childhood in Singapore would be dominated by the savagery of the Japanese, but for the author that was nothing compared to the torment inflicted on her at the hands of her manipulative and violent mother and grandmother. It's told with zero artifice, which only makes it more compelling.

**Michael Wise** (ed) *Travellers' Tales of Old Singapore*. A diverse collection of anecdotes and recollections covering the colonial period up to World War II.

## HISTORY AND POLITICS

**Munshi Abdullah (aka Abdullah bin Kadir)** *The Hikayat Abdullah* (o/p). Raffles' one-time clerk, Abdullah, kept a diary of some of the most formative years of Southeast Asian history, and his first-hand account is crammed with illuminating vignettes and character portraits.

**Noel Barber** *Sinister Twilight*. Documents the fall of Singapore to the Japanese by reimagining the crucial events of the period.

★ **Victoria Glendinning** *Raffles and the Golden Opportunity*. The first serious biography of Singapore's founder in decades does occasionally get bogged down in a surfeit of detail on Raffles' extended family, but offers plenty of enjoyable insights into the headstrong drive of a generally neglected figure of British colonialism.

**Maya Jayapal** *Old Singapore*. Concise volume that charts the growth of the city-state, drawing on contemporary maps, sketches and photographs to engrossing effect.

**Patrick Keith** *Ousted*. Singapore's unhappy stint as part of Malaysia might seem something from the distant past, but the events of the mid-1960s, recounted in this excellent blow-by-blow account by a former advisor to the Malaysian government, still shape both countries and their relations today.

**Colin Smith** *Singapore Burning: Heroism and Surrender in World War II*. Highly detailed, definitive account of the fall of Singapore, written with a journalist's instinct for excitement.

**Carl A. Trocki** *Singapore: Wealth, Power and the Culture of Control*. A digestible dissection of how the PAP, after co-opting and marginalizing Singapore's Left in the 1960s and then allying "with international capital to create a workers' paradise", acquired its present grip on all aspects of life on the island.

★ **C.M. Turnbull** *A History of Modern Singapore*

*1819–2005*. Mary Turnbull had barely completed a major update of this standard work when she died in 2008, and what a fine legacy: the new edition is lucid, thorough, nearly always spot-on in its analysis and, as always, utterly readable.

## ARCHITECTURE

★ **Julian Davison and Luca Invernizzi Tettoni** *Black & White: The Singapore House* and *The Singapore Shophouse*. *Black & White* celebrates the island's surviving colonial "Anglo-Malay" residences– one now houses the *Flutes at the Fort* restaurant (see p.122), and there's another in the Botanic Garden (see p.82) – which marry mock Tudor and Southeast Asian elements. Even better is *The Singapore Shophouse*, dissecting its subject through the lens of stylistic era, district and so forth, with a cornucopia of dazzling photos of interiors as well as exteriors.

**Peter Lee and Jennifer Chen** *The Straits Chinese House*. Packed with old photos, this book on Peranakan homes, domestic artefacts and vanishing traditions makes an excellent memento after you've visited the Baba House or the Peranakan Museum.

**Wan Meng Hao and Jacqueline Lau** *Heritage Places of Singapore*. A compact, full-colour catalogue of the hugely diverse pre-independence architecture of Singapore, from Palladian colonial buildings to overlooked Art Deco edifices as well as traditional temples and shrines.

## CULTURE AND SOCIETY

**James Harding and Ahmad Sarji** *P. Ramlee: The Bright Star*. An uncritical but enjoyable biography of the singer, actor and director sometimes described as the Malay world's Harry Belafonte. More importantly, it's a window onto what seems like a different era, only half a century ago, when Singapore was the centre of the Malay entertainment universe.

**Leslie Layton** *Songbirds in Singapore*. A delightful examination of the local penchant for keeping songbirds, detailing all facets of the pastime, from its growth in the nineteenth century to its most popular birds.

**Gerrie Lim** *Invisible Trade: High-Class Sex for Sale in Singapore*. This exposé of the local escort industry makes for an entertaining but somewhat unsatisfying read, its basic flaw being the idea that it's a big secret that Singapore might be less squeaky clean than it appears.

**Ilsa Sharp** *Path of the Righteous Crane*. Eu Tong Sen, after whom one of Chinatown's main thoroughfares is named, was the founder of the Eu Yan Sang emporia of Chinese herbal medicines. This new biography not only recounts the many successes of this prewar tycoon in Singapore and Malaysia but also unwraps migrant Chinese society of the time.

## FOOD

**Aziza Ali** *Aziza's Creative Malay Cuisine*. For many years the author ran one of the best Malay restaurants in Singapore, and her recipes are intended more to impress at dinner parties than to reflect what's served on the street. Don't expect Thai-influenced dishes from the northern part of the Peninsula either; the emphasis here is on Singapore and the south.

★ **Sylvia Tan** *Singapore Heritage Food*. This book begins a

little unpromisingly with passé colonial-era dishes – prawn cocktails and the like – but then comes a romp through all manner of classic Singapore restaurant and hawker food, from Hainanese chicken rice and chilli crab to less familiar standards that visitors seldom notice, such as *oh luak* (scrambled egg with oysters) and *chap chye* (Peranakan mixed veg and fungi braised in soy sauce). Plenty of vintage photos of now-vanished pushcart food stalls, too.

## NATURE

**M. Strange and A. Jeyarajasingam** *A Photographic Guide to Birds of Peninsular Malaysia and Singapore*. User-friendly and with oodles of glossy plates, this should help even the bird-blind sort out a black-naped oriole from a white-rumped shama.

**Tee Swee Ping** (ed) *Trees of our Garden City*. A guide to Singapore's diverse flora is something local publishers haven't properly addressed. This book does at least cover one of the most impressive aspects of that flora, from the majestic rain tree to the red-flowered flame of the forest.

## FICTION

**Alfian Sa'at** *Malay Sketches*. Not so much short stories as vignettes, Sa'at's miniature tales – collected here under a title that deliberately echoes that of a classic work by a nineteenth-century British colonial official – attempt to capture the bittersweet experience of Singapore's Malay community. The

stories aren't always brilliantly executed, but when they work they do pack a punch, exposing home truths concerning religion, ethnic stereotypes and competition with the Chinese.

**Noel Barber** *Tanamera*. Romantic saga set in mid-twentieth-century Singapore and dramatized for TV in the 1980s.

★ **Anthony Burgess** *The Malayan Trilogy*. Published in one volume, *Time for a Tiger*, *The Enemy in the Blanket* and *Beds in the East* provide a witty and acutely observed vision of 1950s Malaya and Singapore, underscoring the racial prejudices of the period.

★ **James Clavell** *King Rat*. Clavell spins a gripping tale of survival in the notorious Changi Prison during the Japanese occupation.

**Joseph Conrad** *Lord Jim*. Southeast Asia provides the backdrop to the story of Jim's desertion of an apparently sinking ship and subsequent efforts to redeem himself; the main protagonist was modelled on the sailor A.P. Williams, who lived and died in Singapore.

★ **J.G. Farrell** *The Singapore Grip*. Lengthy wartime novel, the last of Farrell's empire trilogy, in which real and fictitious characters flit from tennis to dinner party as the countdown to the Japanese occupation begins.

**Shamini Flint** *Inspector Singh Investigates: The Singapore School of Villainy*. Meet the rotund Sikh police detective, the creation of a Singapore-based Malaysian writer, as he probes a murder at the Singapore offices of an international law firm. It's a passable whodunnit, though with all the depth of characterization of *Murder She Wrote*; don't expect deep insights into Singapore society either.

**Paul Theroux** *Saint Jack*. The compulsively bawdy tale of Jack Flowers, an ageing American who supplements his earnings at a Singapore ship's chandlers by pimping for Westerners. The 1979 movie adaptation, filmed in Singapore behind a smokescreen of subterfuge – the crew knew the sleaziness of the plot would never pass muster with the authorities – has only recently been unbanned on the island.

# Glossary

**Baba** Peranakan male, usually someone of mainly Chinese heritage.

**Bukit** Hill.

**Bumboat** Small cargo boat.

**Cheongsam** Tight-fitting Chinese dress with long slit up the side.

**Expressway** Motorway/freeway.

**Five-foot way** Recessed ground-level walkway, substituting for a pavement; a standard feature of rows of shophouses

**Godown** Riverside warehouse.

**Gopuram** Pyramid of sculpted deities over the entrance to a Hindu temple.

**Haj** Major annual pilgrimage to Mecca.

**Halal** Something permissible in Islam.

**Hawker centre** A cooked-food market containing a cluster of stalls under one roof and sharing common tables.

**Istana** A Malay palace.

**Jalan** Road or street.

**Kampong/kampung** Village.

**Kavadi** Steel frames hung from the bodies of Hindu devotees during Thaipusam.

**Kempeitai** The much-feared military police during the Japanese occupation.

**Keramat** Auspicious Malay site.

**Kongsi** Chinese clan association.

**Kopitiam** Inexpensive diner like a mini-food court, with up to half a dozen "stalls" serving a range of dishes and snacks.

**Kris** Wavy-bladed Malay dagger.

**Lorong** Lane.

**Mahjong** A Chinese game played with little brick-shaped "tiles".

**Masjid** Mosque.

**Nonya** Peranakan female (from the Malay nyonya).

**Padang** Field; used also for grassy town squares.

**Pasir** Sand, often used in names of areas with beaches.

**Peranakan** Person of mixed culture and/or race, born in the territories around the Straits of Malacca.

**Pulau** Island.

**Ramadan** Muslim fasting month.

**Rotan** Rattan cane used in the infliction of corporal punishment.

**Sari** Traditional Indian woman's garment, worn in conjunction with a choli (short-sleeved blouse).

**Shophouse** Townhouse-like building, the oldest examples of which had living quarters upstairs and a shop space at ground level.

**Songkok** Stiff drum-like cap worn by Malay men.

**Sook Ching** The name of the military operation under which the occupying Japanese rounded up and killed thousands of Singapore ethnic Chinese whom they saw as opposed to their presence.

**Sultan** Ruler.

**T'ai chi** Chinese martial art, commonly performed as an early-morning exercise.

**Tanjong/tanjung** Promontory.

**Telok/teluk** Bay.

**Temenggong** Chieftain.

**Tongkang** Chinese sailing boat.

**Trishaw** Three-wheeled cycle-rickshaw.

**Wayang** Theatrical show; in the Singapore context, Chinese opera.

# Small print and index

**A ROUGH GUIDE TO ROUGH GUIDES**

Published in 1982, the first Rough Guide – to Greece – was a student scheme that became a publishing phenomenon. Mark Ellingham, a recent graduate in English from Bristol University, had been travelling in Greece the previous summer and couldn't find the right guidebook. With a small group of friends he wrote his own guide, combining a highly contemporary, journalistic style with a thoroughly practical approach to travellers' needs.

The immediate success of the book spawned a series that rapidly covered dozens of destinations. And, in addition to impecunious backpackers, Rough Guides soon acquired a much broader readership that relished the guides' wit and inquisitiveness as much as their enthusiastic, critical approach and value-for-money ethos.

These days, Rough Guides include recommendations from budget to luxury and cover more than 200 destinations around the globe, as well as producing an ever-growing range of eBooks and apps.

Visit **roughguides.com** to see our latest publications.

## Rough Guide credits

**Editor**: Steven Horak
**Layout**: Pradeep Thapliyal and Jessica Subramanian
**Cartography**: Katie Bennett
**Picture editor**: Tim Draper
**Proofreader**: Karen Parker
**Managing editor**: Keith Drew
**Assistant editor**: Jalpreen Kaur Chhatwal
**Production**: Charlotte Cade
**Cover design**: Nicole Newman, Dan May, Pradeep Thapliyal

**Editorial assistant**: Olivia Rawes
**Senior pre-press designer**: Dan May
**Design director**: Scott Stickland
**Travel publisher**: Joanna Kirby
**Digital travel publisher**: Peter Buckley
**Operations coordinator**: Helen Blount
**Publishing director (Travel)**: Clare Currie
**Commercial manager**: Gino Magnotta
**Managing director**: John Duhigg

## Publishing information

This seventh edition published May 2013 by
**Rough Guides Ltd**,
80 Strand, London WC2R 0RL
11, Community Centre, Panchsheel Park,
New Delhi 110017, India
**Distributed by the Penguin Group**
Penguin Books Ltd,
80 Strand, London WC2R 0RL
Penguin Group (USA)
345 Hudson Street, NY 10014, USA
Penguin Group (Australia)
250 Camberwell Road, Camberwell,
Victoria 3124, Australia
Penguin Group (NZ)
67 Apollo Drive, Mairangi Bay, Auckland 1310,
New Zealand
Penguin Group (South Africa)
Block D, Rosebank Office Park, 181 Jan Smuts Avenue,
Parktown North, Gauteng, South Africa 2193
Rough Guides is represented in Canada by Tourmaline
Editions Inc. 662 King Street West, Suite 304, Toronto,
Ontario M5V 1M7
Printed in Malaysia by Vivar Printing Sdn Bhd

© Rough Guides & Richard Lim, 2013
Maps © Rough Guides
No part of this book may be reproduced in any form
without permission from the publisher except for the
quotation of brief passages in reviews.
192pp includes index
A catalogue record for this book is available from the
British Library
ISBN: 978-1-40936-282-1
The publishers and authors have done their best to
ensure the accuracy and currency of all the information
in **The Rough Guide to Singapore**, however, they
can accept no responsibility for any loss, injury, or
inconvenience sustained by any traveller as a result of
information or advice contained in the guide.
3 5 7 9 8 6 4 2

MIX
Paper from
responsible sources
FSC™ C018179

## Help us update

We've gone to a lot of effort to ensure that the seventh edition of **The Rough Guide to Singapore** is accurate and up-to-date. However, things change – places get "discovered", opening hours are notoriously fickle, restaurants and rooms raise prices or lower standards. If you feel we've got it wrong or left something out, we'd like to know, and if you can remember the address, the price, the hours, the phone number, so much the better.

Please send your comments with the subject line "**Rough Guide Singapore Update**" to ✉ mail @uk.roughguides.com. We'll credit all contributions and send a copy of the next edition (or any other Rough Guide if you prefer) for the very best emails.

Find more travel information, connect with fellow travellers and book your trip on ⓦ roughguides.com

## ABOUT THE AUTHOR

Not to be confused with the Singapore Straits Times journalist, **Richard Lim** works as a freelance editor and writer in London. He returns regularly to his native Singapore and also has a penchant for wandering around the Middle East. When not writing guidebooks, he can be found editing science and technology articles and noodling on the guitar.

## Acknowledgements

Thanks, first and foremost, to my family in Singapore for leads, helping with reviews and for being there. At Rough Guides, thanks to Steven Horak for being a great editor, Katie Bennett for excellent maps, and Pradeep Thapliyal and Tim Draper for layout and images. Thanks also to Susanah Toh from the Singapore Tourism Board, World Nomads travel-writing competition winner Hanna Butler for helping with research, plus Ridwan, Tony T, Jennifer and Tien, Sybil Chiew, Fabian Foo, Grace, Cheryl, Aik Wee, Joel, Ernest, Hidayah Amin, Victoria Glendinning, Jeanette Wong, Shreelatha, Lily, and David Leffman. Special thanks to John Gee, Ang Swee Chai, Kevin Tan, Jim M, Joe Ng, Dina Senan, John and Maggie Liebmann and Ooi Kee Beng.

## Readers' letters

Thanks to all the readers who sent valuable feedback on the guide's last edition, in particular John Adams, Gerry Barton and Gary Birse.

## Photo credits

All photos © Rough Guides except the following:
(Key: t-top; c-centre; b-bottom; l-left; r-right)

**p.1** Getty Images, Peter Adams
**p.2** Getty Images: Nathaniel Gilera Hayag Photography
**p.4** Corbis: Gavin Hellier
**p.6** Corbis: How Hwee Young
**p.7** Getty Images: Alex Mares-Manton
**p.8** Getty Images: Jean Brooks
**p.10** Getty Images: MIXA
**p.11** Alamy: EIGHTFISH (c). Andrew Woodley (b)
**p.12** Corbis: Luca Tettoni (t). Getty Images: Timothy Corbin (b)
**p.13** Getty Images: Klaus Vedfelt (t)
**p.14** Corbis: How Hwee Young (t)
**p.15** Alamy: Aurora Photos (br). Corbis: How Hwee Young (bl)
**p.16** Corbis: Stephen Morrison (b). Andrew Watson (t)
**p.17** Getty Images: Heinrich van den Berg (b). Tibor Bognar (t). Bloomberg (c)
**p.18** Getty Images: Jonathan Chiang Scintt
**p.32** Getty Images: David Lomax
**p.53** Alamy: Arcaid Images (b). travelbild (t)
**p.57** Getty Images: Travelpix
**p.69** Corbis: Robert Such
**p.73** Getty Images: Kenny Teo
**p.78** Getty Images: Heinrich van den Berg
**p.83** Alamy, Maximilian Weinzierl

**p.89** Alamy: Johnny Jones (t). Corbis: Vivek Prakash (b). Getty Images, Roslan Rahman (c)
**p.91** Alamy: JS Callahan
**p.98** Alamy: John Lander
**p.105** Corbis: Charles Pertwee
**p.109** Alamy: Neil Setchfield (t). Getty Images: Klaus Vedfelt (b)
**p.112** Getty Images: Bloomberg
**p.120** Corbis: Steve Vidler
**p.129** Alamy: Peter Horree (t). iklimfotostock (b)
**p.143** Getty Images: spintheday
**p.147** Getty Images: Shilpa Harolikar
**p.150** Alamy: Paul Kingsley
**p.153** Alamy: Travelscape (t). Getty Images: Shirlyn Loo (b)
**p.156** Alamy: Paul Kingsley

**Front cover** Sri Mariamman Temple © Getty Images, John W. Banagan
**Back cover** Tan Teng Niah Residence © Getty Images, Gavin Hellier (br); Orangutan family in Singapore Zoo © kenny photography (bl); Singapore skyline from Marina Bay © Travelpix Ltd (t)

# Index

Maps are marked in grey

# Maps

## Index

## Listings key

■ Accommodation

● Eating

■ Drinking and nightlife

● Shop

# City plan

The **city plan** on the pages that follow is divided as shown:

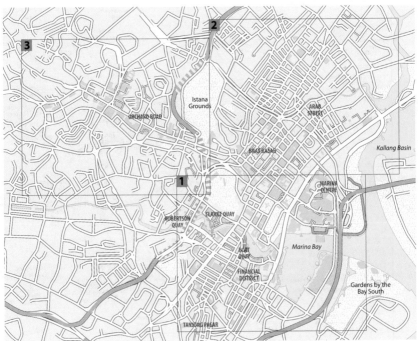

## Map symbols

| | | | | | | |
|---|---|---|---|---|---|---|
| ✈ | Airport | ♦ | Place of interest | 🐘 | Zoo | ▦ Building |
| ⊖ | MRT station | ♦ | Nature park | ▲ | Hill | ⊡ Church |
| ★ | Transport stop | ✡ | Synagogue | ⚡ | Lighthouse | ▢ Market |
| 🚢 | Ferry terminal | ☪ | Mosque | ▨ | Expressway | ◯ Stadium |
| ✉ | Post office | ⛩ | Hindu/Sikh temple | ▧ | Pedestrianized road | ▨ Park |
| ⓘ | Tourist office | ⛩ | Chinese/Thai temple | ⦚ | Steps | ⌇ Swamp |
| ✚ | Hospital/clinic | ≈ | Swimming pool | --- | Ferry | Christian cemetery |
| ⊙ | Statue | ⛳ | Golf course | ⊷ | Railway | Muslim cemetery |
| P | Parking | ⊠ | Gate | --- - | Cable car | |

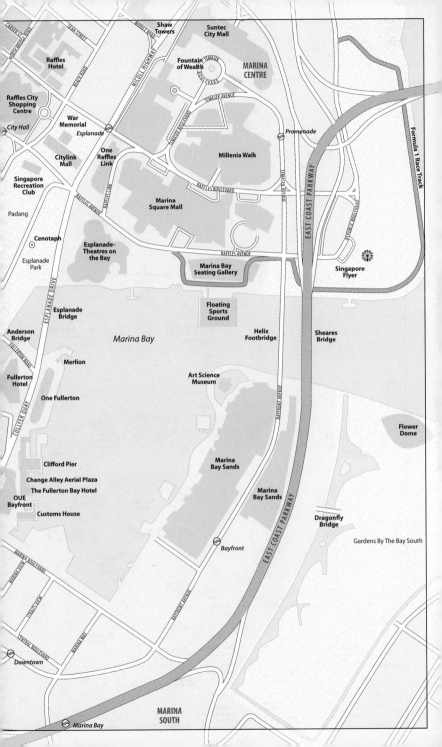

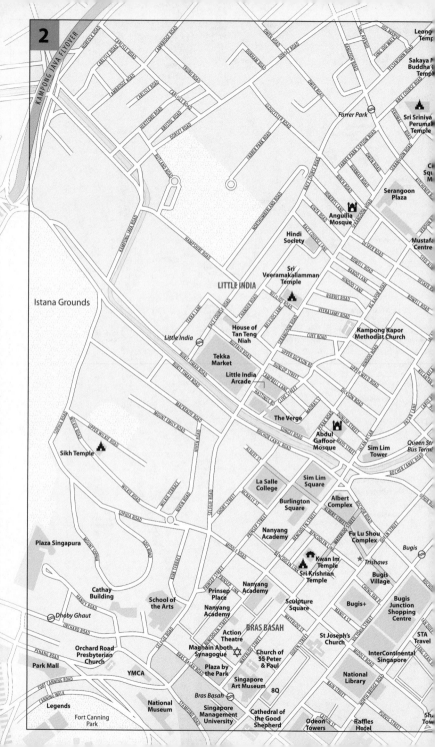

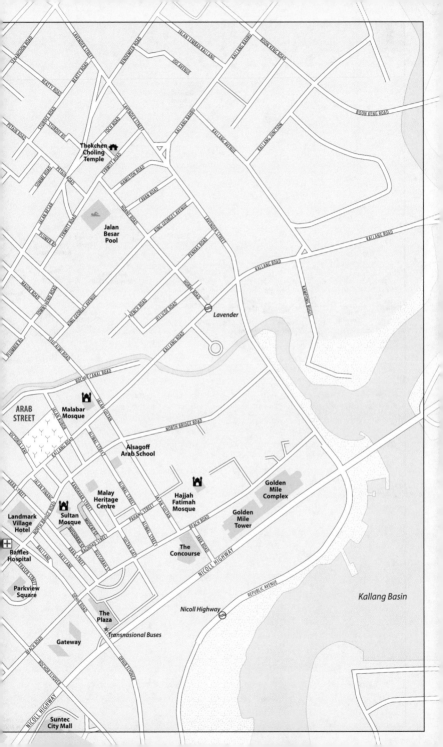

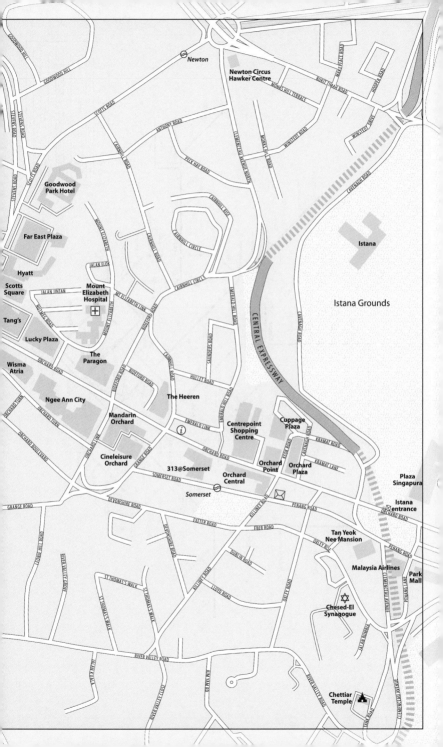

# THE MRT SYSTEM

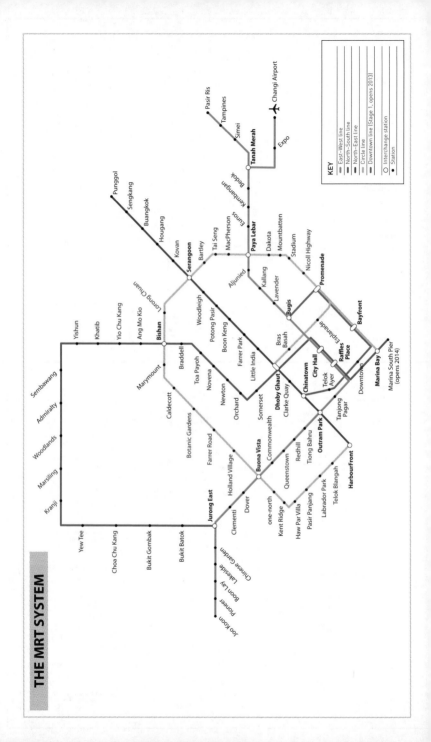

Published in 1982, the first Rough Guide – to Greece – was a student scheme that became a publishing phenomenon. Mark Ellingham, a recent graduate in English from Bristol University, had been travelling in Greece the previous summer and couldn't find the right guidebook. With a small group of friends he wrote his own guide, combining a highly contemporary, journalistic style with a thoroughly practical approach to travellers' needs.

The immediate success of the book spawned a series that rapidly covered dozens of destinations. And, in addition to impecunious backpackers, Rough Guides soon acquired a much broader and older readership that relished the guides' wit and inquisitiveness as much as their enthusiastic, critical approach and value-for-money ethos.

These days, Rough Guides feature recommendations from shoestring to luxury and cover more than 200 destinations around the globe. Our ever-growing team of authors and photographers is spread all over the world, particularly in Europe, the US and Australia.